Russia 2025

Russia 2025

Scenarios for the Russian Future

Edited by

Maria Lipman
Editor-in-Chief, Pro et Contra *Journal, Carnegie Moscow Center, Russia*

and

Nikolay Petrov
Professor, National Research University Higher School of Economics

First published 2013 by
PALGRAVE MACMILLAN

Palgrave Macmillan in the UK is an imprint of Macmillan Publishers Limited,
registered in England, company number 785998, of Houndmills, Basingstoke,
Hampshire RG21 6XS.

Palgrave Macmillan in the US is a division of St Martin's Press LLC,
175 Fifth Avenue, New York, NY 10010.

Palgrave Macmillan is the global academic imprint of the above companies
and has companies and representatives throughout the world.

Palgrave® and Macmillan® are registered trademarks in the United States,
the United Kingdom, Europe and other countries.

ISBN 978–1–137–33690–3

This book is printed on paper suitable for recycling and made from fully
managed and sustained forest sources. Logging, pulping and manufacturing
processes are expected to conform to the environmental regulations of the
country of origin.

A catalogue record for this book is available from the British Library.

A catalog record for this book is available from the Library of Congress.

Contents

v

Tables and Figures

Tables

Figures

Preface

This project is a collective effort of over a dozen authors from Russia, the United States, and Great Britain, who look at the perspectives on Russia's future through to 2025. This project was preceded by an earlier work of a similar kind, titled *Russia 2020* and published in both Russian and English in 2011–12. The new attempt to envision Russia's future was inspired by the mass protests in late 2011 and the creeping political crisis that accompanied Vladimir Putin's comeback to the presidency in 2012. These developments corroborated our earlier analyses – Russia reached an important crossroads described in our project, and facilitated a revision of the earlier outlined scenarios. While we drew on our previous scenario exercise, this time the number of contributors is smaller and the scenarios are more generalized. This volume evolved from a series of expert discussions and seminars held in Russia, several European venues and Washington DC. Earlier versions of some chapters appeared in *Pro et Contra*, a Russian-language journal published by Carnegie Moscow Center.

Acknowledgments

As editors of a collected volume we have been extremely lucky with our team of contributors – each of them a top authority in his or her field. We are deeply grateful for their contributions, for being cooperative and patient with our suggestions and comments and for being terrific company during our joint discussions.

Our colleagues at the Carnegie Endowment for International Peace and at the Carnegie Moscow Center were helpful and supportive at all the various stages of this project. Our special thanks go to Carnegie Endowment's Thomas Carothers and Carnegie Moscow director Dmitry Trenin for their interest in our work and for being thoughtful and encouraging critics.

We would like to express our gratitude to Lenny Benardo of the Open Society Institute for support and encouragement during the early stages of our work.

We would like to thank all those at Palgrave Macmillan who contributed to the production of our volume (particularly) Andrew Baird and Amber Stone-Galilee.

We are grateful to Ivan Krastev of the Vienna Institute of Human Sciences for moral support and academic advice, as well as his assistance in organizing the events our team held in Vienna. Gertraud Borea d'Olmo at the Bruno Kreisky Forum was a most generous and enthusiastic host for our discussions. We highly appreciate the hospitality of Gertraud and her colleagues at the Forum and the excellent organization of our meetings, which made our stay both productive and enjoyable.

Many colleagues at various times took part in our discussions and shared their expertise and their thoughts. We are especially thankful to Sergey Aleksashenko, Pavel Baev, Harley Balzer, Aleksey Berelovich, Timothy Colton, Georgi Derluguian, Thomas de Waal, Boris Dubin, Clifford Gaddy, Alexandr Golts, Lev Gudkov, Thane Gustaffson, Stephen Holmes, Barry Ickes, Alexandr Kynev, Alexey Malashenko, Vladimir Milov, Arkady Moshes, Robert Orttung, Alexey Sidorenko, Jens Siegert, Daniel Treisman, Immanuel Wallerstein, and Igor Zevelev.

Tatiana Barabanova and Yelena Sheetova, our assistants at the Carnegie Moscow Center, have done tremendous work to help this project happen. We are deeply indebted to them for their commitment and tireless effort in the preparation of this book for publication.

Notes on Contributors

Mikhail Denisenko, deputy director of the Institute of Demography, National Research University Higher School of Economics, Moscow.

Vladimir Gel'man, Professor at the Department of Political Science and Sociology, European University at St Petersburg, and Finland Distinguished Professor at the Aleksanteri Institute, University of Helsinki.

Thomas Graham, analyst, served on the US National Security Council staff in 2002–07.

Samuel Greene, director, King's Russia Institute, London, UK.

Boris Grozovsky, economic observer, *Forbes* (Russia).

Henry Hale, associate professor of Political Science and International Affairs, Elliott School of International Affairs, the George Washington University.

Maria Lipman, editor-in-chief, *Pro et Contra* journal, Carnegie Moscow Center.

Fyodor Lukyanov, editor-in-chief, *Rossiya v global'noy politike* (*Russia in Global Affairs*) journal.

Boris Makarenko, chairman of the board, Center for Political Technologies.

Nikolay Petrov, professor, National Research University Higher School of Economics, Moscow.

Kirill Rogov, leading research fellow, Ye.T. Gaidar Institute for Economic Policy, Moscow.

Richard Sakwa, Professor of Russian and European politics, University of Kent.

Natalia Zubarevich, professor, Moscow State University; director, Regional Program, Independent Institute for Social Policy.

Introduction

Maria Lipman and Nikolay Petrov

The mass protests that started in December 2011 signaled the beginning of the period of change for Russia. Although there were no apparent external causal factors, this change was not entirely unexpected, and resulted primarily from the actions of the system itself. First, the regime undermined itself in the fall of 2010 by discrediting one of the most powerful figures in the country, Moscow mayor Yuri Luzhkov. Then, at the United Russia party convention on 24 September 2011, Vladimir Putin and Dmitry Medvedev demonstrated their utter disregard for the Russian electorate by revealing their decision to swap their jobs of president and prime minister. Finally, regional authorities unabashedly abused their powers in an attempt to secure United Russia's convincing victory in the 4 December Duma elections. The newly appointed Moscow mayor Sergey Sobyanin was acting with particular zeal. Mass electoral fraud is not a new phenomenon in Russian politics, and the authorities would have gotten away with it at another time. But a change in the country's political and social climate, along with people's pent-up discontent, produced a mass protest reaction.

Even as late as the spring and summer of 2011, the inertia scenario seemed like a long-term fixture; the regime did not appear to be poised for decisive steps which would make radical change possible. However, the reality turned out to be different. The gradually increasing social tensions and complaints directed against 'Putin's order' (see the chapter by Kirill Rogov in this book) set off the process of internal change, which requires a mere nudge for the change to crystallize and become visible.

The political turmoil of December 2011 has made the regime far more internally unstable. The global economic crisis has also created external instability: economic uncertainty threatens Russia's raw material export revenues, while political uncertainty may bring conflicts in close proximity to Russian borders.

With crisis being a starting point, predicting further developments becomes difficult, since the situation looks increasingly uncertain. The entire system has become fluid, and retaining the status quo no longer appears to be a viable option.

While there are powerful impulses prompting internal system changes, the general framework within which the system operates is also undergoing radical change. Some important long-term trends have been reversed:

> *Original redistribution of property to benefit Putin's elites is over*: 'no one's' assets are largely nonexistent. A redistribution mechanism needs to be developed, whereby young hungry elites are fed while the old ones remain unaffected, and internal elite conflicts are not excessively provoked. One such mechanism consists of blood-letting of sorts: the conditions that enrich the elites have to be changed, and all the elite clans are to be 'taxed' as part of the state's anti-corruption campaign.
>
> *'Nomenclature' vs. 'Elite': one of these models has to be chosen*. The current elite–nomenclature hybrid lacks a mechanism of reproduction. For a period of time, the system could function without it, but now its effectiveness has started to decline drastically. Aging and drastic decline in personnel effectiveness necessitate the construction of a working reproductive mechanism. Thus, a choice has to be made: the nomenclature reproductive bloc requires massive personnel purges, which the elite will never freely accept; an elite reproductive bloc, on the other hand, will introduce greater political competition and weaker manual control over political process, which is not acceptable to the ruling group.

The neo-nomenclature system is also vulnerable to external factors. The 'Magnitsky Act' adopted by the US may serve as an illustration: it undermines one of the regime's basic principles that guarantees immunity for the officials in the power vertical in exchange for unconditional loyalty and obedience to the top leadership. Thus, a personalized power crisis is created, which is especially dangerous under a weak institutional framework. At the same time, there is also a crisis of delegative democracy that occurs as the person in power loses his credibility.

The pendulum of the relations between 'The Center' and the 'Regions' had swung too far toward the center until the middle of 2011, and has been coming back toward the regions ever since. Therefore, regionalization will be an extremely important trend in the next decade. No serious economic or political action on the national level is possible without substantially increasing the role played by regions. Nevertheless, the Kremlin appears to resist the trend instead of accommodating it.

The federation of corporations begins to morph into a corporation of regions. Putin's power 'verticalization' has reached its logical limit; now the time for horizontal structures has come. This change will bring radical transformation of political elites, dismantle corporate 'principalities' and replace them with regional ones.

The crisis of energy geopolitics and a fundamental change of external environment. Gazprom expansion and the idea of turning Russia into the 'energy superpower' were essentially stopped in their tracks by revolutionary changes in gas extraction technologies. Two overlapping factors affect Russia's standing in the global arena: world public opinion, which plays an increasingly important role in times of crisis, considers Putin's 'return' to be a step back; however, Putin cannot alter his 'bad cop' image acquired during the power sharing arrangement with Medvedev.

These trends make inevitable a substantial overhaul of the system. It should also be pointed out that there are two personalized power regimes in Russia, which further weakens the already fragile institutions: Chechnya's Ramzan Kadyrov regime increases the risks posed by Putin's personalized regime.

Not only experts, but the decision-makers themselves realize that the economic growth model used in the 2000s is no longer applicable. Also, there are fewer opportunities for investment: weak institutions stand in the way of creating a favorable investment climate. The government talks of the need for a new economic model and an improvement of the investment climate, while it refuses to acknowledge that any serious economic modernization is impossible in the absence of political modernization.

The increased instability of the last few years has boosted the interest in scenario analysis, in which possible scenarios are not looked at as an attempt to divine the future, but rather as a way to understand the present by constructing integral models that concern every major sphere of life in Russia.

Some of the best-known scenario studies produced during this period are: 'Finding of the Future: Strategy 2012' by Institute of Contemporary

Development (March 2011),[1] which was followed by more concrete thematic studies; the Economic Development Strategy-2020 commissioned by the government and conducted by a large expert team (2011);[2] Valdai Club-2012 projects; the 2011–12 CSR report;[3] the 2012 Institute of Socio-Economic and Political Studies (ISEPS) report;[4] 'Scenarios for the Russian Federation' report at the World Economic Forum in 2013.[5]

The above-listed projects are mostly focused on political dynamics (2011 INSOR report) or economic developments (Strategy-2012, Valdai-2012, and WEF-2013); the 2011 and 2012 CSR reports deal primarily with social aspects.

Our project used a broader, interdisciplinary approach; we did not limit ourselves to just politics and economics but sought to connect them to other aspects of Russian development. We were interested in identifying the trends in political, economic, demographic, and social developments and discovering possible triggers for the system's autonomous development. It was also important to us to analyze the potential impact of both the government and its opponents as they seek to change the objective trends in pursuit of their respective goals.

Such scenarios resemble an impromptu jazz performance more than that of a symphony orchestra, in which every musician is assigned a particular role. This approach is characterized by greater flexibility of the system and higher autonomy for each of its components.

The choice of baseline and time horizon is a key element of scenario analysis. The year 2025 is sufficiently far removed from today that the experts would not become captive to the trends of the political moment. At the same time, the date is close enough to the present day that the scenarios would not seem overly utopian. Besides, if the year 2013 is chosen as a frame of reference, this enables us to discuss 12 years of Putin's actual rule and almost 12 more years of his potential rule.

Scenario structure

Two dominant ideas that find different reflections in a number of chapters are the cyclical pattern of Russia's post-Soviet development (the 1990s–2000s–2010s) and the heterogeneity, or mosaic pattern, of Russia's socioeconomic structure. The first idea is expounded upon in Kirill Rogov's and Nikolai Petrov's chapters. The second concept became particularly popular in 2012 as the concept of 'several Russias'. It was developed by Natalia Zubarevich; in her chapter she analyzes the problem of human capital from the standpoint of economic and geographic diversity. Rogov and other experts also address the subject of 'several

Russias'. Public opinion dynamics and the character of state–society relations are discussed in Sam Greene's chapter. Mikhail Denisenko explores demographic trends which play a major role in socioeconomic and eventually political development and are easier to predict than socioeconomic and political ones. Economic development scenarios are examined in Boris Grozovsky's chapter, while Henry Hale's chapter deals with political aspects. Heterogeneity in time and space – the factor that virtually all our authors allude to – will become much more pronounced in Russia's near future. As a consequence of uneven geographic and power-hierarchy development, spatial contrasts and conflicts are bound to intensify. These conflicts, along with the development of the above trends, will serve as major drivers that will determine system change in a given timeframe.

We examined two extreme options, labeled *optimistic* and *pessimistic* scenarios. Under the optimistic scenario, political modernization begins at the top and gradually intensifies. Under the pessimistic scenario, the authorities do not want to, or simply cannot, make any changes, which leads to increasing public discontent that at some point replaces the 'Putin-style order' with the 'Yeltsin-style democratization'. The two continue to alternate in the future.

As was evidenced by the events of the second half of 2012 and early 2013, neither the optimistic nor the pessimistic scenario is likely to occur. A reactive modernization scenario seems more likely. Under this scenario, the regime does not have a 'grand plan' but merely reacts to new challenges, without adhering to a particular vector.

Elections, which play a key role in determining the vector of political development, may illustrate this scenario. On the one hand, the Kremlin restores direct elections of regional leaders (+), while, on the other, it creates municipal filters that allow the incumbent to remove any unwelcome candidates from the ballot (−). On the one hand, single-mandate districts are restored and party competition is encouraged (+); on the other, all elections are scheduled for the same day and moved to the early fall in order to play down election campaigns, reduce voter turnout and generally breed popular indifference toward the electoral process (−). When choosing between effectiveness and controllability, the Kremlin almost always picks the latter. As a result, elections do take place, but they increasingly cease to perform the only function they had accomplished in the past – that of strengthening the regime's legitimacy.

In order not to focus exclusively on the elites' behavior, it may be more appropriate to look at evolutionary and revolutionary scenarios. The evolutionary scenario calls for a more complex political system, which would ensure its own survival under the changing circumstances. However, the regime has neither strategic vision nor political will to implement the necessary improvements. The segment of the population that wants change is atomized and does not conceive of itself as a counterforce that has the means to put pressure on the authorities. Is the system then doomed to get out of control, and lead to a large-scale revolution? Apparently not: political development can occur through a series of microrevolutions. To ensure such development, the system has to shift from its current 'manual mode' to an 'automatic' one. Political dynamics should become more multistep and detailed and include regular elections.

External influences and internal factors

Two major factors are the drivers of change. These are: the price of oil, which determines the financial might of Putin's state; and the state's administrative effectiveness. Relations between federal and regional 'corporate' elites, as well as public activism, are derived from these two factors but play an important role of their own. All four are nonlinear and are not completely interrelated. If the oil price rises or remains stable, the administrative effectiveness is most likely to decline. This happens because the system, whose planning horizons are short, has no stimulus to undertake administrative (and, broadly speaking, political) modernization. Generally, declining oil prices should encourage the system to modernize structurally. However, the character of this modernization is largely dependent on the trajectory of such decline. Sharp decline will force the regime to search for additional reserves in order to fulfill its social obligations and thus avoid social instability. Only a relatively slow decline in oil prices over a long period of time may prompt the system to undertake structural reforms in order to raise effectiveness.

> *Oil prices rise* – everyone is happy; the elites get along fine. The administrative effectiveness declines, hence the increased risk of power crisis, which, in turn, may lead to increased public protests. The protests may accelerate regime evolution or even its change, if the crisis enters its acute phase.
>
> *Oil prices are stable or decrease gradually* – with social obligations becoming more of a burden to the Kremlin, it has to check elite appetites more strictly; thus, the elites' internal frictions intensify, and the authorities lose some of their support from the elites; reform plans

are postponed. Breaks within the elites and their appeals to public constituencies (disgruntled citizens) may lead to the dynamics described in the previous scenario.

Oil prices decline sharply – the elites' internal struggle becomes extremely intense, public discontent increases. The system is not ready for either of the challenges, and its collapse is only a matter of time. The elites – provided they manage to consolidate – replace the leader, thus erasing all his prior obligations, which will provide some stability to the system for a limited period of time.

All of these scenarios carry the risks of administrative crisis, elite squabbles, and confrontation between the people and the regime.

Until the late 2000s, the degradation of the political system was accompanied by economic growth, which in part allowed the damage to be concealed. However, since the economic growth model put to use during Putin's rule has exhausted its potential, serious internal restructuring is inevitable even if the price of oil keeps going up. Putin's advantages over Yeltsin have stopped working in his favor; he now competes against a younger, energetic, and luckier version of himself. The question is how long the reserves are going to last. Thus, the oil price levels cannot prevent serious economic and political crisis – they simply delay or hasten its arrival. At any event, even in the absence of an acute administrative crisis, it is a matter of two to three years.

It is common to describe Russian development in terms of inertia and path-dependence. However, under current conditions, the inertia scenario is likely to evolve as a phased transition rather than progressive movement. There are two explanations for this phenomenon. First, many of the development trends discussed above have reached their turning points, so it would be more appropriate to compare the current trend trajectory to that of a pendulum that stops right before our eyes, beginning its reverse movement. Second, the system has largely exhausted its resources. The recovery economic growth has ended; the utility and social infrastructures inherited from the Soviet era no longer exist; the personnel reserve formed at the time of active public politics is depleted; the overall political model that came about in the years of plenty is too primitive under the new conditions. All of this spells the end for inertial movement unless there are serious shifts and upheavals within the system.

The objective problems facing the system are exacerbated by the fact that the Kremlin and Putin for the most part continue to operate under the old paradigm. They are not able to fully comprehend the character of the new social mechanisms; nor can they react to the rapidly changing circumstances adequately and in a timely manner; therefore, they are bound to make mistakes. Thus, the regime's wishes and declarations clash with the trends of political and economic development. In this case, the regime's inadequate reaction may have even greater destructive effects, given the inflated expectations on the part of a significant segment of the population. These expectations are being eagerly supported by the regime itself, while its capacity to fulfill social obligations keeps declining.

Scenario breakdowns and transitions

Many specific developments can unfold along the general lines of the revolutionary or the evolutionary scenarios. Possible bifurcation points are associated with elections and other political events. Such specific scenarios are the product of external changes, risk factors, or system breakdowns that may be caused by both administrative decisions and unforeseen developments. The likelihood and timing of these 'elements of turbulence' cannot be rationally predicted; nevertheless, they have to be taken into account. Several lines of development are described below.

Another wave of global economic crisis and a decline in raw material prices

The price of oil unquestionably remains the most important factor that determines Russia's fortunes. As Thane Gustafson writes in his recent book on Russia's oil industry, 'Whichever path [Russia] chooses, oil will be a central part of the choice ... nothing so closely predicts the future of Russia as oil prices'.

As we pointed out above, a significant and sustained drop of raw material prices results in budget cuts and a renegotiating of social obligations, since the government will not be able to fully honor them. Both the elites and the public will have to tighten their belts, which will lead to greater internal conflicts within the elites as well as stirring political passions among the public. The economic structure, along with the entire structure of the resource-revenue-dependent system, will be revamped.

The internal elite conflicts will spill over into a public environment that has already displayed some rudiments of political organization. The opposing elite factions will appeal to the public and newly formed political structures; the country will experience a rebirth of genuine political competition. This scenario may lead to a deep political crisis that will force Putin's government to resort to repressive means in order to restore order. As a result, the nationalist elements inside or outside of the elite may remove the government from power. These elements will call for a greater degree of isolationism and dirigisme. The advance of the left and left-leaning liberal forces is also plausible. They will advocate for restoring social justice and accuse Putin's regime of squandering Russia's wealth of natural resources and being unable to roll back the country's decline. But, if the strong hand scenario is to be avoided, Russia might return to the traditional model that features a centralized monopoly on power. Russia's political system was excessively deinstitutionalized in the 2000s, and the public was too far removed from political participation; hence a seamless transition to a moderate and even relatively democratic political process appears impossible.

But, even if raw material (especially hydrocarbon) prices remain stable during the discussed timeframe, the general trend will still be similar, albeit less harsh.

'Russia without Putin'. A regime's stability can be tested by a hypothetical removal or replacement of key players. A year after Putin's return to the presidency, this scenario suddenly does not look all that outlandish. According to the public opinion polls, many Russians are ready for another president in 2018. Although they fail to name any concrete candidate who would be appropriate, the very thought that Putin may leave office no longer seems implausible. Besides, as the resource wealth decreases, so does Putin's role of a supreme benefit distributor and a universal arbiter of elite conflicts. Putin's disappearance can either bring forth a 'new Putin' or cause the elites to split. At any event, his departure from politics, or his drastic weakening and decline of popular support, may prompt a destabilization. Putin's inner circle remains a powerful presence in the (nonpublic) political space. This is a strong and tiered group of powerful players with a security service background who acquired enormous property holdings in the business and financial spheres during Putin's rule. A new ruler cannot afford to encroach on the group's interest. Any such attempts by an 'outsider' threaten to destabilize the country and may lead to a ferocious and possibly bloody fight. A fierce competitive battle over who will take over Putin's authority as supreme arbiter may ensue. Certain institutions may be strengthened as a result of the political struggle. For instance, the armed forces or the parliament's upper house, which were too weak to be considered serious political players, may gain

strength. This scenario somewhat resembles the internal elite power struggle that followed Iosif Stalin's death in 1953, since that period was also characterized by weak institutionalization.

Close or distant neighbors destabilized. Leadership change is almost certain to bring destabilization to Russia's close neighbors – Belarus, South Caucasus, and Central Asian states – given the personalized character of the regimes in these countries. Power transfer may be especially problematic in Central Asian states, where possible civil wars and humanitarian disasters pose direct political and economic threats to Russia. One cannot rule out the possibility of Arab-Spring-like developments in the Central Asian countries. Some of those countries' leaders have been in power for over two decades; they created authoritarian and even despotic regimes there, while failing to improve the harsh socioeconomic conditions. Moreover, radical Islam is on the rise in these areas. Perhaps in anticipation of these developments, Russia is trying to shore up the Collective Security Treaty Organization, whose forces may be used to disperse street protests and suppress other political unrest. Apart from the direct risk of importing instability, there are risks associated with the measures that may be undertaken in order to prevent 'color revolutions'. Especially if such measures fail to maintain stability, the risk of Russia's conflict with both China and the West (both of which are active in this region) will significantly increase. Russia's direct or indirect involvement in the possible use of force on the streets of any Central Asian capital will create serious problems for labor migrants in Russia, particularly in terms of their relations with the local population. A war in the Middle East may lead to a similar scenario, since Iran has a border with Russia in the Caspian; besides, the turmoil in Iran is bound to have an effect on Azerbaijan, which is even closer to Russia. The only difference in these scenarios is the scale of the conflict. The conflict in the Middle East will have global ramifications, thus increasing the dangers of confrontation with the West. The Greater Caucasus region also faces the risks of external destabilization, which probably exceed the internal threats.

'Soft disintegration'. This scenario features uncontrolled or loosely controlled decentralization or regionalization, which can take place if the system continues to decay and the federal center weakens, as happened in the 1990s. This scenario is quite plausible and would mean that the 'Chechen model' (an autocratic regime

operating beyond the Kremlin's control) would spread to other Russian regions. As a result, Chechnya itself can expand and/or similar models can be created beyond its borders. Contrary to popular belief, such changes will not be triggered by separatism. In fact, excessive centralization is a more likely cause: in seeking to expand its control the federal center risks overstraining its capacity.

The de facto, and in some aspects de jure, secession of some regions from Russia's legal and administrative realm may follow (borderline territories in the Far East and North Caucasus pose the highest risk). The federal authorities are aware of such risks, as evidenced by large-scale investment projects in the Far East. However, these measures cannot reverse the region's depopulation. The most energetic and enterprising segments of the population are leaving the Far East for Russia's European region. With the country's resources wearing thin, it will no longer be able to invest heavily in the Far East. This will weaken the region's ties to the federal center, while possibly strengthening its relations with the neighboring states, such as China, that are clearly interested in developing closer ties with Russia's borderline areas. Such 'soft separatism' does not necessarily imply physical separation; some regions in Russia's heartland may choose 'internal insulation', as was done by Tatarstan and Bashkortostan in the early 1990s. If such processes get underway, they may play a role in the elites' internal struggles.

In the long run, this scenario may have three possible outcomes: an actual disintegration, federalization, or recentralization (provided there are external changes). Any of these paths may be associated with foreign policy complications, as a number of more independently minded regions will conduct foreign policies that diverge from Russia's official stance.

'Split within the elites'. While the scenario that we labeled 'soft disintegration' relates to territorial disintegration, the split within the elites will produce corporate and institutional meltdown. Internal conflicts among the elites have intensified and will continue to escalate. Experts talk of elite fragmentation, if not fully developed splits (according to the report by the Center for Political Technologies[6]). The split is quite likely, especially as the supreme arbiter weakens and the competition between corporate political clans for a piece of the shrinking economic pie becomes more intense. The struggle of

verticals (i.e. rivalry between the hierarchical administrative structures within certain institutions, such as ministries and agencies) is already taking place and may well get out of control.

The 'Russia without Putin' or 'Russia with weakened Putin' scenarios exacerbated by resource depletion, further deterioration of infrastructure, and economic mismanagement can also lead to a split within elites. As a result, some elite groups may celebrate victory over others and bring the losing side under their control. Another possibility is strengthening of the corporate state model. In this case, the main elite groups will have to reach a power sharing agreement that will ensure that they receive their share of rent revenues.

> *Large-scale administrative crisis* may result from a vast man-made disaster. This scenario looks probable in the context of accidents and catastrophes that have become more frequent in the last few years. The ineffective state response to emergencies may also provoke a crisis that will feature mass protests and other instances of confrontation between society and the regime. It is easy to imagine that under certain conditions such local crisis will quickly morph into a nationwide one; hence, the decision-makers, and Putin himself, pay close personal attention to large projects, such as the preparation for the 2014 Sochi Winter Olympics. The president is clearly nervous about missing project completion deadlines and substandard quality of the works. Human factors and natural calamities can lead to simultaneous breakdowns in different parts of the country. The authorities may be forced to make crucial decisions in a time crunch in different regions, while they are faced with shrinking resources and gradual decline of public support. It should also be noted that negative factors that were described in other scenario breakdowns increase the likelihood of administrative crisis.
>
> *'Destabilization in Moscow'*. Just like other regions, Moscow is not immune from destabilization caused by inadequate policies of the federal government. However, the destabilization in the capital has stronger effects, since this is where protest activity is concentrated. The country is overly centralized, and Moscow plays a disproportionally large role in economics and other spheres. Consequently, everything that happens in the capital produces huge reverberations elsewhere.

One can safely predict that public discontent and street protests will be triggered in the future by socioeconomic and/or political developments. They may be caused by failing government services, lawlessness, prosecution of high-profile public figures, abuse of power by the police or government officials, such as mass election fraud, or by encroachment on individual freedoms, such as persecution of human rights activists or restrictions on Internet freedom. This scenario may unfold as a sudden avalanche-like reaction, for instance to restrictions on Internet use. Such restrictions, which have intensified since the second half of 2012, can raise the risk of active confrontation between the government and the progressive segment of the Moscow population.

The Moscow Duma election will be a crucial event on the city's political horizon. Currently, Moscow's legislature is totally dominated by 'United Russia', which does not enjoy broad support among the city voters. Thus, the upcoming 2014 election to the city legislature and the subsequent mayoral election will become a serious test for the regime, especially considering the voters' memories of electoral fraud committed during the 2011 parliamentary elections and the experience with volunteer election monitoring gained in 2011–12. Although political organization among the protesters is fairly weak at this point, it will be expected to grow as time passes. The political crisis in Moscow may evolve as a nationwide crisis that will exacerbate the divisions between the regime and society.

> *'The Third War in the Caucasus'.* The Kremlin's politics in the North Caucasus has reached an impasse: in this region violence has become part of everyday life; explosions, terrorist attacks, kidnappings, and summary executions are common, along with a resurgence of Islamic radicalism. The entire country is vulnerable to acts of terrorism; there were two terrorist attacks in Moscow in 2010 and 2011, in the span of less than a year. New armed clashes in the North Caucasus are frequently reported, which suggests that the conflict may expand.

Because of the highly personalized system of federal governance (in the case of North Caucasus, the same is true of regional governance), stability is held hostage to the whims of leaders and their personal relations. This primarily concerns Putin's and Kadyrov's regimes. Putin is forced to rely on Kadyrov, who is entrusted with the task of containing violence within his region. Kadyrov enjoys free rein despite blatant violations of human rights on Chechen territory and inexplicable murders of his rivals and critics across the globe.

The escalation of violence in the North Caucasus confronts the authorities with a difficult dilemma: the use of force will backfire, but a weak federal response may encourage Kadyrov to act even more independently. Xenophobic sentiments in Moscow and other large cities further exacerbate the problem.

A more rational approach to the problem of North Caucasus would be a formulation of a long-term strategy for the region's socioeconomic and humanitarian/cultural development. Although it does not necessarily guarantee success, such an approach could at least prevent the radicalization of the next generation if it is consistently implemented and receives serious financial support. However, the Russian authorities are generally not inclined to make strategic policies; instead, tactical approaches are favored, and solutions are devised as problems arise. We can clearly see this pattern in the North Caucasus, especially as it applies to the preparation for the Sochi Winter Olympics. The Games impose an artificial deadline: peace in the Caucasus becomes the government's major priority and must be secured at any cost in the run-up to the Games. It distracts the authorities from long-term projects; besides, large government investments into the North Caucasus further aggravate local corruption, which is especially vast here even by Russian standards. Corruption, in its turn, stifles any positive initiative.

With the Sochi Olympics fast approaching, the Kremlin puts its trust in the local elite clans and the external power structures, such as special police forces and state security personnel. Such tactics are intended to quell the unrest in the region, but they produce side effects when combined. The reliance on clans ('nativization') makes political life in the region more archaic and pits the clans against the power structures, which are being 'denativized'. The standoff between the two groups threatens a large-scale social explosion. If the situation remains peaceful in the run-up to the Olympics, it may become unstable once the Games are over and the inflated federal subsidies start sagging, forcing the elites to compete for their share of the falling revenues. Finally, the transformation of the presently smoldering civil conflict into an all-out war against the colonial power is also possible, which can upset anyone's calculations.

> *'Nationalist turn'*. In the 2000s, high-ranking federal officials had been cautiously avoiding playing the nationalist card. Ethnic riots in Kondopoga and the anti-Georgian campaign of 2007 are among the few exceptions in which government authorities resorted to

nationalist rhetoric. The majority of Russians harbor some degree of xenophobic sentiments, mostly directed at labor migrants from the Caucasus and Central Asia, which can be exploited by radical nationalists. The regime's attempt to preempt and take control of nationalist activism before it takes some organizational shape at the local level is perfectly understandable. It also makes sense that the authorities try to channel nationalist sentiments and co-opt the supporters of nationalism by replacing ethnic nationalism with state patriotism. As a rule, this technique is anchored in egregious anti-Americanism, explicit repudiation of liberal values, and fostering the public perception of Russia as a besieged fortress. It also signals a rejection of modernization and a turn to political and social conservatism. There is another risk as well: faced with the threat of ethnic nationalism, the government may be tempted to abandon the cautious approach it adopted in the 2000s and try to seize the initiative by playing the nationalist card. In this case, ethnic violence, which periodically spills over onto the streets of Russian cities, may get out of control. This, in turn, will provoke a response on the part of minorities.

The turn to nationalist policies can be either smooth or sharp; it can be active or reactive. It can be provoked by the policies of forcing ethnic Russians out of the Caucasus region and a war in the Caucasus, which we alluded to earlier. Attempts to turn Russia into a nation state, as well as similar processes in a number of ethnic republics, may lead to a conflict between nationalist ideologies. Mass ethnic riots in the Northern Caucasus and Moscow in December 2010 may serve as examples of these dynamics. Certain political developments can also contribute to a nationalist turn: for instance, Vladimir Zhirnovsky, who personified Russian 'nationalism lite', may exit the political scene, leaving it to real, no-nonsense nationalists. Finally, nationalists can be empowered as a result of relatively free elections.

The system's administrative effectiveness is deteriorating. In most cases, wild cards are programmed to cause system breakdowns. A series of simultaneous breakdowns is possible, and so an 'avalanche' effect.

If we are to draw conclusions from the oscillations of the last two decades, in 2013–15 we can expect either gradual or drastic modification of the current model of the state–society and center–periphery relations.

This modification, which will shape the subsequent developments leading to 2025, will be a product of a widening rift between a modernizing, post-Communist part of society and a largely paternalistic and backward state administration system. The elites' relations with Vladimir Putin will change as well. For the sake of preserving the system, different elite groups will try to steer him toward either greater conservatism or democracy; they may decide to cast him away altogether in order to have a free hand.

The problem with Russia's political system is its low level of institutionalization – even as compared with the Soviet system. As a result, business and political elites lack a tangible framework for consolidation and are unable to formulate and present their position to those at the top of the power vertical. The country's leadership closed all the avenues for the autonomous development of the system. They do not allow the system to grow in complexity, which is necessary for its preservation. On the other hand, the leadership is held hostage to a system with rapidly declining effectiveness. There appear to be only two possible exits from the current conundrum: the modernization of the system, which will allow it to survive under the new conditions, or its replacement, if the top leadership entirely loses control of the situation. The time factor will play an important role in determining whether the development will follow an accelerated evolutionary scenario or whether we are in for a revolution with an unpredictable outcome.

Notes

1. Institute of Contemporary Development (Institut Sovremennogo Razvitiya) (2011) *Obretenie buduschego: Strategiya-2012 (Finding of the Future: Strategy 2012)* (Moscow: INSOR, 2011), www.insor-russia.ru/files/Finding_of_the_Future%20.FULL_.pdf, date accessed 5 August 2013
2. Strategy-2020 (2012) *Strategiya-2020: Novaya model' rosta – novaya sotsial'naya politika*, Report (Moscow), http://2020strategy.ru/documents/32710234.html, date accessed 5 August, 2013.
3. 2012 Corporate Social Responsibility Report, http://csr.cisco.com/pages/csr-reports, date accessed 8 April 2013; 2011 Corporate Social Responsibility Report, http://www.cisco.com/web/about/citizenship/reports/pdfs/CSR_Report_2011.pdf, date accessed 8 April 2013.
4. ISEPS (2012) *Pryamye vybory gubernatorov i sistema sborov munitsipal'nykh podpisey v 2012 godu*, Report (Moscow).
5. The World Economic Forum (2013) 'Scenarios for the Russian Federation' report, http://www.weforum.org/reports/scenarios-russian-federation, date accessed 8 April 2013.
6. Center for Political Technologies (2013) *Vlast' – elity – obschestvo: Kontury novogo obchestvennogo dogovora*, Analytical Report (Moscow).

Bibliography

2011 Corporate Social Responsibility Report, http://www.cisco.com/web/about/ citizenship/reports/pdfs/CSR_Report_2011.pdf, date accessed 8 April 2013.

2012 Corporate Social Responsibility Report, http://csr.cisco.com/pages/csr-reports, date accessed 8 April 2013.

Center for Political Technologies (2013) *Vlast' – elity – obschestvo: Kontury novogo obchestvennogo dogovora*, Analytical Report (Moscow).

Institute of Contemporary Development (Institut Sovremennogo Razvitiya) (2011) *Obretenie buduschego: Strategiya-2012 (Finding of the Future: Strategy 2012)* (Moscow: INSOR, 2011), www.insor-russia.ru/files/Finding_of_the_ Future%20.FULL_.pdf, date accessed 5 August 2013.

Institute of Socio-Political and Economic Development (ISEPS) (2012) *Pryamye vybory gubernatorov i sistema sborov munitsipal'nykh podpisey v 2012 godu*, Report (Moscow).

Strategy-2020 (2012) *Strategiya-2020: Novaya model' rosta – novaya sotsial'naya politika*, Report (Moscow), http://2020strategy.ru/documents/32710234.html, date accessed 5 August 2013.

The World Economic Forum (2013) 'Scenarios for the Russian Federation' report, http://www.weforum.org/reports/scenarios-russian-federation, date accessed 8 April 2013.

1
Forty Years in the Desert: The Political Cycles of Post-Soviet Transition

Kirill Rogov

What matters? Public demand and political supply in hybrid regimes

Over the past ten years, the phenomenon of hybrid regimes (electoral authoritarianisms) has become a central problem in comparative political science. The progressivist image of 'Third Wave Democracy' has been replaced by an understanding that, in many of the countries that underwent liberalization at the end of the 20th century, democratic consolidation has been unsuccessful and transitional, hybrid regimes are demonstrating long-term stability. It would not be a stretch to claim that the Russian case, in particular, imparts a particular sense of scale and drama to the problem.

While some authors have sought structural explanations for the failure of democratic consolidation (cultural patterns and traditions, levels of socio-economic development, etc.), others have preferred a more pragmatic, institutional approach, which focuses on the political actors and institutions of the newly formed hybrid regimes.[1]

Proponents of the last instrumentalist approach assume that the stability of such regimes (electoral or competitive authoritarianisms) depends on their ability to create effective institutions, consolidate the elites, marginalize the opposition, and resist external pressure. Essentially, the idea is that weak popular support, which opens the door to the success of the opposition, is due to the regime's own ineffectiveness. The correlation between support for a given regime and the regime's effectiveness is not in doubt, but the question of causality is not so clear. In 2000, Vladimir Putin inherited from Boris Yeltsin an institutionally weak regime that comprised fragmented and competing elites, but, within a few short months, he came to enjoy tremendous support, which became one of the factors that allowed him to embark on his program of regime consolidation.

The Russian case of de-democratization should allow us to examine the more complicated, bilateral interactions between demand (public support) and supply (type of political regime). The high level of political competition in Russia in the 1990s, reflected in the outcomes of the 1993, 1995, 1996, and 1999 elections (no dominant player emerged and separation between the main contestants was negligible), together with the extremely low level of real security and legal protections, allows us to characterize the regime of this period as a competitive oligarchy (Robert Dahl's term).[2] This meant that elite groups that possessed the appropriate resources could form their own 'political representations' (parties, media holdings, Non Government Organizations (NGOs)) and compete for influence and resources in the public domain, by mobilizing supporters from among the citizenry.

In the 2000s, this system was dismantled by Vladimir Putin and replaced by one of 'imposed consensus', which, unlike its predecessor, made the control of resources by various elite groups contingent on their staying out of politics (ceasing to mobilize the electorate on their behalf).[3] This political transformation, along with the transition to a system of 'imposed consensus', served as a background to the famous 'Yukos' case.

This transformation, however, only became possible once support for the presidential office had increased. A system of 'imposed consensus' is not simply a product of 'stick and carrot' politics – the ability to punish the disloyal and reward the loyal. It also rests on the existence of political support 'from below', which raises the presumed costs of a confrontational strategy for elite groups. In the 1990s, an 'anti-Kremlin' stance nearly guaranteed popularity; the fact that, in the 2000s, such a stance returned minimal or negative dividends predisposed the majority of elite groups toward adopting a strategy of loyalty. In this way, the 'supply and demand' model focuses our attention on the interaction of two factors – elite competition and the fluctuation of public opinion. However, it does not appear that changes in public demand directly influence the political process. Rather, these changes influence the strategies of the elites and, consequently, the principles that govern their internal interactions. In other words, the 'instrumentalist' model described above has been turned upside down: strong support for the regime from 'below' contributes to a consolidation of the elites around the incumbent, which, in turn, allows the creation of effective institutions within an 'electoral authoritarianism'. Weak support, on the other hand, encourages the elites to engage in opportunistic strategies in order to exploit the weakness of the regime for their own purposes and increase internal divisions at various levels, thus preventing consolidation and further diminishing the administration's appeal in the eyes of the public. In other words, if support for a regime matters, then so does its value orientation – usually described as support for the principles and values of a regime or political demand.[4]

The supply-and-demand model and the cycles of post-Soviet political history

A quick glance at the public mood and the institutional tendencies of the political regime reflected in these sociological surveys reveals the surprising reversal they underwent in a mere ten years, from the late 1980s–early 1990s to the early 2000s. The wild enthusiasm for reform in the late 1980s had, by the mid-1990s, been succeeded by a sense of disappointment that was just as strong – a disappointment not only in the concept of 'reform', but in the entire complex of political doctrines (elections, independence, separation of powers) that had formed the basis of hopes and expectations at the time of the USSR's collapse. This period of disappointment was followed by an energetic consolidation of society around the ideas of 'stability' and 'order', a return to centralization and vertical hierarchies ('vertical power structure').

This change provoked a wave of pessimistic commentary about how the installation of democratic institutions in Russia in the late 1980s and early 1990s had been an artificial project that was at odds with the true level of societal development. However, toward the end of the 2000s, sociological surveys began to detect a change in the public mood. This led me to speculate about the possible beginning of a new cycle in Russian politics.[5] The idea was that the powerful pro-democracy movement of the late 1980s/early 1990s, together with the anti-democracy rollbacks of the early 2000s, had not been a movement toward a point of equilibrium, but, rather, a vacillation around a sort of trend line, and the shift in public opinion toward the end of the 2000s was an indication that the pendulum had begun to swing back. The events of 2011–12 and, specifically, the mass protests against the falsified elections provided further proof for this hypothesis.

My concept of political cycles is fundamentally different from that proposed by Henry Hale, who (in the spirit of the instrumentalist approach) believes them to be the result of the incompatibility of the principles of inter-elite cooperation, characteristic of hybrid regimes, with their constitutional design.[6] In my view, the oscillations are caused by shifts in public opinion, which influence the strategies of the elites and, as a result, impact the dynamics of the political regime. In developing the ideas of his father, Arthur Schlesinger, Jr relied on Hirschman's *Shifting Involvements*, which used models of consumer behavior to examine shifts in socio-political trends.[7] In this context, the key concepts are those of consumer (public) 'expectations' and consumer (public) 'disappointment', which, together, determine the dynamics of consumer (public) preference. This suggests a slightly different interpretation of the two 'poles' between which the pendulum swings: periods when social problems are at the center of attention and citizens work to find solutions to problems of public good are succeeded by periods of disenchantment and a return to the idea of the private good and a focus on individual life and individual needs. These oscillations determine shifts in political preferences.[8]

What were the defining features of the public mood of the late 1980s/early 1990s? First, a nearly uniform demand for 'independence' and intense criticism of the centralization of the Soviet system; second, a feeling that nearly every aspect of economic and public life should be reformed, that public institutions were dysfunctional and that they should be replaced by 'new' ones; and, finally, a sharp increase in the public's involvement in political life, caused by a disenchantment with the political institutions of the 'Old Regime'. These three main points defined the reformist agenda of the first cycle.

Disappointment in each of the three elements of this agenda over the course of the 1990s provided the basis for the rise of the very different aspirations of the late 1990s–early 2000s. The costs of reform turned out to be unexpectedly high and its results appeared contradictory. The idea of 'reform' quickly lost its appeal. In a setting where the rule of law was weak, decentralization (the realization of the desire for 'independence') led to a decentralization of arbitrariness and exponential growth in the number of conflicts between various members of the social order, each armed with his own authority. These unfortunate results predictably led to a sharp decline in the value of political engagement in the eyes of the public. This disappointment set the stage for the consolidation of the counter-reformist agenda (the stability agenda), which appeared, to a large extent, as the mirror image of its reformist predecessor.

It is worth emphasizing that both agendas are part of the transitional paradigm: both are based on a sense that the political institutions are unsound and that the current state of affairs is in some way unbalanced.

At the same time, the two agendas reflect fundamentally distinct reactions to such conditions: the reformist agenda rests on the belief that society can find a logical solution to the problems it faces; the counter-reformist agenda rests on a distrust of mass actions, an alienation from politics, a concentration on personal problems and personal consumption, and an increase in demand for 'external management' in politics.

The followers of the instrumentalist approach argue that Gorbachev's 'perestroika' and the subsequent collapse of the Soviet system were the result of the breakup of the Soviet elite. In this context, mass actions such as the large-scale demonstrations in Moscow and other cities, worker strikes, and the results of the first competitive elections of 1989–91 are regarded as a function of this breakup. A breakup of the elite takes place when it becomes impossible to reconcile differences within the framework of the old institutions and procedures, and the competing entities expand the circle of actors involved in the conflict, mobilizing their supporters around alternative political doctrines. This, of course, presupposes weakening support for the fundamental values of a regime and a demand for alternative solutions.

The two-sided nature of this process hints at the existence of two phases in the political cycle. The first is characterized by an erosion of the values of the existing regime: during this period, the political regime continues to appear stable (its stability in this phase is usually exaggerated), but support for the regime begins to weaken noticeably at various levels of society, the public begins to perceive political institutions as ineffective, and the basic values and goals of the regime are called into question.

The next phase of the cycle is characterized by a breakup of the elite and the emergence of a consolidated alternative agenda. The demand for change creates, for certain elite groups, a window of opportunity that did not exist under the institutions and practices of the old regime. As the values of the old regime are questioned and rejected, a new system of ideals is formed – a 'road map' for the implementation of new values capable of mobilizing mass support. When a portion of the elite declares its allegiance to the 'new agenda', the opposition gathers strength, while the organizational (mobilizing) potential of the old regime falls abruptly. This leads to a period of crisis and political instability, which is followed by various attempts to implement the new set of political values as part of a program of political reform.

The breakup of the Soviet elite and the heady political developments of the late 1980s are difficult to comprehend without looking a bit further back in time. After Leonid Brezhnev's death in 1982, the long-standing status quo was disrupted. The succession of funerals that followed was greeted with jokes, pointing to a crisis in the ideology of 'stability' and the institutions meant to maintain it. Despite the growing severity of repression against the dissidents themselves, dissident doctrines saw a sharp rise in popularity and entered mass discourse for the first time. The public was soon convinced of the total (systemic) ineffectiveness of the economic and social order and the need for change. At the same time, the elites began to formulate different plans of escape from the institutional crisis of the 'Old Regime' and seek support 'from below'.

In contrast, during the mid-1990s, the difficulties and failures of reform led to the public's profound disappointment in the foundational myths of reformism. An extremely low level of satisfaction with the political regime of the time – its institutions, elites, and leaders – created an increase in public demand for a new agenda, centered around such values as 'order' and 'stability'. At the same time, the institutions responsible for promoting political engagement, so popular in the late 1980s–early 1990s, lost their value in the eyes of a public ready to delegate its political authority to Putin.

In sum, according to the model proposed in this paper, the 'big transition' of Russian political history has entered its fourth decade (1980s–2010s) and, at the moment, appears to consist of the succession of the following phases of two cycles and the beginning of a third:

Cycle 1: early 1980s–1987: an erosion of the values of the Soviet system and a weakening of support for the regime;
1988–1993: a period of turbulence: consolidation of the reformist agenda, breakup of the elites, and political transition (institutional transformation);
Cycle 2: 1993–1999: an erosion of the values of the reformist period and a weakening of support for the regime;
1999–mid-2000s: consolidation of the counter-reformist agenda and an institutional solidification of authoritarianism;
Cycle 3: late 2000s–early 2010s: erosions of the values of counter-reform and a weakening of support for the regime.

Shifting values: 'firm hand', centralization, 'order', and 'human rights'

The instability of the institutional environment and the heterogeneity of social practices associated with different models of political organization are responsible for the inconsistency of survey results regarding Russians' political preferences. Given the difficulty in interpreting political preferences, I will limit the discussion to evidence gathered in response to questions posed over a number of years. This will allow me to evaluate both the stability of distribution and the direction of change (except when explicitly noted, all post-2005 studies are from 'Levada Center' and all pre-2005 ones from the Russia Public Opinion Research Center).

The coexistence of various ideals of social organization in public opinion should lead, it would seem, to a range of answers to similar questions. For example, the traditionally strong support for the idea of a 'firm hand' in Russia should serve as evidence of the consistently high demand for authoritarianism (see Figure 1.1).

The picture becomes less clear, however, when we compare these findings with the answers to a question that also uses 'hand' as a metaphor, but does not refer to the journalistic cliché contained in the previous question: 'should power be concentrated in the hands of one

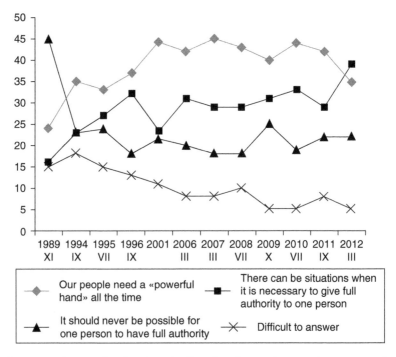

Figure 1.1 Support for the idea of a 'firm hand'. Distribution of answers to the question: 'Are there times in a country's history when society needs a strong and powerful leader, a "firm hand"?'

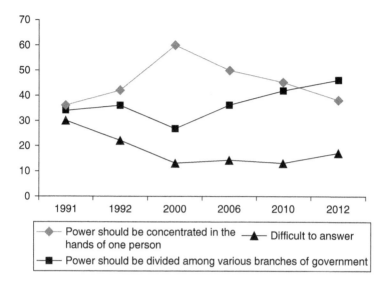

Figure 1.2 Demand for centralization. Distribution of answers to the question: 'What would be best: for power to be concentrated in the hands of one person or for it to be divided among various groups (offices/branches of government)?'

person or should it be divided among various branches of government?' (See Figure 1.2.)

As we can see, in the early 1990s, respondents did not really understand the value of a separation of powers and were confused by the very subject of the question (30 per cent 'could not come up with an answer'); in the late 1990s–early 2000s, they clearly favored 'syncretic' (unified) power; and in the second half of the 2000s and the early 2010s, they actively reconsidered their stance on the issue – close to 50 per cent of the respondents favored a separation of powers. How should we interpret the difference between the two studies?

First, we should note that, despite their common use of the 'hand' metaphor, the studies are asking slightly different questions. The first study is concerned not only with the structure of government, but with the ability of society to self-organize and maintain order ('our people cannot do without...'). Demand for a 'firm hand' is set against lawlessness and anarchy, as well as democratic pluralism, and reflects the public's general skepticism. It appears that demand for authoritarianism in a 'transitional society' is based on distrust of the 'political community' – the entirety of the political process, society, and all of its members – and its ability to self-organize. This may explain the popularity of the idea of a 'benevolent dictator', that is, a political system that promotes the public good despite a society's low capacity for self-organization. This means that demand for democratization will fall as society's skepticism about its own capacity for self-organization increases (as happened in the late 1990s) and rise as skepticism about the desirability of a benevolent dictator increases.

A corresponding trend of increasing demand for centralized government in the late 1990s and early 2000s and decreasing demand in the second half of the 2000s can be seen in the changing distribution of responses to a number of slightly different questions. Take, for example, respondents' shifting attitudes toward the idea of a 'multi-party system' over the past two decades (see Figure 1.3).

The question first posed in 1990 was: 'Do you agree that the Soviet Union needs to adopt a multi-party system?' In the years that followed, four possible answers were provided: (1) Russia needs one ruling party, (2) Russia needs two or three strong parties, (3) Russia needs many small parties, (4) no parties are necessary; the total of answers 1 and 4 represents those opposed to a multi-party system; the total of answers 2 and 3 represents those in favor of a multi-party system.

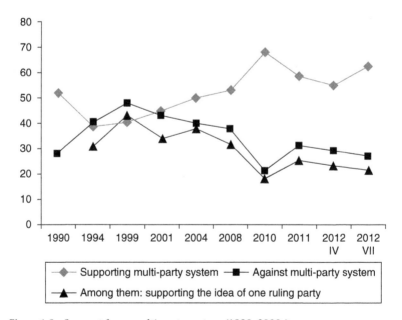

Figure 1.3 Support for a multi-party system (1990–2000s)

In 1990, a multi-party system was favored by a majority of respondents, but by the mid-1990s it had become seriously devalued. By the mid-2000s, however, the proponents of a multi-party system once again gained the upper hand. Finally, in the period following the economic crisis, support for a multi-party system sharply increased, surpassing levels from the early 1990s (more than 60 per cent). Accordingly, the idea of a 'ruling party' became less popular: in the second half of the 1990s and even in the first half of the 2000s, 35 per cent of respondents supported the idea of such a party, but already by the mid-2000s the popularity of this idea had begun to drop rapidly.

The same trend can be seen in the shifting response to similar questions about the necessity (benefit) of political opposition (at the beginning of the 2000s, 56–59 per cent deemed it a necessity; by the end of the decade, the number had risen to 66–71 per cent); opposition parties (at the beginning of the 2000s, around 50 per cent were 'for' such parties; in the mid-2000s, the number rose to around 60 per cent; and in 2010–12, it reached 70 per cent), and the 'freedom to criticize the government' (around 65 per cent in 2006–07 and 75–79 per cent in 2010–11). The idea of centralized and syncretic power started gaining popularity in the mid-1990s and reached its apogee in the first half of the 2000s, at which point its popularity began to decrease, while the perceived value of various balancing mechanisms to combat excessive centralization gradually began to grow.

At the same time, the value placed on 'order' – a key concept of the counter-reformist agenda – began to decrease in the eyes of Russian citizens. For example, there is an observable trend in responses to the question: 'What is more important: order, even at the cost of limiting certain democratic rights, or democracy, even if a certain leeway must be given to destructive elements?'

Even more evident is the shifting distribution of responses to the question: 'What is more important, order or human rights?' The ratio of those who preferred order at the expense of human rights to those who prioritized human rights changed from 2 to 1 at the end of the 1990s to 1.25 to 1 by the beginning of the 2010s (see Figure 1.4).

At the same time, the meaning of the concept of 'human rights' has also changed somewhat.

If we divide the rights listed for the respondents into two groups, basic and social rights (ranked 1–5 in 1994; see Table 1.1) and individual and political rights (ranked 6–10 in 1994; see table 1.1), we see that the first set of 'rights' has traditionally been highly valued and has, despite certain fluctuations, remained at its 1994 levels. The importance of the

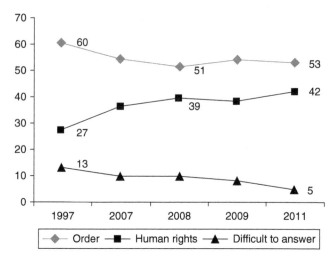

Figure 1.4   Order and human rights. Distribution of responses to the question: 'What is more important: Maintenance of order or respect for human rights?'

second group of 'rights', on the other hand, began to rise dramatically in the late 2000s: over the entire timespan from the mid-1990s to the mid-2000s the proportion of responses favoring rights from the second group was 22–24 per cent and from the first group 76–78 per cent, while in surveys from 2010 to 2011 the proportion was 32–34 per cent and 66–68 per cent respectively.

Note that the rights that have seen the biggest surge (freedom of speech and information) are by their nature passive, although they can clearly be defined as democratic, while the 'active' democratic right – the right to vote – remains less significant.

By no means do the findings listed above represent a fundamental change in the way Russians view the political organization of society; paternalistic models remain dominant and political participation and political rights (and, accordingly, political competition) are considered relatively unimportant. At the same time, certain shifts are clearly observable: strengthening of support for centralized authority and the absolute value of 'order' in the late 1990s and early 2000s was succeeded, in the late 2000s and early 2010s, by growing support for the idea of 'checks and balances', division of powers, and the protection of individual rights. Within the range of individual rights, traditional social rights (associated with 'order') continued to enjoy strong support, but passive political rights began to grow in popularity.

Table 1.1 Which of the following human rights are the most important?

	August 1994	April 1999	October 2003	October 2006	January 2009	October 2010
Basic and social rights (survival values)						
1 The right to have a free education, medical care, maintenance in old age and in illness	64	68	66	74	68	69
2 The right to live	63	57	50	64	58	57
3 Personal immunity, inviolability	55	46	45	50	45	51
4 The right to have a well-paid professional job	49	53	49	56	51	50
5 The right for the 'minimum of subsistence' guaranteed by the state	33	33	38	40	31	36
Individual and political rights (liberal values)						
6 The right to own property	29	23	28	35	33	38
7 Freedom of speech	18	14	19	28	28	34
8 Freedom of religion	14	8	12	17	15	22
9 The right to elect one's representatives to governing bodies	9	8	10	14	13	20
10 The right for information	8	9	15	17	14	22

Erosion of support: Changing appreciation of the quality of a regime and of its institutions

Survey results from the second half of the 2000s show a gradual shift away from the values of the counter-reformist agenda ('centralization', 'hierarchy', 'order'). Results from the early 2010s demonstrate a continuation of this trend. But, although, in 2007–09, when this trend first emerged, the popularity rating of the political regime – its leaders and institutions – was still quite high, the most important development of the post-crisis period has been the decrease on this score, too.

In the early 2000s, the number of people who chose 'increased chaos and anarchy' in response to a question about which direction Russia was headed dropped rapidly, while the number of those who answered positively, choosing 'development of democracy', rose sharply (see Figure 1.5). In the mid-2000s, the number of those who chose 'chaos and anarchy' continued to drop, while the proportion of positive responses

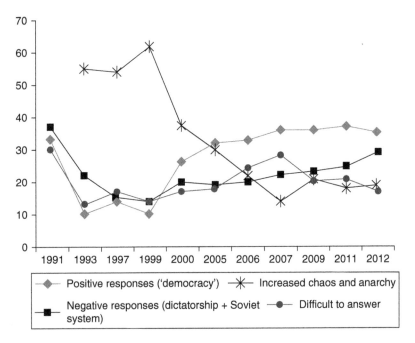

Figure 1.5 What will replace anarchy? Distribution of positive and negative evaluations of the 'new regime'

remained unchanged, with growth only in the 'unable to respond' category. In the late 2000s and early 2010s, a growing percentage chose 'the onset of dictatorship' (from 12–13 per cent to 18–19 per cent). The proportion of positive ('democracy') responses remained at 35 per cent, but the sum of negative responses (dictatorship + Soviet system) grew from 20 per cent to 30 per cent.

In 1991, three possible responses to the question were provided: 'the development of democracy', 'the maintenance of the previous system', and 'the onset of dictatorship'.

The same trend is evident in the changing responses to a question that described the situation in 'terms of development': 'What is happening in Russia today: development and growth, stabilization, or slowing-down and stagnation?' In the early 2000s, 35 per cent of respondents described the situation as one of 'stabilization' and two equal groups of around 20 per cent chose 'slowing-down and stagnation' and 'development and growth'; by 2007, the number of those who chose this last option had risen to 40 per cent, while 'slowing-down and stagnation' remained at around 20 per cent. In the post-crisis period, however, the number of negative responses shot up: in 2011, 36 per cent chose 'slowing-down and stagnation' and only half as many (18 per cent) 'development and growth'.

The fact that an increase in the proportion of positive evaluations of the 'new regime' in the early 2000s (culminating in the mid-2000s) was succeeded by a fairly rapid decrease by the end of the decade reflects a significant reevaluation of the *quality* of the political regime – a reevaluation not just of its values and basic mythologies (which were discussed above), but of its effectiveness (and the effectiveness of its leaders and institutions) in attaining developmental goals. This tendency can be seen most clearly in responses to questions regarding the levels of corruption and bureaucratization (administrative ineffectiveness) under the current government as compared with the 'Old Regime' (see Figure 1.6).

In the early 2000s, around 60 per cent of respondents believed that the level of corruption was the same, around 15 per cent that it was higher, and around 20 per cent that it was lower. In the mid-2000s, the proportion of responses at the extremes ('higher'–'lower') increased in equal measure. The decisive shift took place in the late 2000s and early 2010s, when the number of those who believed that the levels of corruption and bureaucratization had increased reached 50 per cent, while the number of those who thought that they had decreased dropped to a marginal 6–7 per cent.

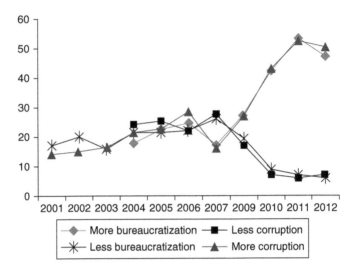

Figure 1.6   Evaluations of corruption and ineffectiveness. Distribution of answers to the question: 'Is the current level of government theft and corruption higher or lower than under Yeltsin/ten years ago?'

The reinterpretation of the hierarchy and importance of the regime's political values ('order', 'centralization', and 'stability') and the increasingly negative evaluation of its quality led to a reevaluation of its central institutional doctrine – 'vertical power structure': in the mid-2000s, those who thought that 'verticality' did more good than harm outnumbered those who held the opposite view; today, those for and against 'verticality', as well as those unable to respond, represent three roughly equal groups (see Figure 1.7).

At the same time, trust in the institutions that embody the idea of 'vertical power structure' – the offices of president and prime minister – began to decrease. Although low levels of trust in government have characterized Russian public opinion throughout the entire transitional period, the institutions that represented 'vertical power structure' stood apart from the rest during the 2000s and inspired considerable levels of trust. By the end of the 2000s and the beginning of the 2010s, this separation had virtually disappeared (Figure 1.8).

The decrease in support for the values of the regime ('order', 'stability', and 'centralization'), followed by a decrease in positive evaluations of the quality of the regime itself, led to a predictable redistribution of preferences for various political systems – the Soviet system, the current Russian system, and the democratic system of Western countries.

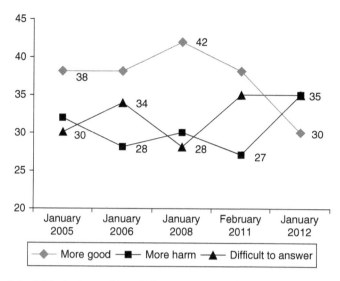

Figure 1.7 Attitudes toward 'vertical power structure'. Distribution over time of answers to the question: 'Vertical power structure...does it do more harm or more good?'

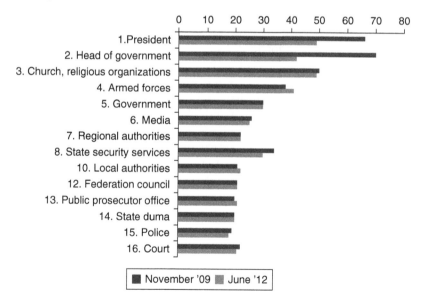

Figure 1.8 Trust in the institutions of 'vertical power structure': Percentage of respondents who answered that the relevant institution 'is generally worthy of trust'

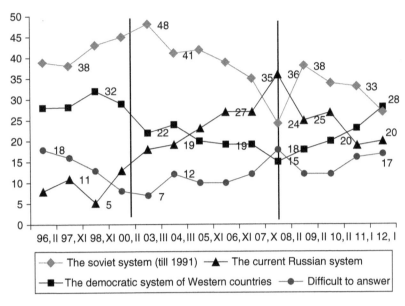

Figure 1.9   Choice of preferred political system over time

Figure 1.9 clearly shows the succession of the three phases. In the late 1990s and early 2000s, the Soviet system was practically without rival in terms of popularity (40–50 per cent support), while support for 'the current system' was at critically low levels. During the 2000s, support for 'the current system' grew rapidly as the number of respondents who favored the Soviet system and Western-style democracy dropped (from 45 per cent to 25 per cent and from 30 per cent to 15 per cent, respectively). The trend was reversed after the economic crisis: the first reaction to the crisis may have been a 'renaissance' in the popularity of the Soviet system, but, in the period of economic recovery between 2009 and 2012, the popularity of both the Soviet and 'current' systems decreased, while support for Western-style democracy increased. To sum up, the situation at the beginning of the 2010s appears fundamentally changed relative to that of the mid-2000s: both the Soviet system and Western-style democracy garner 30 per cent support, the 'current' regime 20 per cent, with 20 per cent undecided.

In this context, the oft-discussed drop in Putin's approval rating in 2010–11 appears not so much as evidence of Putin 'fatigue', but more as part of a gradual process of changing demands and preferences and eroding support for the values and institutions of the political regime. The relative majority that coalesced around the value orientations embodied by Putin in the 2000s broke apart in the late 2000s and early 2010s.

The mobile majority: The *Zugzwang* of 'benevolent authoritarianism'

In the second half of the 2000s, the importance and significance of the values ('order', 'centralization', and 'stability') that formed the core of the counter-reformist agenda of 'Putinism' began to decrease. The erosion of the ideological foundations of the political regime in the post-crisis period (2009–12) was reinforced by a relatively sharp drop in the evaluation of its quality – an attitude manifested in the abrupt increase in the number of those convinced of the regime's corruption and ineffectiveness ('bureaucratization') and the diminishing trust in its institutions (the office of president, the 'vertical power structure') and leaders (Putin and Medvedev's approval ratings).

A perfectly legitimate question is whether this trend is the result of real changes in the functioning of the regime or of a reevaluation of the political system as a result of a 'demand-side' shift in the hierarchy of political values. The answer is not obvious. Did the regime become less effective in 2009–11 or was it the perception of the political system that changed? According to international ratings agencies, Russian governance effectiveness did not drop in the wake of the economic crisis, but, rather, stabilized (or even improved a bit) following a period of rapid deterioration before the onset of the crisis. Corruption ratings are an exception, but they reflect the 'perception of corruption', not actual experience, and are apparently associated with decreasing levels of trust in the political regime and its institutions.[9] With this in mind, the fact that a shift in the corruption and bureaucratization ratings occurred abruptly and in unison seems to indicate that it was largely caused by a change in the perception of the regime and not by any real change in the political system.

Economic factors do not easily explain this shift: the sudden drop in ratings did not occur during the crisis, but afterward, during the post-crisis period of economic recovery and renewed growth (although not as rapid as before) of per capita income. Traditionally, presidential approval ratings and general levels of public satisfaction in Russia strictly correlate with economic performance, but in the post-crisis period this correlation has disappeared.[10] It is quite probable, therefore, that the increasingly negative perception of the regime's quality and the decrease in support for its institutions and leaders are attributable to demand-side changes (the shift in values) described above.

In other words, the decrease in the regime's perceived quality appears to have been caused by its inability to meet a new set of expectations, which accord far less importance to the ideas of 'order' and 'centralization' than to those of 'balance', 'protection of rights', and 'autonomy'. The point is not that corruption has increased, but that its 'negative costs' relative to the new value system have grown (at the height of the regime's popularity, this cost seemed minimal compared with other priorities, particularly those associated with 'restoring order'). Returning to the distinction between a 'firm hand' and 'democracy' in a transitional society, I would suggest that the weakening support for the ideological components of the regime (the values of the counter-reformist agenda) and the decrease in its perceived quality (effectiveness) are two parts of the same process: the gradual disenchantment with the idea of benevolent authoritarianism and the growing sense of its practical limitations. This disappointment in 'benevolent authoritarianism' is evident not only in the diminishing support for a 'firm hand', seen in surveys from 2011–12 (see Figure 1.1), and in the drop in Putin's approval rating, but also in the growing skepticism with regard to the one-party system, associated with the sharp rise in support for a multi-party system in the late 2000s and early 2010s (Figure 1.3).

In October 2011, respondents were presented with a question that used the now familiar 'hand' metaphor, accompanied by a much more starkly formulated alternative:

> Which do you agree with? All power in Russia should be concentrated in the firm hands of one person and elections and so-called democratic freedoms are unnecessary, or – Democratic freedoms should always serve as the foundation of social order; under no circumstances should power be concentrated in the hands of one person.

Thirty-three per cent of respondents chose the first option and 59 the second. It is notable that the percentage of respondents that favored the concentration of power in 'firm hands' is the same as that which opted for 'the Russian people always needs a firm hand' in the traditional version of the survey from March 2012 (see Figure 1.1), and that the pro-democracy majority (59 per cent) is essentially the sum of those (from the same survey) who chose the anti-authoritarian option – 'under no circumstances should power be concentrated in the hands of one person' – and the compromise option – 'there are certain times when it is necessary to concentrate the entire power of government in the hands of a single person'.

Thus, in addition to supporters of a 'firm hand' (authoritarian and hierarchical power) and supporters of democracy (divided and limited power), there exists a third group that prefers democracy, but allows a retreat to the authoritarian model when no other method of meeting pressing public needs is available. This is the group that supports 'benevolent authoritarianism' and is capable of creating either a pro-democracy or pro-authoritarian majority by allying itself with either of the two extreme factions, depending on its opinion of the goals and effectiveness of the current government.

Another conclusion that can be drawn from the data cited above is that, although support for 'syncretic' vertical power structures characteristic of the political system of the 2000s is decreasing, no consolidation around an alternative model of political organization has taken place. The trend, practically across the board, is either an increase in the number of undecided respondents or a parity between the groups that support opposite or incompatible positions. In my view, this is not evidence of a 'polarization' of society, but of the 'transitional' nature of the current situation – the previous coalitions that led to majority support for the counter-reformist agenda and benevolent authoritarianism have collapsed, and new ones have yet to be created.

Returning to the theory of the periodicity of political cycles and their component phases, I would suggest that, over the last few years, a number of signs have pointed to the erosion of support for the current regime, in terms of both its political values and the perception of its quality (of its institutions and leaders). This sets the stage for the transition to the next phase, which, according to this hypothesis, is characterized by a breakup of the elite and attempts to create a new reformist agenda, all in the context of growing disenchantment with the old regime.

At this stage, the threat that Vladimir Putin's political regime is facing is not *Endspiel* (the immediate loss of power), but of *Zugzwang*. The regime is presented with the following dilemma: in order to remain effective and maintain the qualities seen as its main positives by a large portion of the population, the regime must prevent the collapse of its 'imposed consensus' and preserve the consolidation of the elite. But to accomplish this during a time of weakening support, it must heighten the level of authoritarianism (increase the frequency of particular acts of repression). However, such a development is at odds with the change in public demand noted above, which has led to a situation where the citizenry expects precisely the reverse of a crackdown – a softening of the regime, an expansion of the autonomy of various levels of the social hierarchy, and a guarantee of greater security. This contradiction creates new and growing risks.

The cycle hypothesis and the long-term prospects of the political system

Massive political convulsions, which strike outside observers as unexpected, are the result of the painstaking and near-invisible work of the 'mole of history'. At some point, the accumulated tensions between demand (expectations) and supply find an outlet that allows the pressure to flow from one level of the political system to another (as we saw earlier, a decrease in the support for the founding myths and values of the regime is 'translated' into the perception of the quality of the regime, its institutions, and, eventually, its leaders). From the point of view of 'the big transition', Putin's 'stability', itself largely revanchist in nature, was a short respite, not a long-term equilibrium. The fact that several of the key questions of the post-Soviet period (in particular, the problem of the compatibility of political and legal regimes) went unanswered during the last reformist cycle means that they must come up again during the next cycle. In my view, the 2010s are bound to become a period of dramatic new exploration in this direction. Using the duration of the previous cycles as a guide, we can expect the current one to last for most of the decade.

The impossibility of compensating for the observed decrease in support by either substantially increasing the 'rewards' for loyalty or maintaining high levels of repression over the long term suggests a probable democratization of the Russian political regime. A modernization of the regime and moderate democratization involving the introduction of new checks on the overcentralization of power are policies that enjoy a virtual consensus among most of the elite and the centrist majority of the population. Only those from Putin's inner circle, who have enjoyed enormous advantages over the last ten years, would disapprove of such a development. It is impossible to predict when, how, and as a result of what factors (probably accidental) this clash of interests will be resolved. As we have seen, when support for a regime has nearly totally eroded, single episodes such as the murder of a journalist or the self-immolation of a fruit vendor can lead to a complete loss of trust in the regime and its rapid collapse.

At the same time, even if a full-blown crisis of the Putin regime and a subsequent democratization of political life looks likely over the course of the current political cycle, consolidation of a democratic regime in Russia should probably not be expected until the next cycle, in the 2020s. In my view, several factors make democratic consolidation during the current cycle impossible.

First, the availability of substantial rents from the export of raw materials in the context of an incomplete restructuring of industry creates incentives for massive redistribution and greatly expands the government's role in the economy. The formation of multiple redistribution chains in conditions of insufficiently restructured industrial and infrastructural sectors creates a demand for a certain type of regime.[11] At the same time, the rapid growth of average income leads to an expansion in the consumer and service sectors of the economy, creating a demand for alternative political models. The increase in the economic and political influence of these sectors will be the main trend to follow over the course of this decade.

It is clear that a relatively long-term drop in oil prices will lead to a sudden contraction in the size of rent that is available for redistribution and, as a result, to the rapid collapse of the 'imposed consensus' and a transition to a more pluralistic political model. At the same time, experts agree (see, in particular, Zubarevich's chapter in this volume) that an economic crisis and decrease in income would slow the process of urbanization and modernization in those parts of the country that are not yet involved in this process.

In the proposed model, it is important to distinguish between democratization derived from the collapse of the 'imposed consensus', which creates conditions of open competition for the elite, and democratization resulting from demand 'from below'. In the first case, the return to a pluralistic model of competition may not be supported by a strong rule of law and principled protection of rights, leading to a reappearance of 'weak' democracy (competitive oligarchy). Democratic demand 'from below' is more focused on guaranteeing the security of rights, ensuring equality of opportunity, and improving the quality of public services, and considers public competition to be simply a means of achieving these goals. In addition, demand 'from below' entails a restriction on the 'privileges' of the elite, which, for the latter group, is one of the real risks of a democratic system. If, at the moment, demand for democratization comes both 'from below' and from the elite, then the next phase might reveal a stark divergence in the goals of these two groups, leading to a potential increase in leftist sentiment. The existence of two alternatives to the Putin political model – the liberal-democratic and social-democratic options – is clearly evident in the structure of the opposition movement and in the patterns of opposition voting in the parliamentary and presidential elections of 2011–12.

Finally, the differences in socio-economic development and political culture in the various regions of the country pose a serious threat to democratic consolidation in Russia. The managed, unfree elections of the last decade have been associated, paradoxically, with an enormous range in the results in different regions: in the 2003 and 2007 parliamentary elections, the difference between the dominant party's best and worst results was over 50 percentage points; in the 2011 election, the difference was 70 percentage points. Such an artificial distribution is primarily explained by the existence of a 'tail' – a group of regions with anomalously high support for the 'party in power' (Figure 1.10).

If we consider the results of the most recent parliamentary elections, which triggered large-scale protests in big cities, it is possible to divide the regions into three types: in 32 regions, 'United Russia' received less than 40 per cent of the vote (group 1); in 20 regions, it received more than 60 per cent (group 3); and 33 regions fell somewhere in the middle – 40–60 per cent (group 2). It is clear that in the first group, despite

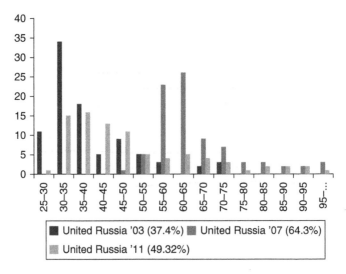

Figure 1.10 Voting for the dominant party by region. Number of regions (vertical axis), voting figures for 'United Russia' that fit the given interval (horizontal axis, %)

the fact that the elections were not free or fair, voters' preference was meaningful and had a substantial impact on the official results. This group is made up of industrial regions with large urban centers and traditional 'red' regions. In any case, elements of a pluralistic political culture can be found here: it is impossible for the federal or regional governments to categorically ignore the preferences of voters or arbitrarily manipulate them. Put together, the population of these regions comes to more than 60 million, although we must add over ten million more for Moscow, which was the site of an unprecedented level of voter fraud for its section of the country ('Russia 1')[12] (exit polls in Moscow had 'United Russia' with 24–27 per cent of the vote). It was this voter fraud that sparked the mass street protests. Thus, over half of Russia's population (more than 70 million) lives in this section of the country. In these regions, 'United Russia' received less than 35 per cent of the vote on average, according to official results (that is a number that was inflated compared with the real results!).

At the other end of the spectrum ('Russia-3'), elections – as in fully authoritarian or totalitarian countries – are not a mechanism for determining the preferences of voters: the final results reflect both the extreme political passivity of the electorate (unmotivated participation – voting for 'the bosses') and the authorities' broad capacity to influence the numbers. This group is mostly composed of national-minority regions and a few Russian districts and has a population of about 28 million people. Finally, around 45 million people live in the regions that make up the intermediate group ('Russia-2'). The intermediate status (from a political perspective) of this group is based on a number of factors: in some places it reflects a long-term equilibrium (i.e. a political culture like that in 'Russia-3'); in others it is the result of temporary and accidental factors; in others yet, it reflects a contrast between the center and the periphery. For example, if we use the conservative official figures, 'United Russia' received 49.5 per cent of the vote in the district of Voronezh (pop. 2.38 million), but only 30.6 per cent in the city of Voronezh (pop. 860 thousand).

The Kremlin is now attempting, with the help of votes from 'Russia-3' and 'Russia-2' (many of them virtual), to impose an authoritarian political system, based on the concept of a ruling party, on a 'Russia-1' that rejected it fairly clearly in the December 2011 elections. It is important to note, however, that, in the case of a liberalization of the political scene on the federal level, the situation will be reversed: 'Russia-3' and, to a certain extent, 'Russia-2' will end up in opposition to the new standards and rules, which the regional elites will try to block from

V. good!!

penetrating into their territory. The existence of this opposition will be another obstacle in the creation of a consensus around playing the game by democratic rules.

In this way, the predicted crisis and subsequent liberalization of Putin's political system appears not so much as a solution to a basic problem, but as the opening of yet another Pandora's box – a cluster of problems that reflect a range of societal and social divisions, predicated on the following contradictions:

1) between the interests of those in the general population and the elite connected to the industrial sector of the economy, formed under the Soviet system, and those connected to the consumer and service sectors of the economy;
2) between the objectives of democratization as understood by the elite and those created by a growing demand for democratization 'from below';
3) between the regions with a patriarchal (and even partly fundamentalist) political culture and those with a nascent pluralistic model of social and political life.

According to our basic script, which presumes a transition back from the counter-reformist agenda of the late 1990s–early 2000s to a new reformist agenda and, consequently, a pluralistic model of political life, all of the contradictions listed above will reveal themselves during the current political cycle and become destabilizing factors. The achievement of stable compromises and the resolution of some of these contradictions should be expected to occur in the next, 'stabilizing', cycle, which should take place in the 2020s. Such, at any rate, are the conclusions that can be drawn from an attempt to project into the future the hypothesis of political cycles, employed in this chapter in an effort to explain the twists and turns in Russia's political history over the last 30 years.

Notes

1. S. Levitsky, L. Way (2002) 'The Rise of Competitive Authoritarianism', *Journal of Democracy*, vol.13, no.2, April; L. Way (2008) 'The Evolution of Authoritarian Organization in Russia under Yeltsin and Putin', Working paper (Helen Kellogg Institute for International Studies) (Issue 352); S. Levitsky, L. Way (2010) *Autocracy by Democratic Rules: The Dynamics of Competitive Authoritarianism in the Post Cold War Era* (New York: Cambridge University Press). On electoral authoritarianism: A. Schedler et al. (ed.)

(2006) *Electoral Authoritarianism: The Dynamics of Unfree Competition* (Boulder: Lynne Rienner); G. Golosov (2008) 'Electoralniy avtoritarizm v Rossii', *Pro et Contra*, vol.12, no.1.

2. R. Dahl (1972) *Polyarchy: Participation and Opposition* (New Haven: Yale University Press).

3. On 'Imposed Consensus', T. Karl (1986) 'Imposing Consent? Electoralism and Democratization in El Salvador' in P.W. Drake and E. Silva (eds) *Elections and Democratization in Latin America, 1980–1985* (San Diego: University of California at San Diego); in the context of Russia: V. Gelman (2003) 'Institutsionalnoe stroitelstvo y neformalnye instituty v sovremennoy Rossii', *Polis*, no.4; V.Y. Gelman (2007) 'Evolutsia electoralnoi politiki v Rossii: na puti k nedemocraticheskoy consolidatsii?', Tretiy electoralniy tsikl v Rossii, 2003–2004 (SPB: Izd-vo Evropeiskogo universiteta v Sankt-Peterburge).

4. P. Norris (1999) 'Introduction: The Growth of Critical Citizens' in Pippa Norris (ed.) *Critical Citizens. Global Support for Democratic Governance* (Oxford: Oxford University Press).

5. K. Rogov (2010) 'Gipoteza tret'ego tsikla', *Pro et contra*, vol.1, July–October.

6. H. Hale (2005) 'Regime Cycles: Democracy, Autocracy, and Revolution in Post-Soviet Eurasia', *World Politics*, vol.58, no.1, October.

7. A. Schlesinger Jr (1986) *The Cycles of American History* (Boston: Houghton Mifflin); A. Hirschman (1982) *Shifting Involvements. Private Interests and Public Opinion* (Princeton University Press).

8. Hirshman's concept of 'disappointment' and shifts between 'private' and 'public' were applied to the Russian developments of the past decades in: E. Chebankova (2010) 'Public and Private Cycles of Socio-Political Life in Putin's Russia', *Post-Soviet Affairs*, vol.26, no.2, April–June. This article, however, deals with social perceptions of the Russian people, rather than an evolution of the political regime.

9. See, for example, R. Rose (2010) 'Experience Versus Perception of Corruption: Russia as a Test Case', *Global Crime*, vol.11, no.2, May.

10. D. Treisman (2011) 'Presidential Popularity in a Hybrid Regime: Russia under Yeltsin and Putin', *American Journal of Political Science*, vol.55, no 3; on the dynamics of the post-crisis period see M. Dmitriev, D. Treisman (2012) 'The Other Russia. Discontent Grows in the Hinterlands', *Foreign Affairs*, vol.91, no.5.

11. See C.G. Gaddy, B. Ickes (2011) 'The Russian Economy through 2020: The Challenge of Managing Rent Addiction' in M. Lipman, N. Petrov (eds) *Russia in 2020: Scenarios for the Future* (Carnegie Endowment); C.G. Gaddy, B.W. Ickes (2011) 'Putin's Protection Racket' in I. Korhonen, L. Solanko (eds) *From Soviet Plans to Russian Reality* (Helsinki: WSOYpro Oy).

12. In her vivid analysis of Russia's socio-geographical differentiation, Zubarevich highlights four Russias (see N. Zubarevich (2011) 'Chetyre Rossii', *Vedomosti*, 30 December). In our case, this framework can be used to distinguish between different types of political culture; the fundamental distinction is between 'Russia-1', where the results of controlled elections nonetheless reflect the priorities of voters, and 'Russia-3', where election results are fully controlled. In the first case, the results of elections reflect the balance between (1) the population and the local government, (2) the

population and the federal government, and (3) the local elite and the federal government. In the second case ('Russia-3'), only the last of these interactions is meaningful. 'Russia-2' is, essentially, an intermediate zone.

Bibliography

E. Chebankova (2010) 'Public and Private Cycles of Socio-Political Life in Putin's Russia', *Post-Soviet Affairs*, vol.26, no.2, April–June.

T. Colton, M. McFaul (2001) 'Verno li, chto russkie ne democraty?', *Vestnik obshestvennogo mnenia*, no. 4.

T.J. Colton, H.E. Hale (2008) 'The Putin Vote: The Demand Side of Hybrid Regime Politics', Prepared for presentation at the conference 'The Frontiers of Political Economics', Higher School of Economics, Moscow, 29–31 May (http://www.hse.ru/data/075/226/1237/paper%20-%20Hale.PDF). Accessed April 5, 2013.

R. Dahl (1972) *Polyarchy: Participation and Opposition* (Yale University Press).

M. Dmitriev, D. Treisman (2012) 'The Other Russia. Discontent Grows in the Hinterlands', *Foreign Affairs*, vol.91, no.5.

C.G. Gaddy, B. Ickes (2011) 'The Russian Economy through 2020: The Challenge of Managing Rent Addiction' in M. Lipman, N. Petrov (eds) *Russia in 2020: Scenarios for the Future* (Washington, DC: Carnegie Endowment for International Peace).

C.G. Gaddy, B.W. Ickes (2011) 'Putin's Protection Racket' in I. Korhonen, L. Solanko (eds) *From Soviet Plans to Russian Reality* (Helsinki: WSOYpro Oy).

V. Gelman (2003) 'Institutsionalnoe stroitelstvo y neformalnye instituty v sovremennoy Rossii', *Polis*, no.4.

V.Y. Gelman (2007) 'Evolutsia electoralnoi politiki v Rossii: na puti k nedemocraticheskoy consolidatsii?', *Tretiy electoralniy tsikl v Rossii, 2003–2004* (SPB: Izd-vo Evropeiskogo universiteta v Sankt-Peterburge).

G. Golosov (2008) 'Electoralniy avtoritarizm v Rossii', *Pro et Contra*, vol.12, no.1.

L. Gudkov, B. Dubin (2007) 'Posttotalitarniy regim: "upravlyaemaya democratia" y apatia mass' in M. Lipman, A. Ryabov (eds) *Puti rossiiskogo postcommunizma. Ocherki* (Moscow: Carnegie Moscow Center), 8–63.

H. Hale (2005) 'Regime Cycles: Democracy, Autocracy, and Revolution in Post-Soviet Eurasia', *World Politics*, vol.58, no.1, October.

H.E. Hale (2011) 'The Myth of Mass Russian Support for Autocracy: The Public Opinion Foundations of a Hybrid Regime', *Europe-Asia Studies*, vol.63, no.8.

H.E. Hale, M. Mc-Faul, and T.J. Colton (2004) 'Putin and the "Delegative Democracy" Trap: Evidence from Russia's 2003–04 Elections', *Post-Soviet Affairs*, vol.20, October–December.

A. Hirschman (1982) *Shifting Involvements. Private Interests and Public Opinion* (Princeton University Press).

T. Karl (1986) 'Imposing Consent? Electoralism and Democratization in El Salvador' in P.W. Drake and E. Silva (eds) *Elections and Democratization in Latin America, 1980–1985* (San Diego: University of California at San Diego).

Latinobarometro, http://www.latinobarometro.org

S. Levitsky, L. Way (2002) 'The Rise of Competitive Authoritarianism', *Journal of Democracy*, vol.13, no.2, April.

S. Levitsky, L. Way (2010) *Autocracy by Democratic Rules: The Dynamics of Competitive Authoritarianism in the Post Cold War Era* (New York: Cambridge University Press).

S. Mainwaring (1989) 'Transitions to Democracy and Democratic Consolidation: Theoretical and Comparative Issues', *Kellogg Institute Working Paper*, no.130, November.

P. Norris (1999) 'Introduction: The Growth of Critical Citizens' in Pippa Norris (ed.) *Critical Citizens. Global Support for Democratic Governance* (Oxford: Oxford University Press).

G. O'Donnell (1994) 'Delegative Democracy', *Journal of Democracy*, vol.5, January.

K. Rogov (2010) 'Gipoteza tret'ego tsikla', *Pro et contra*, vol.1, July – October.

R. Rose (2004) 'New Russia Barometer. XIII: Putin's Re-election', *Studies in Public Policy*, no.388 (Glasgow: Center for the Study of Public Policy, University of Strathclyde).

R. Rose (2008) 'Responses to Transformation and After: Trends in Russian Opinion Since 1992', *Studies in Public Policy*, no.450 (Glasgow: Center for the Study of Public Policy, University of Strathclyde).

R. Rose (2009) 'Russians in Economic Crisis: New Russia Barometer XVIII', *Studies in Public Policy*, no.462 (Glasgow: Center for the Study of Public Policy, University of Strathclyde).

R. Rose (2010) 'Experience Versus Perception of Corruption: Russia as a Test Case', *Global Crime*, vol.11, no.2, May.

R. Rose, W. Mishler, and N. Munro (2011) *Popular Support for an Undemocratic Regime: The Changing Views of Russians* (Cambridge University Press).

A. Schlesinger Jr (1986) *The Cycles of American History* (Boston, MA: Houghton Mifflin Company).

A. Schedler et al. (ed.) (2006) *Electoral Authoritarianism: The Dynamics of Unfree Competition* (Boulder, CO: Lynne Rienner).

D. Treisman (2011) 'Presidential Popularity in a Hybrid Regime: Russia under Yeltsin and Putin', *American Journal of Political Science*, vol.55, no.3.

L. Way (2008) 'The Evolution of Authoritarian Organization in Russia under Yeltsin and Putin', Working paper (Helen Kellogg Institute for International Studies) (Issue 352).

N. Zubarevich (2011) 'Chetyre Rossii', *Vedomosti*, 30 December.

2
After Bolotnaia: Defining a 'New Normal' in Russian Public Politics

Samuel A. Greene

Introduction

None of the following was supposed to happen. United Russia was not supposed to eke out a bare majority of seats in the Russian State Duma on 4 December 2011. Thousands of protestors were not supposed to throng Chistye Prudy and Lubianka in Moscow on 5 December 2011. Thousands more – tens of thousands more – were not supposed to converge on Bolotnaia Ploshchad' on 10 December and on Prospekt Sakharova on 24 December. The protest was not supposed to survive the New Year holiday, and Vladimir Putin was not supposed to have to launch a major mobilizational effort to secure his own triumphal return to the Kremlin.

Aleksei Navalnyi was not supposed to become as popular as he is. Vladimir Ryzhkov and Aleksei Kudrin were not supposed to get second leases on political life. Mikhail Prokhorov was not supposed to get a first. Pussy Riot was not supposed to sing about Putin in Christ the Savior Cathedral, and neither the government nor the Russian Orthodox Church was supposed to react quite as violently when the song was sung.

The difficulty in understanding the significance of such surprises comes when we confuse what is truly new with what is actually old. The conventional view has it that the return of Putin to power (as though he ever left) is the linear process, while the protests marked a deviation from the norm. That, certainly, would upend the contention that Russia's citizens are inert in the face of autocracy, or that they are 'aggressively immobile' in a social, economic, and political context that stubbornly refuses to yield traction.[1] But Putin's rule, and the particular style and aesthetic of governance that accompanies it, is only a dozen years old; the 'inertia' or 'immobility' of Russian society, by contrast, is certainly older. So, wherein truly lies the deviation from the norm?

On the surface, the critical moment seems obvious enough. On 24 September 2011, when Putin and then-President Dmitrii Medvedev announced that the latter would succeed the former and the former the latter – or, rather, that Putin would succeed his successor cum predecessor and Medvedev would succeed his predecessor cum successor – the last thing that anyone in Russia was, was confused. That, surely, was what was supposed to happen, the deconstruction of the artificial 'tandem' and the restoration of the wielder of informal power to the seat of formal office.

But 24 September 2011, in one crucial way, marked a departure from the way the country had been governed before. In declaring that 'nothing changes', that everything returns to the way it was, the regime changed everything. The strength of the post-Yeltsin Russian regime was in its flexibility, in the free orbit of liquid layers of elites, money, property, ideas, and ideals around a small, hard core of concentrated power. Manipulating ideas, people, and property, the regime could change form and approaches, altering the basic chemistry and physics of interaction with its environment without any consequence for the core, so long as it observed one basic rule: no sudden moves. Inertia was the overriding value, and this liquid political economy reacted only to exogenous challenges, avoiding the creation of any challenges of its own.

From this point of view, 24 September was a sudden and entirely unnecessary move, and thus a violation of the rule. Why the decision was made is a question for another author. Suffice it to note that the decision led to the instantaneous calcification of the entire political system. With a new overriding value – the triumph of the leader – it became abundantly clear that all the bits and pieces of the system could now move in only one direction, for the achievement of only one goal. Flexibility was lost. And the liquid, frothy sea of politics that had forever prevented the Russian opposition from gaining its footing suddenly gave way to dry – or, at least, swampy – ground. It was, in the end, Putin who created Bolotnaia Ploshchad.

Or was it? Beginning much earlier, something else changed in Russia, much more subtly, much more slowly, and without fanfare. Briefly put, the structure of Russian public opinion disintegrated. Starting in August 2008, the close correlation of Russian attitudes about politics and the economy with their own welfare began to come uncoupled. The reasons for this are murky and complex. Certainly, the descent of the country into economic crisis, almost a year after the rest of the world, was the overriding factor, sowing a natural anxiety among Russians of all social strata. Perhaps the emergence of the Putin–Medvedev tandem itself had

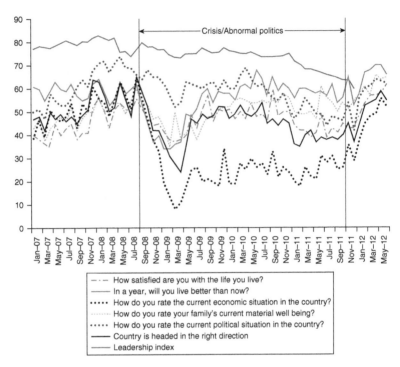

Figure 2.1   Public sentiment in normal vs. abnormal politics

something to do with it, adding uncertainty to the political landscape. Maybe the war in Georgia played a role. It seems unlikely that the failure of Russia's women's gymnastics team to bring back Olympic gold from Beijing was decisive, but neither can it be ruled out. Whatever it was, it went away in September 2011, just as Putin was busy putting an end to the regime of flexible power he had so meticulously created, and order was restored to the structure of Russian public opinion (see Figure 2.1).

These two insinuations – that the regime altered the political landscape, and that something was going on in the public mind that made protest more likely – are not mutually exclusive. In fact, they are complementary, which is fortuitous, given that both phenomena occurred at the same time and place and involved the same people and events. In the remainder of this chapter, I will attempt to show how these two factors may have interplayed by examining what happened to Russian public opinion before, during, and after this period of 'crisis' or 'abnormal' politics. In so doing, I will address three questions. First, I will look at the key ways in which the structure of public opinion differs during 'normal' and 'abnormal' periods of Russian politics. Second, I will look at the ways in which this differentiation between 'normal' and 'abnormal' periods of politics and public opinion forces us to rethink earlier wisdom about the sources of power and legitimacy in Russia. And, third, I will ask whether, after the end of the 'abnormal' period, Russian politics reverted to the pre-crisis status quo, or whether there emerged a 'new normal', which could produce a Russian near future very different from the recent Russian past.

Patterns of public opinion in Russia

Public opinion is a notoriously slippery subject. Despite the tremendous sophistication with which data are collected and interpreted, the data themselves – the answers given by respondents to questions asked by pollsters – are inherently problematic. The difficulties begin with the questions asked and intensify from there. The queries posed by pollsters to respondents are not necessarily the questions about social, political, and economic reality that respondents find most relevant in their own lives, and they are almost certainly not posed in the terms that respondents themselves would have chosen. Moreover, respondents may have any number of reasons for giving a particular answer to a particular question, and only one of those potential reasons is that the response is an accurate reflection of the respondent's opinion. Respondents may lie or dissimulate out of fear, capriciousness, or malice. They may also genuinely not know the answer, a phenomenon which is not the same as answering 'I don't know.' And, even if the answer provides a genuine reflection of a respondent's perceived or experienced life, it is at best only a reflection of the respondent's state of mind at the moment the question was asked; minutes later, that state of mind may be entirely different. For all of these reasons and more, it is a mistake to equate poll results with public opinion. Polls are a very foggy and distorting window through which to view the minds of the public. They are also, of course, just about the only instrument at our disposal.

Issues of quality aside, the data that emerge from polls are of varying types and usefulness, and there are inevitable tradeoffs involved in selecting an instrument for analysis. Panel data provide a cross-section of public opinion at a given moment in time, allowing a close look at what sorts of people gave what sorts of answers. Time series data provide aggregated data – the average temperature in the hospital, to borrow a Russian metaphor – in dynamic perspective. Given the difficulty and expense of collecting and analyzing panel data over time, the tradeoff is usually between dynamism and resolution. For the purposes of this chapter, I have settled for dynamism; further iterations of this research, hopefully, will add the resolution of panel data as a further test of the findings presented here.

As a result, it is important to bear in mind the questions that these data can and cannot answer. We can, using the time series data here, explore aggregate correlations between the answers given by respondents to one question and to another (or more, if need be). We can thus say whether or not the popularity of the regime tends to increase when economic sentiment improves, for example. We cannot say, however, whether an individual's likelihood of supporting Putin depends on his or her personal welfare or even personal perceptions of the economy; the data available for this study are not that fine-grained. More importantly, however, we have to bear in mind that what we are dealing with is the aggregation of reported perceptions of experienced life, a number at least three steps removed from reality. Distortions may occur at any or all of those steps. If we remember that, we will be more circumspect in assigning causality to one factor or another. We will also be more aware of the potential meaning of the distortions themselves.

The data used in this chapter come from several sources.[2] Five questions come from a monthly time series asked throughout the period of study by the All-Russian Center for the Study of Public Opinion (known by its Russian acronym, WCIOM), which are then indexed in such a way that values above 50 indicate positive sentiment, and values below 50 indicate negative sentiment on balance:

- To what extent are you satisfied with the life you are living?
- In a year from now, will your family live better than today?
- How do you rate the material well being of your family?
- How do you rate the current economic situation in the country?
- How do you rate the current political situation in the country?

In addition, I have created several composite indices, drawing on monthly time series provided by WCIOM, the Levada Center and the Public Opinion Foundation (FOM), the results of which are structured identically to the WCIOM indices above:

- the Leadership Index, a composite of the balance between support and non-support for Putin (and, when relevant, Medvedev);

- the National Direction Index, a composite of the balance between answers that the country 'is headed in the right direction' or 'is on the wrong path'; and
- the Political Uncertainty Index, a composite of the proportion of people who expressed neither support nor non-support for the political leadership, controlling for the level of support of that leadership. A discussion of the potential meaning of this index will follow.

Finally, I present four broad economic indicators, as reported by the Central Bank of Russia:

- industrial production, reported as change versus the same month in the prior year;
- inflation, reported as monthly change in the consumer price index;
- unemployment, reported as the monthly rate by International Organization for Labor (IOL) measuring standards;
- real disposable household income, reported as change versus the same month in the prior year (and, thus, discounting seasonal effects).

These data are presented below in two tables. Table 2.1 reports correlation coefficients of various opinion-linked and 'objective' economic indicators with broad measures of political sentiment. Table 2.2 reports correlations of the same indicators with broad measures of economic sentiment. In both of the tables, results are reported in four different iterations:

(1) the full sample, running from January 2007 through June 2012;
(2) the pre-crisis period, running from January 2007 through July 2008;
(3) the crisis period, running from August 2008 through August 2011; and
(4) the post-crisis period, running from September 2011 through June 2012.

A first glance at both of the tables is instructive, in that we see immediately how, while many of the relationships found in the data are stable throughout the various time periods, many of them are not. In some cases, relationships that appear significant in aggregate lose their significance within each of the sub-periods. In other cases, relationships that were salient before the crisis disappear after August 2008, while new

Table 2.1 Correlates of political sentiment

	Leadership Index				National Direction Index				How do you rate the political situation in the country?				Political Uncertainty Index (Controlling for Leadership Index)			
	Full Sample	Pre-Crisis	Crisis	Post-Crisis	Full Sample	Pre-Crisis	Crisis	Post-Crisis	Full Sample	Pre-Crisis	Crisis	Post-Crisis	Full Sample	Pre-Crisis	Crisis	Post-Crisis
How satisfied are you with the life you live?	1.66 (0.12)	0.51 (0.09)	2.89** (0.11)	–	4.34** (0.10)	6.10** (0.13)	4.54** (0.11)	6.75** (0.08)	4.76** (0.13)	5.93** (0.19)	2.48** (0.18)	3.89** (0.22)	3.97* (0.03)	7.15** (0.03)	–1.86 (0.01)	–
In a year, will you live better than now?	–0.27 (0.09)	–0.63 (0.19)	–1.42 (0.07)	–	1.51 (0.09)	0.18 (0.47)	1.01 (0.08)	3.83* (0.14)	0.37 (0.11)	0.09 (0.67)	–0.60 (0.12)	5.26** (0.21)	–2.26* (0.03)	0.84 (0.13)	–2.73* (0.01)	–
How do you rate the current economic situation in the country?	4.48** (0.04)	0.49 (0.09)	1.53 (0.06)	–	6.67** (0.04)	3.70** (0.16)	4.41** (0.06)	6.84** (0.06)	4.13** (0.06)	5.44** (0.19)	2.33* (0.10)	5.62** (0.13)	–2.61* (0.01)	5.94** (0.09)	–0.40 (0.01)	–
How do you rate your family's current material well being?	–1.67 (0.12)	0.64 (0.11)	–1.03 (0.11)	–	1.46 (0.11)	4.25** (0.20)	1.74 (0.12)	1.80 (0.26)	1.18 (0.14)	4.53** (0.27)	–0.52 (0.19)	2.43 (0.40)	0.92 (0.04)	4.26* (0.06)	–2.40* (0.01)	–
Leadership Index	–	–	–	–	7.47** (0.08)	1.68 (0.09)	5.73** (0.11)	–	6.53** (0.15)	0.48 (0.63)	9.43** (0.15)	–	–	–	–	–
National Direction Index	7.47** (0.08)	1.68 (0.09)	5.73** (0.11)	–	–	–	–	–	8.53** (0.11)	6.24** (0.19)	4.95** (0.19)	3.99** (0.42)	1.34 (0.05)	7.85** (0.03)	–2.39* (0.02)	–

Industrial production (y/y)	0.00 (0.09)	1.74 (0.27)	−1.88 (0.07)	—	1.59 (0.09)	−1.82 (0.67)	0.88 (0.09)	0.03 (1.03)	−0.85 (0.12)	−3.04 (0.84)	−1.21 (0.12)	0.07 (2.00)	—	—	—
CPI	3.12** (0.21)	−0.29 (0.21)	2.43* (0.22)	—	3.48** (0.20)	5.99** (0.29)	0.65 (0.29)	−3.10* (0.76)	3.30** (0.26)	9.56** (0.29)	1.33 (0.38)	−3.01* (1.49)	—	—	—
Unemployment	−0.08 (0.63)	1.05 (0.96)	2.86** (0.62)	—	−2.52* (0.64)	−0.28 (2.46)	−0.98 (0.75)	−0.67 (3.82)	−0.10 (0.89)	−1.13 (3.39)	1.86 (1.08)	−0.54 (7.51)	—	—	—
Real disposable household income (y/y)	3.53** (0.10)	1.75 (0.16)	0.50 (0.13)	—	2.89** (0.12)	−1.84 (0.40)	1.47 (0.15)	−0.18 (0.88)	0.76 (0.17)	−2.37* (0.54)	0.73 (0.22)	−1.18 (1.52)	—	—	—

Note: *significant to a 0.05 level; **significant to a 0.01 level; standard errors in parentheses.

Table 2.2 Correlates of economic sentiment

	How do you rate the current economic situation in the country?				How do you rate your family's current material well being?			
	Full sample	Pre-crisis	Crisis	Post-crisis	Full sample	Pre-crisis	Crisis	Post-crisis
How satisfied are you with the life you live?	2.94** (0.27)	5.51** (0.15)	3.34** (0.15)	6.69** (0.18)	7.61** (0.09)	5.56** (0.12)	3.58** (0.15)	3.98** (0.16)
In a year, will you live better than now?	3.80** (0.21)	1.37 (0.49)	1.62 (0.19)	4.11** (0.31)	5.98** (0.08)	1.36 (0.38)	5.49** (0.08)	1.57 (1.57)
How do you rate the current economic situation in the country?	—	—	—	—	2.55* (0.05)	4.43** (0.13)	3.30** (0.08)	3.20* (0.14)
How do you rate your family's current material well being?	2.25* (0.27)	4.43** (0.21)	3.30** (0.26)	3.20* (0.42)	—	—	—	—
National Direction Index	6.67** (0.25)	3.70** (0.20)	4.41** (0.31)	6.84** (0.33)	1.46 (0.14)	4.25** (0.14)	1.74 (0.21)	1.80 (0.46)
Industrial production (y/y)	2.98** (0.23)	−1.89 (0.73)	1.30 (0.19)	−0.06 (2.41)	4.28** (0.09)	−1.83 (0.57)	7.66** (0.07)	−0.21 (1.37)
CPI	0.93 (0.56)	3.88** (0.41)	1.45 (0.60)	−3.03* (1.87)	−3.73** (0.22)	4.43** (0.30)	−3.52** (0.29)	−3.16* (1.06)
Unemployment	−9.21** (1.14)	−1.77 (2.48)	−4.84** (1.40)	−1.82 (8.11)	−3.27** (0.69)	−1.13 (2.04)	−4.28** (0.81)	−1.50 (4.41)
Real disposable household income (y/y)	−3.81** (0.30)	−1.48 (0.45)	−0.02 (0.35)	−0.31 (2.05)	−0.19 (0.14)	−1.71 (0.34)	2.15* (0.18)	0.30 (1.17)

Note: *significant to a 0.05 level; **significant to a 0.01 level; standard errors in parentheses.

relationships arise to take their place. In some cases, relationships in the post-crisis period revert to the pre-crisis norm; in other cases, they do not, or move on to an altogether new state of affairs.

To start at the beginning, it is remarkable how loosely the Leadership Index is correlated with anything at all. In the full period, it displays a strong and robust relationship with how people rate the current economic situation in the country and the National Direction Index. However, the relationship with the economic situation question disappears in each of the sub-periods. Meanwhile, the relationship between the Leadership Index and the National Direction Index pertains only during the crisis period – the period of abnormal politics. The relationship between the Leadership Index and inflation is unexpectedly positive; that is, the higher inflation, the more the support for the regime; and this pertains only during the crisis. The same strange positive relationship pertains to unemployment.

The National Direction Index and the question 'How do you rate the political situation in the country?', by contrast, display strong (and virtually identical) relationships throughout the various time periods with two key indicators: current life satisfaction and rating of the current economic situation. They are, unsurprisingly, closely correlated with each other. They both display a strong relationship to evaluations of current material well being only in the pre-crisis period, a relationship that disappears after August 2008, replaced, evidently, with a relatively strong tie to how people evaluate their material prospects for the future. Interestingly, both of these indicators are linked to the Leadership Index only during the period of abnormal politics. More discussion of the potential meaning of this phenomenon, as well as of the Political Uncertainty Index, will follow later.

Economic sentiment displays a somewhat different logic. Unsurprisingly, how people rate the current economic situation in the country and how they rate their own family's material well being are closely linked in every period, and they are both closely correlated with the degree to which people report being satisfied with their own lives (though the strength of this correlation varies from one period to another). Both are sensitive to unemployment (in the expected direction) only during the crisis. But there are differences, too. While sociotropic sentiment (evaluations of the economic situation in the country) is positively correlated with the National Direction Index in every period, egocentric sentiment (evaluations of one's own material well being) is correlated with the National Direction Index only prior to August 2008. Egocentric sentiment is sensitive to industrial production inflation and changes in household income in the expected directions in the crisis period, while sociotropic sentiment is not.

The picture that emerges is somewhat startling. The initial period of 'normal politics' – up through July 2008 – does not display many of the relationships that we would generally associate with political normalcy. For one, there is no link between support for the regime and whether people think the country is headed in the right direction, or even how people feel about their own lives and welfare or the economy in general; indeed, *prior to August 2008, the Leadership Index is not correlated to anything in the dataset.* Some of the relationships that do exist are bizarre, including what might be termed a 'sociopathic' correlation between egocentric sentiment and objective indicators of unemployment and household income; in other words, the worse off the people around me are, the better I may feel myself. Many of the more intuitive relationships do pertain to the National Direction Index, which is sensitive in the initial period of normal politics to egocentric and sociotropic economic sentiment. The same is true for broad evaluations of the political situation other than those linked directly to support for the country's leaders. This important distinction will be discussed later.

The start of the economic crisis and the arrival of 'abnormal politics', in which the trend lines of public opinion begin to diverge wildly, changes the picture dramatically and, in many ways, actually brings more order to the relationships. Five key changes are worth highlighting:

- First, macro-social and macro-economic factors such as industrial production and unemployment become relevant to both sociotropic and egocentric economic sentiment only during the crisis.
- Second, the crisis eliminates the sociopathic correlations with unemployment and household income and flips the political correlation with inflation from positive (more inflation, more political support) to negative (less inflation, less support).
- Third, during the period of 'abnormal politics' a link appears between welfare and government, including a strong relationship between the National Direction Index and the Leadership Index.
- Fourth, the crisis decouples both political sentiment and the National Direction Index from egocentric economic sentiment, establishing a relationship with sociotropic and forward-looking sentiment.
- And, fifth, the onset of 'abnormal' politics establishes a link between evaluations of the present and the future that was not present before, and that link appears to persist into the post-crisis period.

Reviewing what we think we know

In 1994, Paul Kubicek argued that Russia was sliding into 'delegative democracy' – a system in which voters simultaneously confer democratic legitimacy and the freedom to govern undemocratically on a chosen leader – only a few months after Guillermo O'Donnell had invented the term.[3] Kubicek wrote:

> one can find support for delegative democracy in public opinion surveys. According to polls conducted in November 1993, a month before the election, only 25 per cent of the electorate was familiar with the program of different political parties. Over *half* were not familiar with the platform of the party for which they intended to vote. This means that voters continue to have a personalized view of politics, voting for personalities over policies. This makes accountability more difficult because political platforms become less important. 'Delegates' are not bound to them – since voters do not know about them – so they may do as they want. One survey in May 1993, revealed that 66 per cent of Russians thought Russia needed a strong leader to control parliament. Later, in October, half of respondents to one survey favored the emergence of a 'strong hand' to restore order. This, no doubt, reflects frustration with the existent 'democracy' and a desire for simple and effective solutions to restore social and economic order.[4]

While the term has since fallen out of use, at least in the Russian context – due to the evident abundance of delegation but dearth of democracy – the same basic concept underpins the most widespread assumptions about the nature of legitimacy and power in Russia. The two most recent and authoritative studies on the subject, by Timothy Colton and Henry Hale, on the one hand, and by Daniel Treisman, on the other, conclude separately that Russian voters are content to support Putin in return for perceived economic benefit; both also conclude that such sentiment and support have been broadly genuine, if complex.

Thus, Colton and Hale write:

> Putin wins votes at least partly due to his personal appeal as well as to growing perceptions of economic growth, and ... Dmitrii Medvedev has to a significant extent ridden these same forces to power. Other findings are more unconventional .... Moreover, the relationship between economic growth and the Putin vote is more complex than

often assumed. While we believe economy-related factors do have a major impact, they work through multiple channels and in tandem with other factors.[5]

Part of the complexity that Colton and Hale identify is the mismatch between egocentric economic experience and sociotropic economic sentiment, finding, first, that fewer than a third of Russians ever reported strong personal economic benefit, while votes for Putin were correlated most strongly with sociotropic sentiment.

All of these findings are consistent with an argument that a belief in aggregate economic improvement was creating a glow that initially led Russians not to let dubious policies or perceived failures reduce their overall support for Putin, and that over time came to make even some of the initially disliked policies look good.... At the same time, it is important to remember that actual economic improvement was not personally or consciously felt by much more than a third of the population (and only about 40 per cent of Putin voters).[6]

Treisman is somewhat more strident, writing that 'Putin's unprecedented popularity and the decline in Yeltsin's are well explained by the contrasting economic circumstances over which each presided.'[7]

This statement – and the fact that the data collection in both of the above-mentioned projects ended well prior to August 2008 – begs the question of what would happen were those economic circumstances to change. Given that Putin had presided until then exclusively through good economic times, while sophisticated statistical methods are capable of estimating the relative importance of factors, it remains fundamentally impossible to separate personal factors pertaining to Putin himself from environmental factors involving the economy and public sentiment. The onset of economic crisis provided an opportunity to do so, and initial findings showed a degree of resilience in Putin's poll numbers that would seem to question earlier findings of economically driven legitimization.[8]

Political uncertainty: Extracting truth from falsehood

People lie. Whether or not people lie about politics more than other things is an open question. But the problem of people lying about politics is one that occupies the minds of politicians and political scientists everywhere. In democratic contexts, politicians seeking election must worry about the reliability of voting intentions expressed in polls, or about the true popularity (and potential electoral consequences) of policy choices. In authoritarian contexts, lying – or, rather, the mass transition from lying to truth-telling – is seen as a catalyst for revolution. Because people may lie – or, to use the technical term, falsify their preferences – to pollsters, politicians, police, colleagues, even friends and family, it is impossible to know what the true level of support for a regime is; there is always a gap. This, together with the assumption that the gap is generally larger in authoritarian countries than in democracies, is at the heart of Timur Kuran's theory of cascading authoritarian regime failure. As an insurgency begins to gain momentum, it alters the balance of the variables in the equation that leads people to declare their 'public preferences' (a function of the rewards and punishment for any given public position and the 'integrity' cost of failing to reveal one's private preferences). And the probability of switching sides increases exponentially as the reputational advantages/ disadvantages shift.[9] In other words, the gap between truth and falsehood may close very rapidly. Kuran writes:

> Mass discontent does not necessarily generate a popular uprising against the political status quo. To understand when it does, we need to identify the conditions under which individuals will display antagonism toward the regime under which they live.... The proposed theory treats continuous and discontinuous change as a single, unified process. Private preferences and the corresponding thresholds may change gradually over a long period during which public opposition is more or less stable. If the cumulative movement establishes a latent bandwagon, a minor event may then precipitate an abrupt and sharp break in the size of the public opposition.[10]

The problem, of course, is that you never know whether someone was lying until they've started telling the truth, and by that time it's too late. There are, however, two parts of the data presented here that might provide some insight into the phenomenon of political preference falsification in Russia and how that phenomenon might change from normal to abnormal political periods.

The first of these is the disconnect, already noted, between the trend lines for broad political sentiment on the one hand (the National Direction Index and ratings of the political situation in the country) and leader-specific sentiment on the other (the Leadership Index). As mentioned above, broad political sentiment and leader-specific sentiment become correlated only during the crisis: prior to it, there was no statistically significant relationship at all. Also as noted earlier, while in the

pre-crisis period the Leadership Index seems to have floated freely, correlated exclusively with itself rather than with any other indicators, broad
political sentiment did fluctuate in line with economic and social sentiment, and continued to do so throughout the crisis. Thus, in many
ways, the broad political sentiment indicators would seem to be the
more 'honest' reflection of political preferences. Furthermore, the fact
that leader-specific sentiment becomes correlated with the more honest
broad political sentiment during the crisis adds weight to that argument,
while also suggesting a significant decrease in preference falsification
during the crisis. In other words, as things got worse, people began
telling the truth.

The second set of data that may be relevant to preference falsification is the Political Uncertainty Index. Calculated as the proportion
of people who expressed neither support nor non-support for the
leadership, controlling for the level of support versus non-support,
this Index may capture people who have strong feelings about the
leadership but prefer not to express them (in addition, of course, to
those who do not have such strong feelings). Intriguingly, the correlates of the Political Uncertainty Index shift dramatically from the
normal to abnormal periods of politics. Prior to August 2008, the
Index is positively correlated with both sociotropic and egocentric
economic sentiment, as well as with the National Direction Index.
In other words, the better people's expressed opinions about the state
of their lives and the country as a whole, the greater the number
of people who are hiding their preferences or have no preferences.
After 2008, the Index's correlation with egocentric economic sentiment
turns negative, as does the relationship with the National Direction
Index, while the relationship with sociotropic sentiment disappears.
In other words, worsening economic and social sentiment seems to drive
people out of either uncertainty or preference falsification and toward
a more clearly (and, perhaps, honestly) expressed position vis-à-vis the
regime.

There is no way to know whether this apparent process of preference
de-falsification – or, to use the layman's term, truth-telling – was behind
the unexpected public mobilization that began in December 2011. (Incidentally, the fact that the election protests occurred after the end of
'abnormal politics' need not be seen as problematic. Some perceptions
and sentiments are, presumably, 'sticky', particularly if they coincide
with a preference that is less broadly falsified than before. More on
this possibility in the final section of this chapter.) But such a development would be consistent with existing theory on the emergence of

insurgencies and could help us understand – as Kuran suggests – the ways in which linear processes can give rise to non-linear phenomena.

After 2011: A new normal?

In September 2011, abnormal politics in Russia ended. Order – or something resembling order – was restored to the broad trends in public opinion. Separately, Putin announced his return to the Kremlin, in what I have already argued was an ironic departure from the status quo ante. We already know that, from the institutional perspective, with the focus on how the regime functions and behaves, political life in Russia is no longer quite what it was before. The question remains, however, whether the structure of public opinion reverted to the patterns that held sway prior to the onset of abnormality in August 2008, or whether a 'new normal' began to take hold.

The evidence, one way or another, is incomplete. In each of the given time series, there are only ten possible data points available from September 2011 through June 2012; given gaps in polling, most of the calculations have to rely on an N of no more than eight. In several cases, including all of those involving the Leadership Index, there simply are not enough data even to hint at valid conclusions. Even were there more data, some conclusions would also require more time. But there are some things we can say already with relative certainty.

In some ways, the post-crisis period resembles the pre-crisis period. Broad political sentiment regained and somewhat strengthened its relationship with personal life satisfaction, which had been weakened during the crisis. Relationships that were insignificant pre-crisis – such as industrial production and unemployment – generally remain insignificant after the crisis, even if they were important during the crisis.

In many other ways, though, the post-crisis 'normal' is qualitatively new. The relationship between sociotropic economic sentiment and broad political sentiment is stronger, while the relationship with egocentric sentiment is weaker. Objective indicators, particularly inflation, have taken on the 'expected' signs in their correlation coefficients, meaning that higher inflation is now linked to lower outlook. Perhaps most intriguingly of all, where the important pre-crisis indicator of household material well being has disappeared, political sentiment is now closely linked with thoughts about the future. In other words, the political fortunes of the regime, having been tied in the past to how people thought about their present welfare, now rise and fall as people consider their futures.

t does all of this augur for the next decade of political life in
' This is, of course, an inherently unpleasant game to play, pre-
ᴜᴄᴜᴜɢ Russia's future. Very rarely does anyone do it with much success.
Perhaps it would help, then, to broaden the comparative horizon.

Writing about how 'delegative democracies' emerge, function, and
fail, O'Donnell posited that, faced with crisis, such systems begin to
display dysfunction:

> The longer and deeper the crisis, and the less the confidence that the
> government will be able to solve it, the more rational it becomes for
> everyone to act: (1) in a highly disaggregated manner, especially in
> relation to state agencies that may help to alleviate the consequences
> of the crisis for a given group or sector (thus further weakening
> and corrupting the state apparatus); (2) with extremely short time-
> horizons; and (3) with the assumption that everyone else will do
> the same. In short, there is a general scramble for narrow, short-term
> advantage.[11]

If the period of abnormal politics and the 'new normal' that followed it are indeed characterized by the increasing political salience
of sociotropic sentiment, then that might suggest Russia has moved
beyond delegative democracy to something else. What that something
might be, of course, is another question. Is Russia a post-delegative
democracy, that is, one in which delegation gives way to representation,
or a delegative post-democracy, in which the last trappings of polyarchic
governance may be expected to fall away?

In 1995, Raymond Durch saw the economic chaos that was sweeping
Russia and the rest of the former Soviet bloc and wrote:

> citizens are not likely to abandon democracy and capitalism because
> of economic chaos, regardless of how much information, educa-
> tion, or status the citizen has. In other words, there are no readily
> identifiable pockets of unsophisticated citizenry that will respond to
> economic catastrophe by embracing antimarket or antidemocratic
> solutions.... While they do not abandon democratic capitalism in
> the face of economic chaos, they are likely to punish incum-
> bents for economic hardships. Unlike institutional reform, support
> for particular incumbents was significantly linked to dissatisfaction
> with the economic situation. As a result, the period of democratic
> consolidation is littered with incumbents sacrificed to popular dissat-
> isfaction with economic performance: Ryzhkov and his government
> in 1990; Gorbachev in the aftermath of the failed coup; Gaidar in

1992 and again in 1994 because of his association with a policy that failed to reverse the economic crisis.[12]

A similar line of thought – that, whatever their tolerance for autocracy, Russian citizens had not entirely given up their democratic franchise, and thus their support for Putin could be considered genuine repayment for economic growth – underpins the Colton/Hale and Treisman approaches. At first glance, it might also seem to predict the protests that began in December 2011, if not for one thing: the 2011–12 protests had nothing to do with economics, at least not expressly. The regime, it seems, was being punished for something else.

Putin, having brought the country out of the economic and political turmoil of the Yeltsin period, may well have expected that accomplishment to buoy him for many years to come, just as Yeltsin may have expected to ride indefinitely on the glory of 1991. Research elsewhere, however, suggests that 'when a government effectively combats a severe threat... the salience of the issue diminishes subsequently and people's high appreciation for the president's accomplishment has an even lower impact on their political attitudes and behavior'.[13] Thus, whatever public opinion 'bonus' Putin may or may not have had – and Treisman shows a handful of statistically significant bonuses, including for the second Chechen war, and simply for being nothing like Yeltsin in the early years – may now be assumed to be long gone.

But, again, a broader comparative lens adds other arguments. In particular, it has been shown elsewhere that improving economic sentiment can have wide-ranging and lasting consequences. Investigating Europe, Harold Clarke and colleagues write: 'the effects of economic conditions extend beyond their impact on governing party support to influence feelings of life and democracy satisfaction and demands for radical and reformist social change'.[14] Moreover, turning to Latin America, Karen Remmer finds:

> [Overall electoral change] appears to be far more responsive to economic performance over a two-year period than to fluctuations in the economy immediately preceding elections. These results provide some support for the view that incumbents pay the price for short-term economic setbacks but that deeper crises may be translated into broader political shifts and high overall levels of volatility.[15]

The suggestion is that the important effects are gradual and cumulative, much as Kuran writes of the gradual deterioration of private preferences, even as they are masked by falsified public preferences. Surprises are, by definition, unexpected, but, if we learn to detect and track these underlying trends, then the shock should concern only when surprises occur, not the simple fact of their occurrence.

Are there, then, trends in the making that may provide some clue as to Russia's future? The fact that the future appears more forward-looking than the past – the fact that, post-crisis, the 'new normal' of Russian politics more closely links people's expectations about the future with their feelings about the way the country is governed – appears an important development. If this pattern holds, Russians may pay more attention to what politicians say (and do not say) about policy, in turn encouraging politicians to say more and to mean more (if not actually to do more). This particular shift in the structure of public opinion may not be enough to make public politics meaningful, but attaching public meaning to the practice of policy may not be a bad place to start.

The crisis itself, in establishing a prolonged period of 'abnormal' politics, created three other phenomena that seem to be persisting in the post-crisis period. First, it weakened the anti-social egocentrism that had dominated public opinion previously, opening the door for a more politically salient sociotropism. Second, it established the social meaning of governance, strongly linking sentiment about one's own life and about the state of the country to the act of expressing support for the regime in a way that had not been established before. And, third, it encouraged the de-falsification of public preferences, political truth-telling, narrowing the gap between spoken and unspoken preferences.

Russia's future – immediate, mid-term and, to a great extent, long-term – depends on whether or not these trends persist. If they do not persist, if Russian public opinion reverts back to the status quo ante of 2007, then the events that began in December 2011 will have been a passing episode of no lasting consequence. The habits of egocentrism will return, inertia will prevail, and no new pressures will be placed from below on the country's system of governance.

But if these trends do persist, a calcified and recalcitrant political elite can be drawn back into a political conversation with a newly interested and engaged public, even if within a broadly authoritarian institutional context. What politicians and bureaucrats say and do will matter more, will be more readily punished and, perhaps, even more carefully considered prior to being said and done. Party platforms that speak to people's interests and anxieties may begin to emerge at various points along the political spectrum. The likelihood of liberalization – either through the gradual transformation of delegative democracy into its representative cousin, or through a cascading insurgency – increases.

Notes

1. S.A. Greene (2011) 'Society, Politics, and the Search for Community in Russia' in M. Lipman, N. Petrov (eds) *Russia in 2020. Scenarios for the Future* (Washington: Carnegie Endowment for International Peace).
2. The full dataset, with all of the underlying indicators and index formulae, is available from the author.
3. G. O'Donnell (1994) 'Delegative Democracy', *Journal of Democracy*, vol.5, no.1, 55–69.
4. P. Kubicek (1994) 'Delegative Democracy in Russia and Ukraine', *Communist and Post-Communist Studies*, vol.27, no.4, 429–30.
5. T.J. Colton and H.E. Hale (2009) 'The Putin Vote: Presidential Electorates in a Hybrid Regime', *Slavic Review*, vol.68, no.3, 473–74.
6. T.J. Colton and H.E. Hale (2009) 'The Putin Vote...', 493.
7. D. Treisman (2011) 'Presidential Popularity in a Hybrid Regime: Russia under Yeltsin and Putin', *American Journal of Political Science*, vol.55, no.3, 590–609.
8. S. Greene (2012) 'Citizenship and the Social Contract in Russia', *Demokratizatsiya*, vol.20, no.2, 133–40.
9. T. Kuran (1989) 'Sparks and Prairie Fires: A Theory of Unanticipated Political Revolution', *Public Choice*, vol.61, no.1, 41–74.
10. T. Kuran (1991) 'Now out of Never: The Element of Surprise in the East European Revolution of 1989', *World Politics*, vol.44, no.1, 7–48.
11. G. O'Donnell (1994) 'Delegative...', 65.
12. R.M. Durch (1995) 'Economic Chaos and the Fragility of Democratic Transition in Former Communist Regimes', *Journal of Politics*, vol.57, no.1, 122.
13. K. Weyland (2000) 'A Paradox of Success? Determinants of Political Support for President Fujimori', *International Studies Quarterly*, vol.44, no.3, 481.
14. H.D. Clarke, N. Dutt, and A. Kornberg (1993) 'The Political Economy of Attitudes toward Policy and Society in Western European Democracies', *Journal of Politics*, vol.55, no.4, 998.
15. K.L. Remmer (1991) 'The Political Impact of Economic Crisis in Latin America in the 1980s', *American Political Science Review*, vol.85, no.3, 785.

Bibliography

H.D. Clarke, N. Dutt, and A. Kornberg (1993) 'The Political Economy of Attitudes toward Policy and Society in Western European Democracies', *Journal of Politics*, vol.55, no.4, pp. 99–1021.

T.J. Colton and H.E. Hale (2009) 'The Putin Vote: Presidential Electorates in a Hybrid Regime', *Slavic Review*, vol.68, no.3, pp. 473–503.

R.M. Durch (1995) 'Economic Chaos and the Fragility of Democratic Transition in Former Communist Regimes', *Journal of Politics*, vol.57, no.1, pp. 121–58.

S. Greene (2012) 'Citizenship and the Social Contract in Russia', *Demokratizatsiya*, vol.20, no.2, pp. 133–40.

P. Kubicek (1994) 'Delegative Democracy in Russia and Ukraine', *Communist and Post-Communist Studies*, vol.27, no.4, pp. 423–41.

T. Kuran (1989) 'Sparks and Prairie Fires: A theory of Unanticipated Political revolution', *Public Choice*, vol.61, no.1, pp. 41–74.

T. Kuran (1991) 'Now out of Never: The Element of Surprise in the East European Revolution of 1989', *World Politics*, vol.44, no.1, pp. 7–48.

G. O'Donnell (1994) 'Delegative Democracy', *Journal of Democracy*, vol.5, no.1, pp. 55–69.

K.L. Remmer (1991) 'The Political Impact of Economic Crisis in Latin America in the 1980s', *American Political Science Review*, vol.85, no.3, pp. 777–800.

D. Treisman (2011) 'Presidential Popularity in a Hybrid Regime: Russia under Yeltsin and Putin', *American Journal of Political Science*, vol.55, no.3, pp. 590–609.

K. Weyland (2000) 'A Paradox of Success? Determinants of Political Support for President Fujimori', *International Studies Quarterly*, vol.44, no.3, pp. 481–502.

3
Four Russias: Human Potential and Social Differentiation of Russian Regions and Cities

Natalia Zubarevich

Social differences – understood here as differences in human potential, population quality, and standard and way of living – are especially pronounced in territorially large countries characterized by inequality between regions and ethnic diversity. All these characteristics are intrinsic to Russia, which is why social diversity within the country is vast.

Social differentiation can be measured; quite often it is done in terms of regional differences. Regional demographic differences are well researched.[1] Human potential has been measured since the late 1990s.[2] However, regional perspective is of little use when it comes to analyzing essential social transformations related to changes in a population's way of life and value system. Social transformations do not spread from region to region, but, rather, develop hierarchically – from large urban centers to the periphery. Combining regional and center–periphery perspectives allows a more adequate evaluation of social differences in Russia.

Human development index

The development of human potential that proceeds from higher educational and material levels, better health, and more accessible social services expands the range of choices. The methodology of assessing human potential created by the UN Development Program includes the integral assessment of three essential components: longevity as measured by life expectancy, educational levels,[3] and income measured by per capita Gross National Income.

Russia is 66th in the 2011 Human Development Index (HDI) rating, which includes 187 countries, so it belongs to the group of countries with high human development.[4] In the last ten years, Russia's place in the ratings has not changed significantly, ranging from 60th to 67th. In fact, Russia's index grew steadily in the last decade (from 0.662 in 2000 to 0.719 in 2010, according to the new calculation method);[5] Russia's annual HDI growth was one of the highest among countries with comparable income levels. However, other BRICS countries (Brazil, Russia, India, China, and South Africa), whose original index values were substantially lower, demonstrated faster growth.[6]

Rapid economic growth, brought on by a sharp rise in energy prices, played a significant role in Russia's index increase. An increase in number of college students – educational quality is not measured by the index – was an additional factor, although its impact was much weaker. Russia's most problematic indicator – life expectancy – started increasing only in the second half of the 2000s. HDI dynamics did not allow Russia to assume a higher place in the world rating: other countries that do not possess energy resources had been developing at the same pace due to a higher growth in social indicators.

Russia's population health is the main reason for the low rating. Out of 187 countries, Russia is 120th in life expectancy, despite the fact that this indicator grew by more than 3.5 years in the second half of the 2000s. Russia, Ukraine, and Kazakhstan are the only three countries with high human development levels whose population's life expectancy does not reach age 70. Russia is in 51st–53rd place in other HDI components (income and educational levels).

Imbalance in Russia's human potential development is reflected in the modified index, which is not income-related (only health and educational components are taken into account). Russia falls from the 66th to the 74th place in the non-income-related HDI rating.[7] Such rating decreases are characteristic of oil export-dependent countries where high oil export revenues are not adequately invested in social development.

In case of Russian regions, the old HDI calculation methodology is used, since average and projected statistics on education length are absent. Fewer than ten regions display higher than average indicators – these are the federal cities and the major gas and oil-producing regions.

Not all of them are characterized by high educational and public health levels; they were in the lead mostly thanks to their economic development (the gross regional product (GRP) per capita indicator). The indicators for most regions are below Russian averages and do not differ much. The group of 10 to 15 outsiders is comprised of underdeveloped ethnic republics (with low income indicators) and the depressed regions with low indicators in all categories.

The 2000s trends indicate that countries with dynamic economic growth also displayed the maximum HDI growth. Among them are the new oil and gas-producing regions (the Sakhalin and Arkhangelsk regions, including Nenetski Autonomous District), the federal cities (especially Saint Petersburg, which is now in the second place in HDI in Russia), and the new industrial regions (Kaliningrad). The underdeveloped republics (Dagestan and Ingushetia) and the depressed Zabaikal region have also become HDP growth leaders, but as a result of increases in federal transfers.

Thanks to the economic growth in the 2000s, the proportion of the population residing in the high HDI regions has significantly increased. In 2005, more than 17 per cent of the population lived in the high HDI regions (over 0.800 according to the old calculation method); in 2009, this number had reached 85 per cent.[8] Russia no longer has low HDI regions (the regions in which the indicator is lower than 0.700), although more than 19 per cent of the country's population lived there in 2005. Only the Tyva Republic displayed the index of 0.750. However, the HDI growth in the 2000s can be mostly explained by the sharp increase in oil and gas export revenues, which were redistributed by the state as budget transfers to the less developed regions. Other index components have improved significantly less.

Social differentiation: Four Russias

Regional differences only partially explain social differentiation in the country. Many aspects are better explained through change in perspective and using a center–periphery criterion. In this case, a hierarchical system of populated localities is considered; the localities are divided into the largest, less large, small, and rural periphery. The population size serves as the major criterion for such division. Size matters, since the effect of concentration (the agglomeration effect) actually accelerates modernization. This approach allows three Russias to be identified inside one country. 'First Russia' is comprised of cities with populations of over half a million people; 'Second Russia' includes cities of 50,000 to 250,000 inhabitants (cities with populations of 250,000 to 500,000 are between the first and the second groups); 'Third Russia' is made up of small towns, urban-type settlements and rural territories – although any rigid borders are tentative. The population of the three Russias is

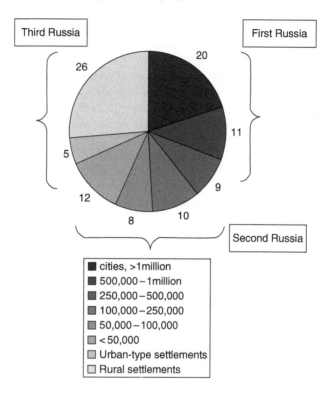

Figure 3.1   Russia's population distribution among towns and rural settlements in 2010, %

Source: 2010 Census data; the author's calculations.

roughly equal, with a third of the country's population concentrated in each of them (see Figure 3.1).

'First Russia'

These are the inhabitants of large urban centers that share higher living and educational standards, a developed university education system, and mass Internet use. 'First Russia' is characterized by a wider choice of employment and consumer opportunities, as well as the youth migration influx from the periphery. The number of such cities is quite small: there are 61 cities with a population of over 250,000 people, and only 34 cities with a population over 500,000 people.[9] Twenty-one per cent of the population, that is, one in five Russians, resides in the 14 cities with over one million people (the number includes the federal cities and is based on mid-2012 data). One in nine Russians lives in Moscow or Saint Petersburg, which is quite substantial for changing political 'climate'.

Russia of the large cities is not homogeneous: the advantages of the large cities are evident. They are the post-industrial economy leaders with high development levels: the per capita GRP is 47,000 dollars in terms of spending power in Moscow and 22,000 in Saint Petersburg, which is comparable to developed countries. The federal cities boast the most educated population: 50 per cent of Muscovites and 44 per cent of Saint Petersburg residents over the age of 15 have higher education. The labor market is most diverse here and provides the largest number of high-paying jobs. At the same time, Moscow is significantly ahead of Saint Petersburg in all economic indicators: more than 5 times in GRP, more than 4 times in total budget (1.5 times in budget per capita revenues), and more than 1.7 times in average per capita income. These differences do not eliminate the main similarity: federal cities' way of living is most modernized. Small business employment, which encourages independence and responsibility, supports this trend (27–30 per cent of all workplaces are in the small business sector). However, the federal cities' population has aged significantly; the proportion of the population above the retirement age has reached 24–25 per cent (31–33 per cent among women); thus, pension increases and other social support mechanisms make a large part of the elderly electorate, as well as public sector employees, dependent on the state.

All cities with population over a million were large industrial centers in the Soviet times, but the situation has changed noticeably in the last 20 years. Yekaterinburg, Novosibirsk, Rostov-on-Don, Nizhniy Novgorod, and Kazan are being rapidly transformed into large centers of the service economy, since they lost their competitive edge in machine building as early as the 1990s. The first three cities have historically developed as inter-regional capitals of the Urals, Siberia, and the South, respectively; higher education is more developed there, which is why they are more attractive to migrants. The economies of Ufa, Perm, Omsk, Chelyabinsk, and Volgograd are still dominated by the Soviet industrial mega-plants (oil-refining and metallurgical), but the service sector is already leading in employment. Post-industrial transformation is the slowest to take shape in Volgograd. This city – a clear illustration of Soviet industrialization – looks like a huge industrial zone stretching for 70 km along the Volga River. The industrial zone consists of large enterprises which for the most part find adaptation to market conditions difficult; they have downsized, but as of yet have not closed their doors. Volgograd has not historically been an inter-regional center, so cultural heritage does not abound there. Similarly to Volgograd, the populations of Omsk, Chelyabinsk, Perm, and Ufa retain an industrial mentality due to their economy's industrial structure. Besides, a large proportion of people with secondary professional education live in the Ural, Volga, and Siberian million-cities (except for Novosibirsk); however, their educational level is insufficient to adapt to the new labor market conditions and social life. Considering all these factors, the way of living in million-cities is slow to change. Another factor that slows down urban modernization is low budget appropriations. Unlike federal cities (the Russian Federation subjects), all other major cities are municipalities, whose budgets receive significantly less in tax revenues, since the major taxes – personal income taxes – are primarily transferred to the regional budgets.

Changes in employment structure and consumer behavior facilitate lifestyle modernization. The percentage of white-collar workers is higher in million-cities, and so is small business employment; there are more qualified employees in budget sectors – thanks to a more developed system of higher education. These cities are first to adopt Moscow's consumer behavior, although local wages are 1.5–2 times lower than they are in the capital. The middle class forms faster there, and 'angry urbanites' appear. However, the majority of the 'angry urbanites' are concentrated in the enormous and super-rich capital, while they are much less active in other million-cities.

Cities with populations over 500,000 also differ, but all of them are regional centers whose economy is polyfunctional.[10] However, they have fewer opportunities to develop market services and white-collar employment in comparison to million-cities. Nevertheless, these cities are capable of fast transformation provided that budget revenues and investments grow. For instance, Krasnodar with its population of 750,000 had for many decades been eclipsed by Rostov-on-Don, but, since the 2000s, it has experienced the active growth of the entertainment industry, restaurant and bar chains, business services, higher education and the Internet. In the late 2000s, Krasnodar was one of the leaders in per capita investment, housing construction, and retail sales among large Russian cities. This can be explained mainly by the fact that some of the means appropriated for the Sochi Olympics have 'spilled over' into the Kuban capital. There is another, longer-term, factor, though: the south provides more comfortable and affordable living; thus, it is attractive to investors. Tyumen, with a population of over 600,000, has been a recipient of large budget investments since the mid-2000s thanks to tax revenue transfers from two leading oil-producing regions – Yamalo-Nenets and Khanty-Mansi. Results have been the same: accelerated development of entertainment and shopping centers, improved higher education, as well as the highest per capita housing construction and retail sales rates. However, the rent life cycle is coming to an end, municipal budget revenues have decreased, and the urbanites' discontent is growing. Krasnodar is likely to face similar difficulties after 2014. In both cases, one can hardly expect a sharp increase in protest sentiment: both cities are surrounded by vast rural peripheries that supply them with politically passive citizenry, while the regional authorities are more authoritarian than those of other regions. However, thanks to higher education, there are more and more young urbanites who demand quality employment and freedom of choice.

Continuous development of higher education and science in urban centers plays an enormous role. For example, Tomsk, with a population of 500,000, is highly urbanized: every fifth city resident is a university student, independent television channels and newspapers exist there, and there is also an active cultural scene and greater civic involvement.

If 'First Russia' is to include all urban centers with a population of over 250,000 (although this is an overly optimistic assessment), the category will account for 37 per cent of Russia's population.[11] According to the geographers' research, cities whose populations were above this threshold turned out to be more socio-economically stable in comparison with smaller cities during the system crisis of the 1990s.[12] However, the modernization processes are quite heterogeneous in these cities, as indicated by the electoral statistics. In some places, modernization is extremely slow: for example, Saransk, as well as the entire Republic of Mordovia, votes exclusively for the United Russia; protest movement is more active in Kostroma, but it is in support of the Communist Party. Meanwhile, in the border cities of Kaliningrad (population 430,000) and Vladivostok (population 590,000), fewer than 50 per cent of the electorate voted for Putin. Moscow registered the same result. The borders of 'First Russia' are tentative; they can be drawn either on the basis of transformational dynamics (then the cities with population over half a million will be included) or on the basis of sustainable city development (then this category will contain cities with population over 250,000, albeit with certain exceptions).

It is evident that, aside from *the basic population factor* (the scale effect), value and lifestyle modernization are also impacted by other factors. Thus, the second tier of the following qualitative modernization factors can be identified:

- *city functions* (post-industrial economic development, especially the development of higher education and market services);
- *geographic location* (modernization takes place faster in the 'contact zones' – large border cities located along major trade routes with developed near-border trade);
- *the length of urbanization processes*, which is partly linked to *the ethnic population makeup* (patriarchal traditions in less urbanized republics, as well as in some semi-agrarian regions, slow down lifestyle and value system modernization);
- *the type of regional political regime* (the degree of authoritarianism and control of civil society), which primarily influences electoral results; however, in a broader context, the authoritarian regimes act as a barrier to modernization of the population value system.

The proportion of 'First Russia' in the country's population will inevitably grow, since migration flows are directed toward the largest cities. The only difference is that the Moscow capital agglomeration and Saint Petersburg along with Leningrad region draw in migrants from the entire country, thus acquiring 60 and 20 per cent of total Russian migration, respectively; while other large cities mostly attract migrants from their own region – primarily young people determined to receive higher education. The growing concentration of active and competitive population in the country's largest cities is an indictment of the 'power vertical'.

It is large cities that are home to the majority of the 50 million of Russian Internet users, which makes information accessible. The white-collar workers and the Russian middle class, who shape the demand for institutional modernization, are concentrated there as well. The angry urbanites' active public involvement is not triggered by the impending crisis, but, rather, by the frightening prospect of a lengthy Putin stagnation with its slowed-down vertical mobility, corruption, investment deficit, and lack of quality employment. The protest energy unleashed by 'First Russia' was not brought on by the oil price collapse; the *homo economicus* reflexes were replaced by moral rejection mechanisms.

What can diminish protest sentiments in 'First Russia'? First of all, the new crisis wave can. It will deal the educated urban population a powerful blow; the mobility and high competitive ability of the city residents will enable them to adapt more quickly to the unfavorable situation, although considerable time and effort will be required to do this. Second, the protest activity may diminish due to a substantial decrease in the number of young people in the next decade (as a result of the demographic wave, the small generation of those born in the 1990s will enter the labor market). It will reduce the competition for high-skilled employment and may also lead to a decline in political activity, since the number of young people – the traditional conductors of the protest sentiment – will diminish. The third factor that may stem the protest activity is the end of the global crisis and the beginning of global economic growth. In this case, emigration from Russia will increase sharply, since it is the educated and competitive youth residing in large cities that generally leaves the country in search of employment opportunities overseas.

'Second Russia'

These are people living in the towns with populations of 20 thousand to 50 thousand – to that of 250 thousand people and in the additional 12 larger industrial towns (see Note 12). A total of 25–30 per cent of the country's population lives in these towns.[13] Not all of the towns have retained their industrial profile in the post-Soviet times, but its spirit is still strong, as is the Soviet way of living. In addition to significant industrial sector employment ('the blue-collar jobs'), many residents of these towns are employed in the public sector and do mostly low-skilled work. As a rule, small business is poorly developed due to the population's low buying power and serious institutional barriers. There are some exceptions, though: for instance, retail, entertainment, and recreational small businesses are much better developed in Magnitogorsk, but their development is directly linked to the economic fortunes of the Magnitogorsk Iron and Steel Works: crisis-period pay cuts to its employees will obliterate the demand for services.

Numerous 'Second Russia' cities can be divided into two groups: industrial, among which there is a large share of monotowns, and the cities that lost a large part of their industrial functions during the crisis of the 1990s and are now being developed as primarily local municipal centers. The latter are generally subsidized; the employment opportunities are mostly concentrated in non-market services of the public sector; market services are poorly developed – although one can find examples of more successful cities. Risks and prospects of local municipal development are contingent upon economic conditions and regional budget, as well as on relations with regional authorities. Protest activity is low in such cities: the population is clinging to its public sector jobs, since there are almost no alternatives on the local labor market. The growing labor migration also diminishes the protest activity. The competitive part of the population opts for jobs in the larger cities, renting housing there (as a rule, men find positions of security guards, while young women get clerical office jobs), or they may work seasonally off the books (in villa construction or house repairs).

The remaining industrial cities, especially the monotowns, are subjected to the most serious development hazards. There are about 150 monotowns in Russia which have stable enterprises and high industrial employment. Nine per cent of the country's population lives there. Other Soviet-era monotowns greatly downsized their workforce back in the 1990s, so it is hard to consider them industrial cities, let alone monotowns. The remaining industrial cities suffer from unstable development, as was highlighted by the 2009 economic crisis. The monotowns specializing in iron works and machine building have been affected the most. The basic governmental efforts were directed at sustaining employment at any cost, regardless of the enterprise's efficiency or competitive ability. The options of part-time employment and public works were widely used; in some regions, an employee could be terminated only after a sanction from the office of the public prosecutor. Despite the large industrial production slump, employment was successfully sustained thanks to the federal budget transfers, but it has remained inefficient. Federal funds for monotowns' support were insignificant, and were 'manually' distributed: in fact, the largest enterprises (AvtoVAZ, Uralvagonzavod) received much greater funds that the cities where they are located.

A new crisis will have a particularly strong impact on the 'Second Russia's' industrial towns, since the old problems are still present there, and the industrial production is decreasing more substantially during the crisis than in other economic sectors. There are almost no other jobs in these cities, and their population's mobility and skills are low (the largest industrial centers and the northern oil-producing towns are the exceptions). In crisis-ridden 2009, the federal budget appropriations for regional subsidies increased by one-third, while the employment support transfers tripled. If the federal budget runs out of cash during a new crisis, the residents of industrial cities will lead the protests demanding work and pay, as previously happened in the town of Pikalevo. Such protests will increase pressure on the federal and regional authorities and will contribute to populist decision-making. Most of the barely surviving enterprises need to be shut down, since they are inefficient and unprofitable, but this was not done in 2009 and is not likely to be done during another crisis wave. Russian authorities realize the dangers of socio-economic protest in 'Second Russia', and are probably capable of

extinguishing it through economic and administrative measures while there is still money in the federal budget. However, during a powerful and lengthy crisis, the financial resources are unlikely to be sufficient.

It is clear that the nature of the protest in large urban centers and industrial cities is different. In the case of new economic crises, 'Second Russia' will fight for employment and wages but will remain indifferent to the issue of bad institutions, which concerns the middle class. The federal authorities understand this well and tried to incite the 'Second Russia's' blue-collar workforce against the 'First Russia's' white-collar workers on the eve of the 2012 elections. Such tactics have proven successful in the short run, since the two Russias speak a different language and have difficulty understanding each other.

However, it will be harder to employ this method in the longer term, since the benefits of large urban centers are growing in number, while the population of industrial cities is aging. Even relatively successful industrial cities are losing their appeal. During the period of economic growth, wages in industrial cities grew more slowly than they did in regional centers, since the state was raising the pay of the public sector and administrative employees by drawing money from its enormous oil revenues, while the industrial business sector was not able to provide pay increases at the same pace. At the time of the crisis, wages in industrial regions fell far more substantially.[14] As a result, the population of most industrial towns is rapidly decreasing as young people are migrating to regional centers and federal city agglomerations. Besides, barring a few exceptions, industrial towns built considerably fewer housing units per 1,000 inhabitants than regional centers did, which also adds to their lack of appeal.

Prospects for 'Second Russia's' urban Development –with respect to both industrial towns and towns that have practically lost this function – depend on where these cities are located. The location in the vicinity of large urban agglomerations accelerates function diversification. Such cities gradually become the agglomerations' external periphery; sustainable enterprises that work for the agglomeration's large market are moved or established there; communications and housing construction also come to these cities. Towns located along major freeways also have favorable development prospects. Unfavorable peripheral location accelerates depopulation; such cities lose their population and industrial specialization more rapidly, becoming small local centers for the surrounding territory. Small resource-extraction localities of the far north might completely vanish off the face of the earth as their resource base becomes depleted.

In the 2010s or even later, one can hardly expect the residents of large urban centers and industrial cities to consolidate their protest activity. The processes are more likely to be in phase opposition: under crisis conditions, the 'Second Russia's' protests demanding work and pay will intensify, while the 'First Russia's' educated urban population will resort to individual job-searching strategies without wasting their time on protests. Unlike the 'angry urbanites', industrial city dwellers have no motive to protest while the economy is stable. This means that with some 'sleight of hand', utilizing the 'carrot and stick' approach, the federal authorities might succeed in isolating different protest groups. Even now, in anticipation of the new wave of economic protests, the 'First Russia's' political field is being cleansed of undesirable elements in order to free the authorities' hands for stopping the crisis-related protest movement in 'Second Russia', where conducting repressive policies is much harder.

'Third Russia'

This is the vast peripheral territory that includes residents of rural villages, numerous urban-type settlements, and small towns. In total, a third of the country's population lives there, but the population is rapidly declining, which is why the populated territory is shrinking like an ice cube in the sink. Besides, the educational level of 'Third Russia's' population is low; it is not mobile, and survives off the land. The periphery's population is most distanced from the state: the natural calendar of agricultural works is not contingent on official policies. Depopulated small towns and urban-type settlements of peripheral 'Third Russia' are scattered around the country, but they are especially characteristic of central Russia, the northwest, and the industrial regions of the Urals and Siberia. Rural population is concentrated in the Southern and North Caucasian federal districts (27 per cent of the total rural population). The southern 'Russian' villages have better retained their demographic potential; there people survive thanks to intensive subsistence farming on the fertile chernozem lands. Large-scale agribusinesses primarily invest in profitable and non-labor-intensive types of crop farming (grain production, sunflower cultivation); that is why many rural area dwellers lose their jobs in the agricultural sector, and young people are moving to the cities. Southern regions are still far from completing the urbanization process.

In more urbanized regions, only villages located in the vicinity of large cities are able to survive. Their population is younger and more mobile, and it earns more. A significant part of the population is commuters working in large cities. The transformation of the rural area within the Moscow agglomeration borders is proceeding especially fast; many non-agricultural jobs have already been created there. More than half of the Moscow region's rural population came from other regions, and the migrants are more active and adaptive. The situation in the depopulating peripheral territories is far worse. For example, more than 40 per cent of women in the Pskov region are seniors; most of the agricultural enterprises are money-losing ventures; the non-agricultural business is very slow to develop in this rural area.

The able-bodied population of the peripheries with low agrarian potential has essentially returned to gathering and earns a living by picking mushrooms, berries, and pine nuts, or by fishing. There are no other jobs beside those in the public sector in some small Sakhalin villages, but people are not leaving, since the shadow earnings from the salmon spawning season provide them with sustenance for the entire year. Shadow employment enables the population of these areas to be independent from the state, while those dependent on the state – the public sector employees and senior citizens – are unable to leave or protest. The 'Third Russia's' protest potential is minimal even if there are crisis-related pension and salary interruptions. The situation is unlikely to change in the foreseeable future – barriers to the modernization of the Russian periphery are too great.

'Fourth Russia'

The three preceding groups were defined in terms of a center–periphery model that explains social differences through a position in the hierarchical system of localities. It encompasses localities ranging from the most modernized large cities to the patriarchal rural periphery. The model is quite applicable to most of the country, but it loses its explanatory powers in the case of the underdeveloped republics of the North Caucasus and South Siberia (Tyva and Altai), where almost 6 per cent of the country's population lives. The center–periphery gradient is weaker in these republics for a variety of reasons. The urbanization process is continuing there; the large Makhachkala agglomeration in Dagestan is being formed – according to statistical data, the city population numbers 580,000 people, but it reaches one million if the densely built-up suburbs are factored in. However, this agglomeration, just like other republican centers, has a scant educated middle-class segment, which is being eroded by migration to the regions with more comfortable living conditions. Besides, the demographic transition is still in progress in the region; the rural population is young and growing, in contrast to other regions of the country. The young adults are actively moving away from the rural areas into the regional centers, but migration serves its 'social lift' functions rather poorly: there is almost no work in the cities. The migrants require help from their clan in obtaining (purchasing) public sector or shadow employment. Shadow economy predominates in the North Caucasus republics; corruption is rampant there. The clan system endures, as do religious and ethnic conflicts and the clans' fierce struggle for resources. The North Caucasus' urban population is not sufficiently modernized to create a modernization trend in the region. All of these factors weaken the typical disparities between center and periphery.

'Fourth Russia's' prospects are widely debated, and among them is its possible disintegration. However, one should remember that, despite the multitude of problems, the overwhelming majority of the North Caucasus' inhabitants consider themselves Russians. Their decision is greatly influenced by federal policies. So far, the policies have been ineffective and directed at pumping money into the politically unstable territories. In 2011, the monetary transfers to the North Caucasus republics, where 5 per cent of the Russian population lives, amounted to 179 billion rubles, or 10 per cent of the total federal transfers to the regions. The transfers are not equally distributed: Chechnya received 39 per cent (68 billion rubles) of the total transfer amounts.

The cited data indicate that the total amount of federal aid to the North Caucasus republics is not that great (except for the Chechen transfers). The federal budget will be able to sustain the current aid levels in order to prevent the rise of social tensions even under the crisis conditions. However, there is no transparency in aid spending, which only exacerbates corruption and social instability. The Caucasus problem cannot be solved unless the entire system of state governance is modernized. Thus, 'Fourth Russia' may long remain a 'trouble spot', capable of provoking social and political instability across the country in the worst-case scenario.

Development scenarios: How will four Russias change?

The institutionally undeveloped democracy creates fewer risks for 'First Russia', since the large cities' actual competitive advantages will facilitate their development. Besides, as a result of decentralized governance – which is inevitable even under a weak democracy – the scale of financial resource redistribution in favor of peripheries will diminish, and money will concentrate in large cities. Thus, the institutional modernization scenario is most advantageous to large cities.

For 'Second Russia', the institutionally weak democracy creates serious short-term risks, since such a regime is unable to assist industrial cities in the time of crisis. However, in the longer term, it will accelerate the reorganization of inefficient enterprises and revitalize Russian industry and industrial towns. Social costs and risks are really high in this case: substantial unemployment growth in many industrial cities, the expansion of economically depressed areas, and the increase in social tensions. Such consequences generally lead to a change of political course and a restoration of the controlled model of the economy, or even to a return of the authoritarian political regime.

'Third Russia' would prefer the authoritarian development scenario, as it provides for financial resource redistribution favorable to the periphery with its controlled electorate. Nevertheless, in the long view, even given institutional weakness, a liberal setting is more conducive to the exit from homeostasis, however insignificant such instances will be. Peripheral territories can be developed and modernized provided that the local authorities and business community are competent and capable of capitalizing on local competitive advantages, while the weak federal center is unable to foil their modernization agenda.

'Fourth Russia' loses under any scenario. Its problems are so severe that they can only be solved through continuous and consistent effort of the competent and authoritative central government aided by regional actors – business, civil society institutions, and elite groups. Under the Latin American model, the North Caucasus will be a constant source of instability (terrorism and violence), thus promoting authoritarianism on the federal level.

Territorial contrasts in population concentration will inevitably intensify, especially between 'First' and 'Third' Russias, where this process has been taking place for years. It will gradually spread to the depopulating cities of 'Second Russia', except for those located within the borders of large agglomerations. At the same time, the completion of demographic transition in 'Fourth Russia' and its population's increased migration to the large cities will result in population deconcentration.

The state's social policy for the next decade is predictable and will encourage the increase in territorial contrasts, but primarily inside 'Third Russia'. Bifurcation in social and regional policies is inevitably created in countries with depopulating peripheral territories: the choice is between supporting the existing rural population distribution and its network of social institutions (schools, hospitals, etc.) and modifying this network to accommodate the changing population distribution.

As a rule, the second option is chosen, since the first one requires greater state budget expenditures.

This choice has already been made in Russia. The program that optimizes the network of social institutions went into effect in the second half of the 2000s. It is reducing the number of small schools and first aid medical facilities in rural areas and small townships; a system of transporting kids to schools is created, and many medical functions are transferred to larger medical centers. When the network of social institutions is territorially concentrated, budget financing becomes most cost effective; at the same time, basic services become less accessible to those living in the peripheral territories, which accelerates the migration of high-skilled workforce and service consumers to larger population centers. Due to the lack of developed transportation infrastructure in Russia and the enormous scale of peripheral territories, transforming the network of social services results in substantial social costs.

The consolidation of social services will continue in the future, but in many respects will be contingent on the nature of the political regime. Under the institutionally weak democracy, the diversity of regional social policies will increase – they may be strictly focused on optimizing the budget social spending or may seek to preserve the existing network of basic services and inefficient social spending, which will imply squeezing the money out of the federal budget. The authoritarian regime is less predictable. It may either suspend the required changes or implement the changes in a rough, Russian-style form of a short-lived campaign that will incur high social costs to the population. For the transformation model to be not only economically but socially effective, regional specifics have to be taken into account. The model has to be developed on the regional level and involve consumer feedback; the network must be modified smoothly with minimal costs to the population. But, even under the 'kind tsar', such an improvement in the quality of governance seems unlikely; it requires developed civil society and an ability to stand up for one's rights and achieve compromise.

The development of infrastructure in general, and the transportation infrastructure in particular, should help to diminish the territorial contrasts. However, there are serious problems in this department as well. In the second half of the 2000s, Russia was building as many kilometers of highway roads in a year as China was in two to three weeks – and this happened despite the enormous budget oil and gas revenues. One of the reasons for this state of affairs is the centralization of road funding and its transfer to the federal level, which led to a threefold decrease in the aggregate road construction. In the early 2010s, the road funding was returned to the regions, but the regional budgets have extremely limited financial resources for road building because of the increased social spending. Public–private partnership in this sphere is not well developed due to the serious institutional barriers. Federal highway construction programs primarily focus on political projects. They invest in road construction in preparation for the 2014 Sochi Olympics and the 2018 Soccer World Cup or try to alleviate Moscow's transportation collapse, which has already become a political problem. The improvement of the road network that links Russia's large cities with other localities is not designated as the first priority. Given the increased budgetary limitations, the infrastructural problems will have negative consequences for the whole of Russia. The country is split into two parts: one has no roads, the other has roads that are impossible to drive on.

The state's economic policies will play a greater role in the development of 'First Russia' and 'Second Russia'. Stimulating entrepreneurial activity and reducing economic dependence on gas and oil revenues will accelerate 'First Russia's' development; at the same time, Moscow and, to a lesser extent, Saint Petersburg will be deprived of the enormous oil and gas rent. To compensate for the losses, the federal cities will have to use their agglomerative advantages (the scale effect) more sensibly and reduce inefficient budget spending, which will only be beneficial. The towns of 'Second Russia' will lose if the economic dependency on oil and gas revenues diminishes. Their enterprises and budgets are being supported by the energy industry's rent revenues and the energy export orders. Meanwhile, the growth of small and midsize business will slow down due to the weakening of the scale effect and declining population quality. The policy of administrative decentralization will accelerate the development of both 'First Russia's' large centers and the more successful 'Second Russia's' industrial towns, which have a significant tax revenue base; however, the policy is to be implemented in terms of both 'federal center–region' and 'regions–municipalities' relations.

Any economic modernization will inevitably cause greater territorial *economic* contrasts, as the scale of the federal and regional financial assistance to the peripheral territories ('Third Russia' and 'Fourth Russia') will be more limited, and their intrinsic developmental capacity is lower than that of larger cities. These risks are substantial. Social contrasts can be mitigated through policy directed at developing human potential, population mobility, and a more effective social safety net in the peripheral territories. However, such a social policy is only possible under effective federal governance, and even under this condition it will not be implemented right away.

Contrasts among the four Russias are great, but the differences between the Russia of large cities and the industrial Russia are most important politically. It is not at all clear that they will increase in the future. In fact, the possible administrative decentralization and the stronger role of municipalities also provide dividends to many 'Second Russia' cities. However, there are rather slim chances for political interest consolidation of the post-industrial large cities and the more traditional industrial towns. 'Second Russia' remembers the socio-economic costs of the past reforms and prefers stability. As of yet, there have been no post-Soviet instances of successfully combining institutional and economic reform with effective policies in the spheres of employment, human capital development, and population mobility. But the meeting points for the two most capable Russias do exist: they are administrative decentralization and fair elections of city governments.

Notes

1. The Institute of Demography at the Higher School of Economics publishes annual *Population of Russia* reports.
2. The *Report on the Development of Human Potential in the Russian Federation* is published annually by The UN Development Programs. The reports are available at: UNDP (2013), http://www.undp.ru/index.php?iso=RU&lid=2& cmd=publications1&id=49 (in Russian).
3. Until 2010 – adult literacy rates and gross enrollment ratio; starting in 2011 – mean and expected years of schooling.
4. UNDP (2011) Human Development Report 2011: *Sustainability and Equity: A Better Future for All.*
5. UNDP (2010) Human Development Report 2010: *The Real Wealth of Nations: Pathways to Human Development.*
6. Gorina E. (2012) 'Indeks chelovecheskogo razvitiya v Rossii i drugikh stranakh mira: obzor po materialam doklada PROON' (Human Development Index in Russia and Other Countries of the World. Review of the UNDP Report), *SPERO (Social Policy: Expertise, Recommendation, Overviews)*, No. 16, 193–98.
7. Gorina E. (2012) 'Indeks chelovecheskogo razvitiya v Rossii...,' 196.
8. A. Auzan, S. Bobylev (eds) (2011) *National Human Development Report 2011 for the Russian Federation* (Moscow: UNDP in Russia).
9. The cited number does not include non-capital industrial cities.
10. The author does include in 'Russia-1' the industrial non-capital cities Tolyatti, Naberezhnye Chelny, and Novokuznetsk.
11. If non-capital industrial cities with a population of over 250,000 (Magnitogorsk, Nizhny Tagil, Volzhskiy, Cherepovets, Surgut, Sterlitamak, Komsomolsk-on-Amur, Taganrog, Nizhnevartovsk) and the three larger cities Tolyatti, Naberezhnye Chelny, and Novokuznetsk are included, the proportion increases to 40 per cent.

12. T. Nefedova, A. Treyvish (1998) 'Sil'nye I slabye goroda Rossii' in Y. Lipets (ed.) *Polyusa i tsentry rosta v regional'nom razvitii* (Moscow: Institute of Geography, Russian Academy of Sciences).
13. Given the lower threshold of 20,000 for the 'Russia-2' city population.
14. N. Zubarevich (2010) *Regiony Rossii: neravenstvo, krizis, modernizatsiya* (Russian Regions: Inequality, Crisis, Modernization) (Moscow: IISP).

Bibliography

A. Auzan, S. Bobylev (eds) (2011) *National Human Development Report 2011 for the Russian Federation* (Moscow: UNDP in Russia).

E. Gorina (2012) 'Indeks chelovecheskogo razvitiya v Rossii i drugikh stranakh mira: obzor po materialam doklada PROON' (Human Development Index in Russia and Other Countries of the World. Review of the UNDP Report), SPERO (Social Policy: Expertise, Recommendation, Overviews), no. 16.

T. Nefedova, A. Treyvish (1998) 'Sil'nye I slabye goroda Rossii' in Y. Lipets (ed.) *Polyusa i tsentry rosta v regional'nom razvitii* (Moscow: Institute of Geography, Russian Academy of Sciences).

UNDP (2010) Human Development Report 2010: The Real Wealth of Nations: Pathways to Human Development.

UNDP (2011) Human Development Report 2011: Sustainability and Equity: A Better Future for All.

UNDP (2013) http://www.undp.ru/index.php?iso=RU&lid=2&cmd=publications 1&id=49 (in Russian). Accessed September 2, 2013.

N. Zubarevich (2010) *Regiony Rossii: neravenstvo, krizis, modernizatsiya* (Russian Regions: Inequality, Crisis, Modernization) (Moscow: IISP).

4
Russia's Population until 2025

Mikhail Denisenko

The main demographic phenomenon in developed and many developing countries is population aging. It is underlain by two longstanding trends – sustained life expectancy growth for older ages and birth rate decline, when generations of children do not replace those of parents in terms of numbers. Demographic projections indicate that in the long view the aging process will not just intensify but will also be accompanied by population decline (depopulation). As for Russia, according to the calculations made by the Central Statistical Administration of the Russian Soviet Federative Socialist Republic (RSFSR) (renamed as Russian Federation by the special law in December 1991)[1] as early as the 1980s, the process of depopulation was projected to start in 2001. However, as in a number of Eastern European countries, the severe socio-economic crisis of the 1990s accelerated the onset of depopulation. Numerical and age–gender population changes present a challenge for public institutions that have formed under the dominant presence of younger generations: how to ensure economic growth given a declining and aging population? As of yet, a satisfactory answer to this question has not been found.

Considering high mortality rates and uneven territorial population distribution, the cited tendencies make demographics 'the most serious problem of today's Russia', to use Vladimir Putin's phrasing.[2] Reacting to the unfavorable situation, the state stepped up its efforts to change the demographic trends, formalizing them in 2007 as the 'Concept of Demographic Policy of the Russian Federation until 2025'.

This work focuses on the current state of demographic indicators and their expected changes by 2025.

The population numbers and demographic balance in Russia

In 1950, in the aftermath of World War II, the Russian Federation was the fourth in the world in population (103 million people) behind only China, India, and the US. The country reached its historic maximum of 148.6 million people in 1993. By the start of 2011, population numbers had shrunk to 142.9 million people; Russia slipped to the ninth place in the world in population rankings, overtaken by Indonesia, Brazil, Pakistan, Nigeria, and Bangladesh.

Prior to the 1990s, the main source of population growth was natural increase (see Table 4.1). However, as a result of a sharp decrease in birth rates and an increase in death rates, the natural population decline began in 1992. It still continues, and had reached 13 million people by 2011. Migration growth for this period had added 7.5 new residents, but this only partially (57 per cent) compensated for the losses from the negative birth and death rate balance.

The data for the last two years indicate a decline in natural losses. Moreover, thanks to migration that compensates for the losses, the population of the country has started growing, prompting optimistic assessments of the demographic situation by officials. The 'Concept of the State Migration Policy' adopted in June 2012 maintains that 'according to the Federal State Statistics Service (Rosstat) prospective population estimate until the year 2030 (high and medium variants), factoring in the Russian Census results and the demographic process dynamics of the recent years, the country's population will be 142.8–45.5 million people at the start of 2025'.

Table 4.1 Russia's demographic balance in the inter-census periods (in thousands)

Period, years	Population at the start of the period	Total increase	Natural increase	Migration increase
1959–69	117,534	12,545	14,272	–1,727
1970–78	130,079	7,472	7,330	142
1979–88	137,551	9,471	8,029	1,442
1989–2002	147,022	–2,058	–7,554	5,496
2003–10	144,964	–2,098	–4,536	2,438
2011	142,866	–	–	–

Source: Calculated based on Rosstat data.

Table 4.2   Prospective Russian population estimates (in millions)*

Source	Variant	2010	2015	2020	2025	2030
Rosstat (2012)	Medium	142.8	...	...	142.8	...
	High		...	...	145.6	...
Institute of	Low		142.2	139.5	135.7	130.9
demography NRU	Medium	142.8	143.2	143.0	142.2	140.8
HSE (2012)	High		144.1	146.5	148.7	150.7
UN Population	Low		140.9	137.7	133.6	129.1
Division (2010)	Medium	142.9	142.2	141.0	139.0	136.4
	High		143.6	144.3	144.5	143.7
US Census Bureau (2012)	Medium	142.5	142.4	141.7	140.1	138.2

Note: *Rosstat and the Institute of Demography NRU HSE – 1 January estimates; UN Population division and US Census Bureau – 1 July estimates
Sources: The concept of the state migration policy; UN Population Division: World population prospects: The 2010 revision (http://www.unpopulation.org/); US Census Bureau: (http://www.census.gov/ipc/www/idb).

Actually, a few variants of demographic estimates are always developed. The so-called 'medium variant' is considered the most likely or expected. Low and high variants denote the limits of possible demographic indicator changes. By 2025, according to the medium variant of Rosstat's estimate, the country's population will remain practically unchanged (see Table 4.2). An insignificant decrease (one million people) by the same year is predicted by the specialists from the National Research University – Higher School of Economics (HSE).[3] Foreign experts predict more substantial depopulation (from 2.2 to 4.4 million people). Population growth has been noted only in high variants. However, after 2025, all estimates project the intensification of the depopulation process, except for the high variant estimate by the NRU HSE.

The main reason for the estimates' discrepancies lies in the size of the projected migration increase, since all of the estimates project the current or even higher natural population decrease. For instance, NRU HSE demographers believe that from 2012 to 2014 the migration increase in Russia will amount to at least 3 million as per the low variant, up to 4.2 million as per medium variant, and 5.5 million as per high variant. The UN experts' estimates put the number at 1.8 million people. A negative natural increase is part of nearly all of the estimates, even taking into account the increased birth rate. Thus, population stabilization or increase is significantly related to the migration policy pursued.

The compression of Russian demographic space

Up until the end of the Soviet era, a slow population shift to the east, and to a lesser degree to the north and south, had been taking place. As a result, the percentage of population residing in the Asian part of Russia had increased from 13.1 per cent in 1926 to 21.8 in 1989. While migration was the main component of the population growth beyond the Urals and in the far north, high natural increase accounted for the population growth in the North Caucasus and several autonomous regions of Siberia and the Far East, as well as in the Volga region a little earlier. Demographic transition, that is, birth and death rate decline as part of the transition from traditional to modern society, reached the indigenous peoples of the Russian autonomous regions half a century later than it came to the ethnic groups of European origin. Consequently, the regions of Central Russia had an earlier onset of demographic aging, which was exacerbated by migration from the rural areas. Hence, children below age 15 comprise 12 per cent of the population of Ryazan and Tula Oblast, while those above age 60 constitute 23 per cent. In contrast, the same indicators for Dagestan equal 25 per cent and 9 per cent respectively; for Chechnya, they are 33 per cent and 9 per cent.

After the dissolution of the Soviet Union, migration flows reversed from east and north to west and south.[4] As a result of 'the western drift' of migration, the eastern part of the country has lost almost 1.5 million people to the population exchange with the European part. The process of compression of 'social geospace'[5] has been taking place. In this particular case, it is a depopulation process affecting vast territories of the country (compression of demographic space). For instance, from 1989 to 2010, the population of Chukotka Autonomous Okrug had declined by almost 70 per cent; that of Magadan Oblast had fallen 60 per cent; those of Murmansk and Kamchatka Oblasts and the Komi Republic had decreased by 30 per cent. Apart from the eastern regions, natural population decline had markedly reduced the population of many Central Russia regions as well as those of the Volga and the northwest. At the same time, people were actively moving to the Moscow region, the oil-rich provinces of western Siberia and southern Russia. For example, in the period from 1989 to 2011, Moscow Metropolitan Area (the capital and the Moscow Oblast) had registered a migration increase of 5.2 million people, while the population of Moscow had grown 28 per cent: from 9 to 11.5 million people. The proportional share of the North Caucasian Federal District has grown thanks to the high natural increase (see Table 4.3). In the last 20 years, Dagestan, the

Table 4.3 Population of Russian regions, 1989–2011

Region	Population (in thousands)			Growth (percent)		Population proportion (percent)		
	1989	2003	2011	from 1989 to 2003	from 1989 to 2011	1989	2003	2011
Russia	147,022	144,964	142,865	98.6	97.2	100	100	100
Moscow and Moscow Oblast	15,522	17,004	18,647	109.5	120.1	10.6	11.7	13.1
Saint-Petersburg and Leningrad Oblast	6,644	6,324	6,618	95.2	99.6	4.5	4.4	4.6
Central F.D.	22,418	20,943	19,798	93.4	88.3	15.2	14.4	13.9
Northwestern F.D.	8,592	7,625	7,008	88.7	81.6	5.8	5.3	4.9
Southern F.D.	13,252	13,954	13,851	105.3	104.5	9.0	9.6	9.7
North Caucasian F.D.	7,284	8,938	9,439	122.7	129.6	5.0	6.2	6.6
Volga F.D.	31,765	31,105	29,880	97.9	94.1	21.6	21.5	20.9
Urals F.D.	12,526	12,361	12,087	98.7	96.5	8.5	8.5	8.5
Siberian F.D.	21,068	20,031	19,252	95.1	91.4	14.3	13.8	13.5
Far Eastern F.D.	7,950	6,680	6,285	84.0	79.1	5.4	4.6	4.4

Source: Rosstat (1989) – 12 January estimates (date of the census 1989). 2003 and 2001 – 1 January estimates

F.D. – Federal District

(РОССТАТ РЕГИОНЫ РОССИИ. СОЦИАЛЬНО- ЭКОНОМИЧЕСКИЕ показатели – 2012, http://www.gks.ru/bgd/regl/b12_14p/IssWWW. exe/Stg/d01/03-01.htm; РОССТАТ РЕГИОНЫ РОССИИ. СОЦИАЛЬНО- экономические показатели – 2003, http://www.gks.ru/bgd/ regl/B03_14/IssWWW.exe/Stg/d010/i01009r.htm)

district's most populous republic, has seen its population grow 1.7 times to 3 million people.

At the present time, population is decreasing faster in the traditionally well-populated regions of the central and northwestern federal districts than it is in most Siberian and Far Eastern regions. In these territories, the Russian rural space has compressed into detached pockets and areas, with a socio-demographic desert separating them.[6] A record of sorts has been set by the Kostroma Oblast, which lost a quarter of its rural population in the period from 2003 to 2011. Every third village of the Kostroma Oblast has no residents now.

During the two post-Soviet decades, the number of city dwellers has shrunk by 2.6 million, while the rural areas have lost 1.6 million people. As a result of economic and demographic upheavals, administrative and territorial changes, and the municipal government reform, there are 950 fewer urban-type settlements now, and more than 20,000 rural settlements have ceased to exist. At present, almost 19,500 rural settlements exist only nominally – they are actually completely depopulated. Some urban-type and rural settlements have received town privileges, thus increasing the total number of towns.

According to Natalia Zubarevich's political geographic typology, the vast territorial periphery consisting of village residents, urban-type settlement residents, and small town dwellers comprise 'Third Russia'. This part of the Russian population survives off the land; it is outside politics. Its share in Russia's population is about 35 per cent and is decreasing in both absolute and relative terms. 'Second Russia', according to Zubarevich, comprises towns with between 20,000 and 500,000 inhabitants; 34 per cent of the country's population lives there. 'First Russia' encompasses cities with more than 500,000 inhabitants. This cluster's share has increased from 26 to 31 per cent. More than half of this growth came from Moscow. A different type of population resides there: it is more educated, young, and mobile; the middle class is also concentrated there.

It is safe to predict that the proportion of urban population will not change much by 2025, and the population redistribution in favor of large and largest cities – in both absolute and relative terms – will continue. In large part, the process will be facilitated by Moscow's territorial expansion.[7] As per our estimates, the additional growth of the capital region's population may reach at least 2 million people by 2025. Thus, Moscow will absorb the remaining part of the young and educated population from many of the Russian regions, including the regions bordering Moscow Oblast and the Far East. The process's negative consequences for both demographic and socio-economic development of the 'remaining' Russia are evident. At the same time, the new workplaces in the capital region's expanding economy (in construction, service industry, trade, and transportation) will attract labor migrants from labor-surplus republics of the North Caucasus and abroad.

By 2025 the western migration drift from the eastern Siberia and Far East regions will diminish, but only due to the depletion of local demographic resources. High-profile government officials voice concern over the territory's depopulation, but few real steps are taken to broaden economic opportunities and raise living standards. For example, in unemployment indicators for May 2012, the eastern regions were ahead of only some North Caucasus republics. In crime statistics, the Far East and eastern Siberia are in the lead, while being at the bottom of the list in life expectancy figures. Even if the regime discards its consumer-like attitude toward the regions, the 'redirection' of migration flows from large cities back to the eastern regions appears to be virtually unfeasible. Nikita Mkrtchyan of the Institute of Demography at NRU HSE believes that the growth of certain population centers in the east is possible, but only at the expense of the peripheral areas of the given region. The development of these centers and the accelerated creation of a comfortable urban environment there might stem the tide to the west and generally reduce population losses in Siberia and the Far East.

Russia: Neither young nor old

A simple visual analysis of Russia's age and gender population structure at the beginning of 2011 reveals two groups of factors that affected its formation (see Figure 4.1). The first group is associated with a logical birth and death rate decrease as a result of the demographic transition. Compared with 1897, the pyramid base has narrowed significantly, which is a direct effect of the birth rate decrease. Fewer children were born in 2011 in comparison to 1897, although the country's population at the end of the 19th century was 1.5 times lower that it is now (at that time, it consisted mostly of children). The proportion of children below age 15 was approaching 40 per cent,[8] while in 2011 it was equal to 15.4 per cent. At the same time, the top part of the pyramid has grown heavier: the proportion of those older than 60 has grown from 6.5 per cent to 18.5 per cent. As Figure 4.1 indicates, by 2025 the proportion of the elderly will increase in both absolute and relative terms.

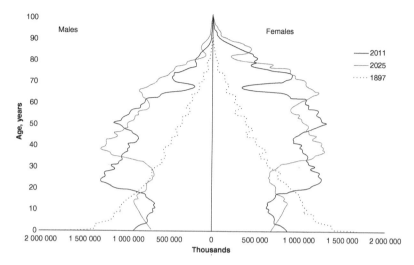

Figure 4.1 The Russian population age distribution in 1897, 2011, and 2025

The large deformities (depressions and bulges) in the age pyramid are associated with the second group of factors: military and socio-economic upheavals, as well as demographic policy measures that caused temporary birth rate spikes. The latter include the abortion ban of 1936 and the efforts to increase birth rates in the 1980s. The wave-like changes in the numbers of certain age groups are related to these disturbance factors. The demographic 'war echo' is a clear example of this phenomenon: the sharp birth rate decline of 1942–45 has echoed in later years as the 'children' or 'grandchildren' of war entered active reproductive age. It is precisely these large deformities that make Russian age distribution structure different from that of European countries. There is a 1.5 to 2 times difference in the number of births at the wave's lowest and highest points. Even Poland and Germany, which suffered heavy human losses in World War II, have not demonstrated such fluctuations.

The Russian demographic wave was intensified by the 1980s increase in birth rates as large generations of women born in the 1950s and early 1960s were taking advantage of the benefits provided in accordance with the demographic policy of the day. Numerically smaller generations that followed entered the active reproduction period in the years of economic crisis and postponed childbirth for this reason. Hence, the anticipated demographic wave fluctuation between the birth rates in the mid-1980s and mid-1990s was further intensified. A similar situation is

Table 4.4   Large and small generations in Russia

Large generations, birth years	Number of births, in millions	Small generations, birth years	Number of births, in millions	Ratios
1	2	3	4	[2]/[4]
1936–40	16.1	1942–46	7.5	2.1
Max 1939	4.5	Min 1943	1.1*	3.8
1951–60	14.1	1966–70	9.4	1.5
Max 1954	2.9	Min 1968	1.8	1.6
1983–88	12.2	1994–2000	6.3	1.9
Max 1987	2.5	Min 1999	1.2	2.1
2007–11	8.7	1994–2000	6.3	1.4
Max 2011		Min 1999	1.2	

Source: Rosstat data, *author's estimate.

emerging today as the new childbirth stimulus measures, which may prove to be temporary, affect primarily the large generations of the 1980s. Thus, the demographic wave is not losing but gaining in strength (see Table 4.4). In the long-term perspective, demographic waves have negative effects, since they are followed by sharp fluctuations in supply and demand of various goods and services, forcing the restructuring of various economic and social institutions.

Generations and social movements

Due to the demographic wave, Russian generations[9] differ greatly in size. Thus, the generation of those born in 1939 is more than 3.5 times larger than the generation of people born in 1943. The 1987 generation is twice as large as the smallest post-war generation, those born in 1999 (see Table 4.4). Scientific research has frequently indicated that generational size affects its members' biographies. But is there a relation between generational size and mass social movements? In the post-war period, we can pinpoint three such movements: Khrushchev's Thaw (1956–64), Gorbachev's Perestroika (1985–91), and the events of late 2011–early 2012. The movements' inceptions are separated by periods of 29 and 26 years, which is approximately equal to the span of one generation.[10] On average, approximately similar time intervals separate large generations. At the height of mass public movements, members of large generations happened to be at young ages (see Table 4.5, page 95). Besides, they were at higher educational levels than members of older generations.

Table 4.5 Social movements and age of large generations

Generation, birth years	Khrushchev's Thaw (1956–64)	Perestroika (1985–91)	Protest movements (2011–12?)	Future (around 2035)
1936–40	16–28 years old	45–55 years old	71–77 years old	–
1951–60	–	25–40 years old	51–61 years old	–
1983–88	–	–	23–29 years old	50–55 years old
2008–12	–	–	–	23–28 years old

Aging will accelerate

Almost all estimates project noticeable and virtually identical changes in population distribution by the year 2025 (see Table 4.6), which cannot be corrected by any demographic policy measures. The proportion of those over age 65 will increase by more than 35 per cent, thus increasing the burden on the working-age population, which will have to support large numbers of the elderly. Nearly every fifth Russian will be over 65 in 2025.[11]

Russia's population is aging only 'from the bottom' due to a low birth rate. For as long as three decades, the aging process in most developed

Table 4.6 The Russian population age distribution in 2010 and 2025 (%)*

Source	2010			2025		
	0–14 years old	15–64 years old	Over 65 years old	0–14 years old	15–64 years old	Over 65 years old
Rosstat (2010)	15.1	72.0	12.9	16.6	66.0	17.5
Institute of Demography NRU HSE (2012)	15.1	71.9	13.0	16.7	65.4	17.8
UN	15.0	72.2	12.8	16.8	65.8	17.4
US Census Bureau	15.1	71.7	13.2	16.3	65.7	18.0

Note: *Rosstat and the Institute of Demography NRU HSE – 1 January estimates; UN Population Division and US Census Bureau – 1 July estimates
Sources: The concept of the state migration policy; UN Population Division: World population prospects: The 2010 Revision (http://www.unpopulation.org/); US Census Bureau: (http://www.census.gov/ipc/www/idb).

countries has also come 'from the top' thanks to longer life expectancies in the oldest age groups.

The decrease in working-age population

In 2006–07, the number of potential members of the workforce reached its historic peak of 90.1 million people, or 63 per cent of the total population of the country. Prior to that, such a positive market trend was seen only at the turn of 1980. At the same time, due to the low birth rates of the 1990s and the retirement of people from small war-time generations, by 2006 the demographic burden on the workforce on the part of children and the elderly had fallen to the all-time low of 580 dependents to 1,000 potential workers. It thus brought about a uniquely favorable condition for economic development: a maximum number of workers with a minimum number of dependents. Such changes in age distribution during a period of economic growth precipitate a demographic dividend that consists of a more rapid per capita income increase. According to the received estimates, in the period from 1998 to 2008, per capita GDP had been increasing at an average rate of 7,3 per cent a year. The working-age population had been growing at an average rate of approximately 0.9 per cent a year, while number of those employed had been rising by 2.2 per cent a year.[12] All in all, for the period discussed, approximately 17 per cent of per capita GDP growth was related to favorable changes in age distribution.

The period of low demographic burden on the workforce has opened a window of opportunity for various types of reforms related to the living conditions of the elderly. However, this window was shut by another demographic wave: by 2025 the working-age population will fall by 10 million people, and this trend cannot be reversed. It can be somewhat weakened by reducing the mortality rates of those in the working-age category and by more active recruitment of migrants.

There will be fewer students, but more educated people

Secondary education has long become virtually universal in Russia. After the completion of the ninth grade, 90 per cent of children continue their studies in high schools and professional educational institutions of different kinds. However, the school cohort itself (children ages 7–17) fell to a historic minimum of 14.9 million in 2011. The projected growth will be quite moderate (up to 3.5 million people by 2025).

From the late 1980s until 2007, the student cohort (ages 18 to 24) had been steadily increasing, reaching 17.6 million. In the immediate future, this age cohort will also markedly diminish and in 2021 will fall below the mid-1960s historic minimum of 10 million people (at that time, the war generations had reached college age).[13]

According to the Organisation for Economic Co-operation and Development (OECD) estimates, Russia is the world leader in the proportional share of individuals ages 25 to 65 with complete secondary education (54 per cent). As for college education, Russia (22 per cent)[14] is behind only the US (30 per cent), Israel (27 per cent), Norway (31 per cent), the Netherlands (28 per cent), New Zealand, Denmark, and Canada (all three at 25 per cent).[15] Provided past trends continue into future demographic changes, the number of individuals with full or incomplete college education will grow as the economically active part of the population decreases in number. This will primarily happen due to the lower numbers of those receiving professional and complete secondary education. The proportion of individuals with less than complete secondary education will become insignificant. This trend certainly reflects the growing accumulation of human capital and the expansion of the middle class. At the same time, future shortages of lower-skilled labor are to be expected. Under such conditions, the increased demand for low-skilled workers may be offset by introducing labor-saving technologies or met by importing low-skilled workers from abroad or through sizable wage increases that will attract relatively well-educated individuals to low-skilled labor.

Fertility prospects

'The Concept of Demographic Policy of the Russian Federation until 2025' has a unique characteristic: it stipulates the values of birth rate and other demographic indicators. Neither the Soviet Union nor any other country (France, Sweden, Australia, and so on) have ever formulated their family policy goals in such a way. In many respects, it proceeds from the lack of evidence that links pronatalist measures and long-term increase in birth rates. Nevertheless, many state institutions work toward meeting the objectives set forth in the 'Concept'.

The recent increases in the number of births were caused both by the increase in the number of women of child-bearing age (ages 20 to 40) and by the actual increase in birth rate. The country owes such positive shifts in population age distribution to the 'children' of the Soviet demographic policies – the large generations of the 1980s. However, as early as 2012, Russia will enter a period when the number of potential mothers will start declining rapidly. By 2025, the number will decline by almost half a million people. The number of births will decrease even as birth coefficients increase. Hence, in the absence of radical changes in mortality rates' dynamics, natural population loss will rise.

The Soviet family policies have substantially affected the birth rate dynamics. In the 1980s, spurred on by financial incentives, a significant number of married couples accelerated the achievement of their reproductive goals. But the instituted measures did not affect the goals themselves: the goal of having one or two children was prevalent. Therefore, as a result of scheduling births for an earlier date (birth calendar shift), fewer children were born in the following years. Total fertility rate started declining while still in the Soviet era: from 1987 to 1990, it fell 15 per cent.

Another reason for the 1990s birth rate decline has to do with the economic crisis. Potential parents had to postpone both creating a family and childbirth due to a sharp decrease in living standards, unemployment, diminished assistance from relatives, and the destruction of a social safety net that included housing benefits. Some of these postponed births have never materialized.

The third reason is related to a change in the demographic behavior of the young generations entering reproductive age in the late 1990s–early 2000s. Relative to their predecessors, they were getting married later and less frequently; they were also postponing births until older ages.

Based on stability of reproductive goals, as well as changes in economic conditions and young people's behavior, Russian and foreign demographers projected a birth rate increase as early as the start of the new century. For instance, according to the projection of the Center of Human Demography and Ecology at the Institute of Economic Forecasting of the Russian Academy of Sciences, total fertility rate was projected to increase from 1.32 births per woman in 2003 to 1.43 in 2010 and 1.51 in 2015.[16]

The UN experts produced a similar estimate of birth rate increases in 2004. According to the statistical data, the birth rate increase started in 2006 – a year before birth rate stimulus measures went into effect. Thus, the implementation of pronatalist policy coincided with the increasing birth rate trend. In Sergei Zakharov's opinion, 2007–10 data (the years the new socio-demographic policy measures were in effect) fit perfectly into the trend that took shape in 2000.[17] Thus, it is incorrect to attribute the observed birth rate growth exclusively to the demographic policy measures.[18]

In most experts' opinion, the results of the Russian financial-incentive-based pronatalist policy will be mixed in the next decade: the monotonous development of birth rate processes is likely to be broken. As was the case in the Soviet era, the birth rate increase may be followed by a compensatory decline. One of the conditions for overcoming such a decline and maintaining a relatively high birth rate (in comparison to developed countries) is a comprehensive improvement of the socio-economic environment and an implementation of a time-stable policy directed at creating favorable conditions for every family's development. Family policy measures that are directed at increasing birth rate should not be reduced solely to financial support. In a number of European countries, these measures are being implemented in the following ways:

- more family and children-friendly social environment is created;
- conditions for parents' participation in their professional and parental roles are created;
- financial support for families with inadequate resources is provided;
- gender equality, which includes equality in employment opportunities and family life, is promoted.[19]

However, even given the implementation of all the possible and impossible positive changes in the country, the Russian birth rate will not exceed the total fertility rate of 1.9 births per woman. In any event, it is insufficient to provide prospective population growth in the absence of migrant flow.

The issues of life expectancy

The transition to market economy in the former Soviet republics has sparked a sharp increase in mortality rates. In 1994, life expectancy in Russia fell to its lowest point since the second half of the 1950s: 57 years for men and 71 for women. As a result, the country joined the club of less advanced states of the developing world. Only in 2003 did the death rate start falling, and life expectancy increased. By 2011, life expectancy in the Russian Federation had risen to 64.3 years for men and 76.1 years for women, averaging 70.3 years.

By 2011, some success in preserving life had been achieved: the country returned to (for women) and approached (for men) the highest indicators registered in 1965 and 1987. But the world has advanced further since then. While in the mid-1960s Russia was between the 20th and 30th top countries on the life expectancy list, with neighbors like

Austria, Finland, and Japan, in 1987 it slipped below the 70th country, ending up below 120 countries in these rankings next to Iran, North Korea, and Bangladesh in 2011. Russian women are twenty places higher than the men, who were in the company of men from Madagascar, Laos, Pakistan, Ghana, and Yemen.

Currently, 70 per cent of deaths are explained by cardiovascular diseases and external causes such as road accidents (according to official data, from 1990 to 2010, 790,000 people died as a result of road accidents in Russia). Other causes include murder (620,000 people for the same period), suicide (890,000 people), and accidental alcohol poisoning (610,000 people). These numbers greatly exceed the estimates of the Soviet Union's human losses in all its post-war conflicts or allied military personnel losses in World War II. Moreover, Russians die of cardiovascular diseases 10–15 years earlier than people in Western countries.

In keeping with education and GDP to life expectancy ratios observed around the world, Russia's life expectancy should be equal to at least 75 years for both genders. However, such numbers are not observed. One of the main reasons for this discrepancy is seen in high levels of economic inequality in Russia, which are approaching those of Latin American countries.

Economic inequality is one of the reasons for inequality before death. Another factor is different self-preservational behavior of particular population groups. Behavioral factors are especially significant in studying gender differences in health attitudes and causes of the excessive death rate for men in Russia. The phenomenon of inequality before death engenders protest against the socio-economic relations that condemn people to premature death.[20] Therefore, health care policy in a large number of states is primarily directed toward eliminating this inequality, specifically the inequality between certain provinces and population groups. Social differentiation in mortality rates also existed in the pre-reform Soviet era, but its scale was completely different, and it apparently was not such a significant factor characteristic of Russian mortality rates.[21]

Russian regions differ profoundly from each other in mortality rates. On one end of the spectrum lies Moscow, with life expectancy of 69.5 years for men and 77.7 years for women, according to Rosstat's estimates for 2009. It is on the level of the Eastern European countries. On the other end is the Tyva Republic, with life expectancy of 54.4 years for men and 66 years for women. This mirrors the indicators of the poorest African nations. The profound differences in mortality rates are also observed inside the regions between the regional centers and the periphery. As an illustration, life expectancy in the city of Kostroma was 62.4 years for men and 74.6 years for women in 2008–10. Meanwhile, in the majority of Kostroma Oblast rural municipalities, it equaled 55–58 years for men and 70–72 years for women.

As a number of study findings indicate, low educational level, marital status, poverty, and underemployment are the main preconditions for premature death.[22] Alcohol is a powerful mortality factor, but it is closely related to the above-mentioned variables of poverty, unemployment, and low educational level. A number of scientists believe that two types of mortality can be identified in Russia. One of them is characteristic of socially adapted,[23] comparably well-educated, and fully employed individuals with an income level at or above average. This population comprises a significant part of those living in 'First Russia'. High mortality rates are characteristic of the socially inactive part of the population dominated by blue-collar workers of lower educational and income levels. Such a population is more prevalent in the 'Second Russia' and especially in the 'Third Russia', which exhibits higher mortality rates than major cities.

The goal of 'increasing life expectancy to age 70 by 2016' was declared in the 'Concept of Demographic Policy'. The goal was achieved earlier, in 2011. However, there is no basis for linking its achievement with the state's targeted efforts. Russia lags behind most developed countries with respect to health care expenditures. In absolute terms, the Russian state spends 3.9 times less on health care per capita than the EU members do, on average. The quality of medical care and its accessibility have not increased. The state's steps directed at promoting healthy lifestyle taken prior to 2011 (various health centers and programs, tobacco and alcohol excise tax increases, and so on) were cautious and insufficient in both substance and financing.[24] Of all the state policy measures, birth allowances instituted as part of the 'Health' national priorities project are worth a special mention; they had a positive effect on the infant mortality rate dynamics and the health of newborn babies and their mothers.

The decreased mortality rates are to an extent a byproduct of changes in a whole host of public life spheres, which are not directly related to health or demographics. Among them are reduction in army draft, better quality of automobile fleet, changes in traffic regulations, and adopting amendments to the federal law on government regulation of ethyl alcohol production and sales. The main factor of life expectancy growth, though, is change in the population itself. Part of the population is changing its self-preservational behavior on its own accord in the direction of greater conformity with the standards of developed countries. These shifts were facilitated by increases in income and educational levels among the Russians. In particular, a number of researchers stress a possible decrease and positive changes in alcohol consumption.[25] Road etiquette has clearly improved as well. Moscow school students have initiated a grass-roots movement for healthy lifestyle, which calls for complete abstinence from alcohol and tobacco and regular physical exercise. However, the Soviet-era lifespans that were attained again are unlikely to be surpassed in the future without active state support. As evidenced by the experience of developed countries, without a significant increase in government spending, the health care system cannot be reformed, nor can the public attitude toward personal health be substantially changed.

Reducing the high mortality rate should be among the first priorities of Russian government policy. Despite the achieved success, the country continues to suffer heavy losses from premature deaths. Economic, social, and demographic consequences of these losses are enormous, and, unfortunately, they are still not fully recognized by Russian society. One of these consequences is human capital devaluation: substantial investments in professional training end up being lost as a result of high mortality at young ages. High mortality complicates the implementation of pension reform and renders the concept of continuing education meaningless. Intensifying efforts directed at the rapid reduction of mortality rates and improvement of the health care system will lead to population growth whose demographic effect is as significant as that of the targeted birth rates stipulated by the 'Concept of Demographic Policy until 2025'. However, the economic and social effect of mortality rate reduction will be greater. Since this reduction will primarily affect certain high mortality risk age groups, that is, those who are in the workforce, the number of potential workers will increase under the conditions of declining labor supply. In addition, the number of nuclear families and births will increase, and the number of widows and orphans decrease as a direct corollary of a reduction in excessive male mortality rates. A reduction in mortality rates is an essential precondition for Russia's modernization. The technological and economic lag can hardly be overcome given a population whose lifespan is equal to that observed in developed countries half a century ago.

Notes

1. The Russian Soviet Federative Socialist Republic is the name of Russia during the Soviet period. RSFSR was renamed into the Russian Federation by the special law on December 25, 1991.

2. 'President's Address to the Federal Assembly of the Russian Federation', *Rossiyskaya Gazeta*, 11 May 2006.
3. One of the first working versions of prospective estimates is presented here. The estimates were completed at the Institute of Demography NRU HSE before the final results of the all-Russian census of 2010 were released.
4. It is commonly known that, at the initial stage of implementing market reforms, most state projects concerned with developing the northern and eastern territories were cut back or eliminated. Generous incentives that attracted labor force to the far north and the localities of equal status were devalued; the social infrastructure that required significant investments was destroyed.
5. A. Treivish (2012) 'Szhatie Sotsial'nogo Geoprostranstva: Mezhdu Real'nost' yu i Utopiey", *Demoscope Weekly*, no.507–08. http://demoscope.ru/weekly/2012/0507/tema01.php.
6. T. Nefedova (2010) 'Sel'skaya Rossiya: Prostranstvennoe Szhatie i Sotsial'naya Polyarizatsiya', *Polit.Ru*, Public speech, http://polit.ru/article/2010/08/05/countryside/
7. N. Zubarevich (2012) 'Sovremennaya Rossiya: Geografiya s Arifmetikoy', *Otechestvennye Zapiski*, no.1.
8. In the modern world, such a high proportion of children can be found in countries like Bolivia, Nepal, and Sudan.
9. In this case, generation is understood as an aggregation of people born in a particular period.
10. An average time interval that separates parents' generation from children's generation.
11. Russia trails developed countries in aging rate by almost a quarter of a century. The proportion of people aged 65 and over currently observed in Russia was recorded in Germany in the late 1970s, Japan in the late 1990s, and Sweden in 1975.
12. V. Bessonov, V. Gimpelson, Y. Kuzminov, and G. Yasin (2009) *Proizvoditel'nost' i Factory Dolgosrochnogo Razvitiya Rossiyskoy Ekonomiki* (Moscow: HSE – GU).
13. According to different projections, the number of 18-year-old males will only reach approximately 650,000. Given this number, reforming the educational system (greater diversification of professional education and raising the quality of education) is inevitable. The army will also require reform (reducing size of the draft and transitioning to professional armed services).
14. According to the 2010 census.
15. OECD (2009) *OECD at a Glance 2009: OECD Indicators*.
16. A. Vishnevsky, ed. (2004) *Naselenie Rossii 2002* (Moscow).
17. S. Zakharov (2012) 'Kakoy Budet Rozhdaemost' v Rossii?', *Demoscope Weekly*, no.495–96, http://www.demoscope.ru/weekly/2012/0495/tema01.php.
18. Despite the increased birth rate, Russia has not joined the category of developed countries with high 'low birth rate'. It is worth noting that this category includes both the countries where active family policies are pursued (France, Sweden, Denmark) and the countries that have no such policies (the US, Great Britain). Birth rates did not guarantee simple reproduction (parents' generations' replacement by children's generations) in any of the developed countries.

19. UNECE (1993) European Population Conference Recommendations, March 1993, http://www.unece.org/pau/epc/epc1993_recom.html. Subsequently, these recommendations were included in other UN documents.
20. E. Rosset (1981) *Prodolzhitel'nost' Chelovecheskoy Zhizni* (Moscow: Progress), 282.
21. A. Ivanova, V. Semenova, and E. Dubrovina (1994) 'Marginalizatsiya Rossiyskoy Smertnosti ', *Demoscope Weekly*, no.181–82. http://demoscope.ru/weekly/2004/0181/tema01.php.
22. E. Andreyev, V. Shkolnikov, and T. Maleva (eds) (2000) *Neravenstvo i Smertnost' v Rossii* (Moscow: Signal); V. Shkolnikov, V. Cherviakov (eds) (2000) *Policies for the Control of the Transition's Mortality Crisis in Russia* (Moscow: UNDP).
23. See Note 22.
24. Strategy-2020 (2012) *New Growth Model – New Social Policy*, the final report of the expert work results on the current problems of socio-economic strategy until 2020 (Moscow).
25. D. Khalturina, A. Korotayev (2008) Alkogol'naya Katastrofa: Kak Ostanovit' Vymiranie v Rossii. In: D. Khalturina, A. Korotayev (eds) Alkogolnaya Katastrofa i Vozmozhnosti Gosudarstvennoy Politiki v Preodolenii Alkogolnoy Sverkhsmertnosti v Rossii (Moscow:URSS); A.Vishnevsky (ed) (2011) *Naselenie Rossii 2009* (Moscow: HSE Publishing House).

Bibliography

E. Andreyev, V. Shkolnikov, and T. Maleva (eds) (2000) *Neravenstvo i Smertnost' v Rossii* (Moscow: Signal)

V. Bessonov, V. Gimpelson, Y. Kuzminov, and G. Yasin (2009) *Proizvoditel'nost' i Factory Dolgosrochnogo Razvitiya Rossiyskoy Ekonomiki* (Moscow: HSE Publishing House).

Ivanova, V. Semenova, and E. Dubrovina (1994) 'Marginalizatsiya Rossiyskoy Smertnosti', *Demoscope Weekly*, no.181–82. http://demoscope.ru/weekly/2004/0181/tema01.php. Accessed August 2013

D. Khalturina, A. Korotayev (2008) Alkogol'naya Katastrofa: Kak Ostanovit' Vymiranie v Rossii. In: D. Khalturina, A. Korotayev (eds) Alkogolnaya Katastrofa i Vozmozhnosti Gosudarstvennoy Politiki v Preodolenii Alkogolnoy Sverkhsmertnosti v Rossii (Moscow:URSS).

T. Nefedova (2010) 'Sel'skaya Rossiya: Prostranstvennoe Szhatie i Sotsial'naya Polyarizatsiya', *Polit.Ru*, Public lecture, http://polit.ru/article/2010/08/05/countryside/. Accessed August 2013.

OECD (2009) *OECD at a Glance 2009: OECD Indicators* (Paris).

'President's Address to the Federal Assembly of the Russian Federation', *Rossiyskaya Gazeta*, 11 May 2006.

V. Putin (2008) 'Stroitel'stvo Spravedlivosti: Sotsial'naya Politika Dlya Rossii', *Komsomolskaya Pravda*, 13 February.

E. Rosset (1981) *Prodolzhitel'nost' Chelovecheskoy Zhizni* (Moscow: Progress), 282.

V. Shkolnikov, V. Cherviakov (eds) (2000) *Policies for the Control of the Transition's Mortality Crisis in Russia* (Moscow: UNDP).

Strategy-2020 (2012) *New Growth Model – New Social Policy*, the final report of the expert work results on the current problems of socio-economic strategy until

2020 (Moscow: NRU HSE). http://2020strategy.ru/documents/32710234.html August 2013

Treivish (2012) 'Szhatie Sotsial'nogo Geoprostranstva: Mezhdu Real'nost'yu i Utopiey', *Demoscope Weekly*, no.507–08. http://demoscope.ru/weekly/2012/0507/tema01.php. August 2013

UNECE (1993) *European Population Conference Recommendations*, March 1993 http://www.unece.org/pau/epc/epc1993_recom.html. Subsequently, these recommendations were included in other UN documents. August 2013

Vishnevsky (ed.) (2004) *Naselenie Rossii 2002* (Moscow: CDU).

A. Vishnevsky (ed) (2011) *Russia's Population 2009* (Moscow: HSE Publishing House)

S. Zakharov (2012) 'Kakoy Budet Rozhdaemost' v Rossii?', *Demoscope Weekly*, no.495–96, http://www.demoscope.ru/weekly/2012/0495/tema01.php. August 2013

N. Zubarevich (2012) 'Sovremennaya Rossiya: Geografiya s Arifmetikoy', *Otechestvennye Zapiski*, no.1.

5
Government Interference: An Institutional Trap

Boris Grozovsky

In the spring of 2007, few supposed that the US mortgage crisis would lead to a global crisis of sovereign debt that could last a decade. Five years earlier, Russia Prime Minister Mikhail Kasyanov sought to prepare the country for 'the debt problem of 2003', not knowing that there would be no such problem, because 8–10 years later oil prices would settle at around 100 dollars per barrel. From August to October 1998, nobody could have expected that a country that had defaulted on its debts and devalued its currency, whose economy was based on barter and missed payments, would see a decade of stable GDP growth. And, in late 2010, experts were not predicting an explosion of political activity and did not foresee that, a year and a half to two years later, a fairly large percentage of the urban population would begin to perceive the Russian political system as hopelessly archaic. The number of such examples is limitless, and any attempt to predict economic developments nearly 20 years ahead of time is truly a thankless task.

In hindsight, the country's economic development seems to have followed the most obvious and probable trajectory – 'this is where we were always headed'. It is possible to examine the gradual accumulation of changes in the past and discover many symptoms, signs, and hints of what was to come. But 'in the moment' they are not so apparent. The seemingly eternal Soviet system fell apart in a matter of years, while the socio-economic and political infantilism that, in the euphoria of the perestroika, seemed a passing phase persists as the most basic aspect of social consciousness. It is this infantilism that lies at the source of public demand for socio-economic paternalism and leads to the absence of a coherent value system even among the elites. Under such conditions the government can give handouts to the public and elite groups, while focusing on its own goals behind their backs.

There is no crystal ball that would allow us to predict the future of the economy or the financial markets. As University of Chicago professor Eugene Fama said about the credit bubble: 'After the fact you always find people who said before the fact that prices are too high.... When they turn out to be right, we anoint them. When they turn out to be wrong, we ignore them. They are typically right and wrong about half the time.'[1]

Determining factors

The long-term outlook of the Russian economy depends on two factors. The first is the price of oil and other natural resources exported by the country. The second is whether Russia will be able to escape the shackles that interfere with the development of a diversified economy and get out of the institutional trap that keeps it in a rut of non-competitive growth, based on the extraction and distribution of oil and gas wealth.

Both of these factors are quite uncertain. The current high price of oil is based on a considerable increase in demand in developing countries, as well as a massive weakening of currencies in developed countries as a result of the global financial crisis. Cheap money always finds its way into the natural resource market and prices rise as a result.

But there are reasons to believe that gas and oil prices will fall. The principal causes are:

- The rise of **unconventional oil and gas**: oil shales, associated gas, oil sands, shelf extraction, and so on. As a result of the exploitation of new sources, the US could become the biggest oil producing country in the world by the end of the decade.[2] The prospect of increased oil production in the US once again disproves the 'peak oil' theory, which argues that global oil production has reached its peak, that the discovery of new reserves is slowing, and that oil will last for x more years.[3] This idea has been repeatedly disproven: improvements in technology allow us to find fossil fuel in places where we could not see it before.
- Increased **energy efficiency**. In developed countries, energy use per unit of GDP has been steadily dropping. By this measurement, Russia does about half as well as the US and about one-third as well as Europe and the Organisation for Economic Co-operation and Development (OECD).[4] Many countries are pushing to decrease fuel consumption in the most energy intensive segment of the economy – transportation.[5] From 2001 to 2011, consumption of primary energy,

calculated according to the oil equivalent, fell by 3.7 per cent in Europe and increased by a mere 2.2 per cent in the OECD.[6]

- The growth of **alternative energy**. Over the last 11 years, the worldwide production of renewable energy (wind, sun, biomass, and so on) has increased by a factor of 3.6. For now, only 1.6 per cent of global energy consumption comes from renewable resources (according to figures from BP), but the rate of growth is increasing. In anticipation of a gradual decrease in the cost of 'ecological' energy from alternative sources, developed countries have been supporting its production with substantial subsidies.

The high cost of oil and gas prompts consumers to try to economize by seeking other sources of energy and causes suppliers to increase extraction and diversify it by type of energy. Taken together, these factors will cause oil and gas prices to fall in the medium term (2020–30). Of course, it is true that three factors point in the opposite direction. First, fuel consumption will continue to grow in developing countries; second, the extraction of fossil fuels from new sources (shelf, oil sands, and so on) is quite expensive; and, third, the prospects of shale gas are not altogether clear because of the ecological risks associated with its extraction (water contamination).[7] This means that we should not expect an extreme decrease in the price of oil and gas.

In Russia, the outlook for natural gas is worse than it is for oil. The prospects for a return on Gazprom's substantial long-term investments in pipelines have become less and less clear as a result of a decrease in the dependency of natural gas consumers on their suppliers. This is due to the increasing importance of shale gas (the distance between the location of production and consumption can be small) and liquefied natural gas (LNG). Costly investments in pipelines that tie the consumer to the producer for a long period of time are becoming unnecessary: in a few years, gas companies from Norway, Qatar, and Russia will be competing in the same markets. According to Citi's perfectly sensible prediction, oil and gas prices will drop by about 15 per cent (to around $65–90 per barrel) as early as 2020.

Russia is less prepared than ever for such an eventuality. From 2005 to 2012, the price of oil that allows Russia to maintain a balanced budget has risen from $20 to $117 per barrel. That is the highest value among the world's largest oil exporters (not counting Nigeria). Russia is more vulnerable to economic crises than other countries, and not only to oil crises. Financial disturbances in Europe and the US immediately deprive our major corporations of financial stability because of their high debt load.

Russian politics in the 2000s was essentially based on the government's 'purchase' of various social and elite groups. Political leaders grew used to the idea that discontent within any socio-economic group could be cut short through the offer of material benefits. This logic was responsible for the valorization (substantial growth) of pensions in 2010, the offer of living space to members of the military, and the considerable increase in the salaries of government employees, law enforcement officials, and judges. Beginning in the mid-2000s, the government had money for everything: welfare politics, the promotion of industry, increased funding of the military, and law enforcement. The end of the cycle of high oil prices will deprive Russian politicians of such possibilities.

An examination of institutional traps – the second factor determining the potential growth of the Russian economy – is the subject of the rest of the article.

Joining the world economy

An increase in the price of oil, gas, and metals, in addition to the effect of transitional and post-crisis growth (as businesses and the public adapted to the markets), led to impressive growth rates in the 2000s (see Table 5.1). GDP, investment, and income increased by a factor of 4–5 in dollar amounts (1997, before the crisis and the devaluation of the ruble, is used as a point of comparison).

The figures above do not only reflect quantitative growth. Important changes also took place in quality of life, personal experience and habits, and consumer markets.

Table 5.1 GDP, investment, and income of the population in 1997 and 2011

$ Billion	1997	2011	Growth factor
Gross Domestic Product (GDP)	393	1844.1	4.7
Capital investment	68.6	364.1	5.3
Export	86.9	522	6
Import	72	323.8	4.5
Foreign Direct Investment (FDI)	2.6	52.9	20.3
Average income ($/month)	157.8	699.3	4.4

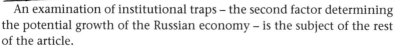

Source: Rosstat, central bank of Russia.

Let us take the automotive market as an example. From 1994 to 2002, an average of 115,000 cars were imported into the country per year for an average value of $0.915 billion. In 2005–11, import figures grew by an order of magnitude – up to an average of 1.101 million cars per year. In dollar terms, the market grew by a factor of 16, to $14.6 billion per year. These statistics do not include domestic assembly of foreign cars – another segment that has grown significantly (the percentage of such 'domestic foreign cars' exceeds 60 per cent in the Russian light automotive industry). In today's Russia, the number of cars per thousand people has reached 250 (Ernst & Young).[8] This is roughly equivalent to analogous figures in South Korea. As recently as 2000, there were only 130 cars per 1000 people and in 1990 there were 58.5. A country where every fourth person has a car (essentially one per family) has little in common with one where the figure is one in 17.

This fourfold increase in the number of cars per capita over a period of 20 years is not just a statistic. It represents a qualitative jump in mobility and a new urban reality – a burden that is too much for traffic infrastructure designed for a world where there were 5.5 cars per 1000 people (the figure from 1970).

Other markets changed in exactly the same fashion. A person from Moscow or St Petersburg who had lived in Germany from 2004 to 2011 would not recognize Russian retail upon returning home: the shelves are now stocked with the same goods available in Europe – goods that were nowhere to be found in the stores of Russia's two main cities in the 1990s. And the stores themselves have changed completely. Russia is now part of the global consumer goods market. People in Russian cities eat and dress in nearly the same fashion as citizens of European countries. They drive the same cars and use the same services. None of this would have been possible without a four or fivefold increase (in dollars) of per capita income.

The world of business and corporate management saw similar changes. In the 1990s, work in a foreign company differed qualitatively from work in a Russian company. In foreign companies, there was an established system, a clear division of labor and responsibilities, and a project-oriented attitude. Russians who went to work for foreign companies were surprised by this precision and structure, and not everyone was able to adapt. The newly created Russian companies offered an entirely different employee experience: an upswing of creativity, complete financial and managerial confusion, and an attitude of 'everybody does everything'. And the old industries existed in an atmosphere of total apathy and do-nothingness.

Today these distinctions are gradually disappearing. The managers of Russian and 'Western' companies speak the same language, use the same administrative techniques, create identical systems of corporate accountability, discover the same information, use similar technologies of production and quality control, the same methods for improving the efficiency and cost-effectiveness of business, and so on.

The local business environment is gradually approaching Western standards.[9] And, in terms of the concentration of corporate capital, the Russian model is becoming more and more like that of a majority of countries.[10] The direct participation of shareholders in the management of corporations is becoming less and less frequent. This creates incentives for using standard corporate procedures to control the activity of hired management. The 'wild' corporate wars of the late 1990s have receded deep into the past, as have the gangster get-togethers that could decide the fate of a large factory.

To use the words of Vladimir Potanin (in 2013 – No 7 in Forbes list of country's richest people). Russia's main economic goal before the crisis of 2008 was to 'return to the premier league' of the world economy – a place it had lost in the 1990s. The fact that it did return there is supported by a wealth of evidence, from the decreased levels of poverty and a modern style of consumption in cities to the 'refinement' of corporate culture. In the 2000s, Russia did what it had dreamt of doing in the 1980s – it regained its place in the global economy, and reintegrated itself into the outside world after a 70–80-year absence. As Daniel Treisman noted, this is evident in the increase in the number of Russian students studying abroad, in the growth of international tourism and telephone calls, and in the purchase of inexpensive real estate abroad. Russia has begun to transform itself into a 'normal country'.[11]

A modern way of life, of corporate management and consumption, is taking hold of an ever-growing segment of the country's big city population – a 'modernized Russia' that is gradually entering into more evident conflict with the country's outmoded system of government. Today's urban citizens will not stand for a social system built on castes, where respect for human rights and consequences for crimes committed depend on a person's socio-professional and family ties. They are no longer willing to live in the suffocating atmosphere of lies, paternalism, lawlessness, and limited civil liberties. The lifestyle adopted by a modern society demands a new relationship with the government.

The dead weight of the state

Not only champions play in the premier league of the global economy – it is only with this qualification that Potanin's metaphor can be of any use. You have the middleweights and the obvious outsiders who are in danger of relegation. Having made it back to the premier league, we have yet to make the position permanent and are balanced somewhere in the bottom half of the table. The public sector is pulling us down most. If the country's urban dwellers are already living in the 21st century, then some elements of the government – the police, for example – have barely exited the Middle Ages. It is enough to remember the systematic police torture and the thousands in jail because of slander by a competitor.

This does not only concern the public sector. The municipal and financial sectors, government industries, monopolies and their various offshoots stand apart and play no role in the reintegration of Russia into the global economy. They exist in their own time and even speak their own language. Over the last 20 years, the language of legislation has deteriorated irreversibly: laws and resolutions are written in a complex bureaucratic Newspeak, which no normal person is capable of understanding.

The public sector is very large. In July 2012, nearly 1.1 million people worked in the civil (federal and regional) and municipal service. Together with service personnel, the number of those working in government or municipal agencies reaches 1.65 million people, according to Rosstat. Over the course of the 2000s, the number of people working in federal or regional governmental agencies increased by a factor of 1.7, while the number of public officials per thousand has grown from 15 to 25 since 1994. According to Rosstat, 14.7 million people work in the public sector as a whole. That is 22 per cent of the entire workforce. Putin and Medvedev's repeated, but halfhearted, efforts to reduce the size of the state administration have been unsuccessful.[12] Consequently, the number of people directly or indirectly working for the government is no less than 35–40 per cent of the entire Russian workforce. This rough estimate points to the share of the electorate (including pensioners) that benefits from the existing state of affairs and the size of the non-modernized public sector.

The public sector still does not think of itself as a service. A decade and a half of state administration reform has not meaningfully improved the situation for Russian citizens or business. In fact, these reforms have gone practically unnoticed. The civil service and the entire public sector still work for themselves, not 'for the customer'. They work to prove their own usefulness within a vertical bureaucratic structure by drafting meaningless reports, responding to inquiries, organizing events, and carrying out instructions. They are busy building administrative barriers, imposing unnecessary services on the public, and extracting profits from wherever possible. Government employees think of their work as an opportunity to apply pressure to the section of the economy that they regulate with the goal of extracting profits. The extremely low quality of the civil services has a harmful effect on business, investment, and entrepreneurship and gets in the way of social reform.[13]

The following example provides a perfect illustration of the attitude of government employees.[14] In a remote region of Russia, a single bus took children to school (6 km). When the number of schoolchildren grew to the point that not all of them could fit on the bus, the local administration decided that all those over the age of ten would walk instead – in any weather, through the dirt, along highways filled with 18-wheelers. Although the bus route took only five minutes, the municipal government could not afford to pay for another trip. The situation was described in a TV program and a local official was asked what would happen next. His response was pure bureaucratese: 'we will create a committee, pay close attention to the issue, and attempt to determine the burden on the transportation system and [attention!] the legitimacy of refusing service'. Of course, any issue connected with potential payments or kickbacks (selling or leasing land for the construction of a store) would have been resolved far more quickly and productively.

Nearly 100 per cent of the time, a government official will receive a far lighter punishment than a normal citizen would for the same crime (for example, a traffic violation that results in casualties). In addition, high-placed officials continue to move about the city in cars with flashing lights, accompanied by security details with little regard for those around them – a practice that has long been the subject of considerable frustration on the part of normal citizens. The demand for fairness and equal rights and opportunity was one of the principal driving forces of the 2011/12 protest movement that enveloped Russia's bigger cities.

It is highly likely that Russia's next political cycle ('after Putin') will respond to this specific need. This does not bode well for the political 'right', which has been historically perceived as reflecting the interests of the ruling class. In free elections, the 'left' could gain a considerable presence in parliament. But these would likely be representatives of a modern 'left' who understand how to use new media technology to engage broad sections of the population in the administration of the federal and municipal governments.

The government in the economy: A cost center

Unlike managers from privately owned companies, managers of government-owned corporations are not directly motivated to increase the value of shares or dividends. The profits they generate will be incorporated into the federal budget, and will only marginally improve the evaluation of any specific person – for example, a director of a school or a hospital. On the other hand, they can earn extra income by lowering the official revenue figures for their institution, giving 'discounts' to business partners, and pocketing the difference between the official and market price of renting out facilities under their management.

For public officials and employees of state-owned companies, expenses represent the principal source of income. Overstating the price of goods and services, ensuring their provision by friendly companies, unofficially redistributing profits between the contractor and the client – these are the rule, not the exception, for Russian state purchase contracts.

There are several reasons for this. First, no limits are imposed by reputation (a public official who spends several million dollars on a ridiculous government purchase will not be sent packing or refused further government positions, and, frequently, will escape without any administrative sanction). Second, enforcement of the law is political: cases are investigated when it is necessary for political objectives. In such an environment, fighting corruption and cleaning up government purchases is impossible.

State-owned enterprise makes up a sector of the economy that is essentially isolated from the market. Its management can run these companies without facing the risk of bankruptcy. If the economy takes a turn for the worse, state-owned companies and banks are the first to receive credit from public funds, along with any number of government guarantees and exemptions. Since it is shielded from competition, the public sector begins to expand and reproduce itself. This increases the political base of the ruling regime, but limits the economy's potential for growth. State officials, along with all those who work in the public sector or for state-owned companies, owe their security to the country's political leaders. They understand that almost any other administration would subject the government sector to harsh reform – reducing the number of special privileges, letting go of excess personnel, demanding more focused work. For this reason, Putin is rushing to raise salaries in the public sector as a means of increasing loyalty to the regime.

Friends of Putin – friends of state-owned companies

Companies that are not state-owned, but that make most of their money on contracts from government-owned companies or the government itself, represent an intermediate, 'buffer' zone between the public and commercial sectors. These are companies that do support work for the big monopolies and government-owned corporations – they supply materials, build roads and pipelines, sell oil abroad, and so on Some of these companies were created from nothing, while others may have previously formed part of Gazprom, for example, before being sold off to businessmen with close connections to the political leadership of the country. A number of Gazprom assets were sold off according to this model as early as the 1990s under Rem Viakhirev. Putin later reintegrated them into the company. In the 2000s, new management started selling off secondary assets even faster than before. Only, this time, the buyers were friends of Putin.

The government and state-owned corporations (Gazprom, The Russian Railway System, Olympstroy, Transneft, and so on) are extremely picky in their choice of suppliers and contractors. According to Forbes Russia, in the period of 2008–11, of the $170 billion worth of state purchases and contracts entered into by monopolies and state-owned corporations, over half went to only ten people (Arkady and Boris Rotenberg, Gennady Timchenko, Oleg Deripaska, Ziyavudin Magomedov, Ziyad Manasir, and others).[15] This is an enormous sum – over 26 times more than the yearly revenue of Russia's 30 top Internet companies and only 2.5 times less than the turnover of Russia's 200 largest private companies put together.

These contractors have played an active role in all of the large government construction projects of the last few years – the Olympic site in Sochi, gas and oil pipelines, the site of the Asia-Pacific Economic Cooperation (APEC) summit in Vladivostok, and so on. All of these projects are based on personal agreements between representatives of these companies and the government. The creation of infrastructure in Russia is very expensive – 1 km of one lane of the Moscow–St Petersburg highway (which is being built by a company in which Arkady Rotenberg is a shareholder) will cost $4.8 million. Analogous highways in China, India, and Sweden cost five to eight times less ($0.73–1 million). As with all projects of this kind, road construction is primarily financed by the government and federal banks.

None of the state corporations and monopolies companies could exist outside of the preferential network – where large contracts are awarded to 'friends' on a non-competitive basis and criticism is not expected from government officials. In a different political and economic situation, these companies would soon 'disintegrate'. Instead of collecting the economic rent through taxation or simply leaving it with the fuel and energy companies, the government forces them to share their excess returns with metalworkers, railway employees, and even soccer players. But this is only possible during a period of rapid growth, such as the mid-2000s. As soon as rents drop, there will be nothing left to redistribute along the production chain. Both the owners and employees understand that any political shift would end up having a negative effect on them personally. The country's political leadership deliberately supports this ineffective segment of the economy, knowing that all those associated with it, as well as their families, provide support for the regime.

An unsustainable model

Within the Russian economy is a powerful cluster of businessmen and companies concerned with maintaining the status quo. These are companies that are protected from competition (foreign and domestic) by the government and companies whose primary business comes from government contracts. Further development within this framework will inevitably reduce efficiency: the elimination of competition removes any possibility of rapid growth. The monopolies do not have any incentive to control their costs, and will continue to raise prices. This will affect the entire economy (through the price of energy and transportation) and Russian industry will become uncompetitive.

The economy ends up in a vicious circle: expensive oil leads to a general price increase (through state spending), with basic goods such as energy and transportation experiencing the biggest jump. The monopolies are not answerable to the public and are only loosely regulated by the government. Combine this with the fact that they are expected to spend money on 'socially responsible' projects (for example, the financing of soccer teams, building athletic complexes for the Sochi Olympics, and so on) and the result is an increase in prices and prohibitive costs for infrastructure improvement. Essentially, any project that the government considers important, but would rather not finance with public funds, is carried out by state-owned or private companies.

There is enough 'long' money in the budget for infrastructure investment, thanks to the economic policies of the mid-2000s and the pension
system. But investing these resources in the construction of roads, railways, and other infrastructure projects makes no sense given the current
level of costs and kickbacks.

Paternalism as a social practice

The goals of macro-economic stabilization set by economists at the
beginning of Putin's first presidency were mostly met by the end of the
decade.[16] Russia found itself with a stable economy based on the high
price of gas and oil. The country's economic policies also became more
'civilized' – inflation no longer exceeds 10 per cent, the political authorities understand the danger of running a high deficit, and it is impossible
to imagine the government taking loans directly from the Central Bank,
as it did in the 1990s.

But social policy managed to make it through the 2000s unchanged.
The Eastern European countries that managed to complete a series of
successful reforms in the 1990s rejected the Soviet system of social guarantees in the very first stages of their transformation and established a
new social contract that was then used as the basis for a new system of
education, health care, and social security.[17] In Russia politicians tried
to leave this system untouched, fearing social unrest and active opposition from interest groups. As a result, social assistance remains largely
untargeted (not all who need assistance get it, while some of those who
do receive aid would be quite well-off without it).[18] Instead of funding a
particular social service itself, the government continues to support an
inefficient network of state-sponsored organizations that are granted a
monopoly on providing these services.

If the government were not afraid to purchase the care necessary for
the elderly on the market – from non-profits and businesses – it could
substantially cut the cost of supporting public social security institutions. And whatever is saved could then be poured directly into social
security proper. The need to transition to such an approach has been
discussed for years, but any possibility of reform butts up against the
government officials working in the social security system, for whom the
purchase of the necessary services 'on the market' appears far less attractive than the direct financing of public institutions. And, even when
volunteer organizations provide social services independently, the government perceives them not as allies, but as hostile observers who could
'air the dirty linen in public'.

It is impossible to modernize this system from the inside – the internal incentive structure works against any potential overhaul. Entrusting the reform of the social security system to those currently running it makes no more sense than asking a wolf to guard a flock of sheep. Every government institution has its own micropolitics designed to block reform. The goal is to preserve the status quo and to increase the influence of the given institution by taking advantage of a climate of weak administrative control and a general attitude on the part of the government that any public oversight is an unacceptable interference in its internal affairs.

This system is supported by an electorate (especially in smaller towns and villages) that is receptive to the paternalistic setup cultivated by the government. The conservative majority is ready to accept the illusion of social guarantees, along with strong government interference in all socio-economic processes, and does not believe in the possibility of a more effective system of self-regulation through public involvement and the workings of the market. Paternalistic economic policies that benefit the recipients of special exemptions and the distributors of public funds are more popular than more 'adult' alternatives based on the independence and responsibility of economic agents.

Surveys of values show that elderly Russians are far more committed to 'preservation' (conservatism) and 'security' than their European peers, while young Russians place a higher value on 'self-realization' than their European counterparts and express less 'concern for people and the environment'.[19] This is a result of the socio-economic transformations of the 1990s and 2000s, which led to an increase in atomization and egoism. The elder generation, in large part, remains nostalgic for the lost Soviet collectivist values, while Russia's youth, on the other hand, has shifted along the value scale toward egoism and openness to change. This ideology, based on self-realization and asocial egoism at the expense of a concern for others, is only very gradually being replaced by a resurgence of solidarity and a readiness to invest one's time and money in public initiatives.

According to the value structure along the entire range of the sample (disregarding age distribution), Russia is far less committed than Europe to risk-taking and innovation and attaches considerably more importance to self-realization at the expense of a concern for others. At the same time, the value placed on wealth, power, and personal success markedly outstrips the importance attached to courage and a readiness to make independent decisions. The centrality of self-realization does not leave room for concern for others, tolerance, and so on.

Overall, the value system described above points to the likelihood of fairly substantial socio-economic transformations within the next ten years. After all, the older generation, with its attachment to tradition, is gradually disappearing. But what will these transformations look like? If altruistic values manage to gain a foothold before the beginning of the period of political upheaval, it is possible that Russia might transform into a European-style social democracy. But if not (a far more probable scenario), the evolution of the country's political system will likely follow the Latin American model.

Possible scenarios

The scenarios listed below are constructed based on a number of different possibilities: (1) Does the price of gas and oil remain high or does it fall? (2) Will the urban population's dissatisfaction with the ruling regime grow quickly? (3) Will the regime find the resources to gradually modernize from within and find solutions to the most pressing social issues, and will the 'security forces' elite yield power to the public and accept democracy? If the second question is answered with 'no' and the third with 'yes', then Russia could develop according to scenario 1 (see below). A sharp increase in dissatisfaction will make a 'revolutionary' scenario (2) inevitable, regardless of the regime's willingness to change and the future price of oil. A drop in oil prices would increase dissatisfaction, hastening the advent of the 'revolutionary' scenario.

But expensive oil would not necessarily guarantee the preservation of the ruling regime. On the one hand, it would provide the government with the resources to purchase the loyalty of various social groups and (given the desire) allow the possibility of modernization. On the other hand, a gradual growth in general prosperity would allow a shift in the lifestyle of Russia's urban population and an expansion of the middle class, resulting in decreased support for authoritarian rule. The range of possible scenarios, based on the forks described above, can be described in the following manner: possibilities one and two are basic, while three and four could only temporarily delay their realization.

1. **Forced modernization and a soft transition of power.** By the late 2010s/early 2020s, the price of oil falls to $70–90/barrel, while gas remains cheap thanks to an increased supply of LNG and the extraction of shale gas. The government can no longer support an enormous army of security forces, civil servants, and ineffective state companies. Even the current plateauing of oil and gas prices has

forced the government to economize by choosing between the development of human capital (education, medicine) and the funding of the army and security forces. For now, the political leadership clearly prefers the second option. Increased dissatisfaction with the regime (spurred on by a decrease or stagnancy in the price of oil and gas and, consequently, a shrinking of 'the redistributive pie') forces the elites to find a new leader and change the developmental paradigm.

This will be followed by a removal of excess government structures and a transfer of all functions that do not necessarily have to be carried out by the state to the market or the third sector. The economy will gain new incentives for development. Essentially, this would be 'Putinism without Putin' – a preservation of preferences for big business and a liberalization of civil and, to a certain extent, political freedoms. But defense and security would remain untouchable – the 'reformers' would not have a mandate to make changes in these sensitive areas. This is more or less what liberals were expecting from Medvedev in 2008.

2. **An uprising of the urban population – the hardcore scenario.** If the modernization scenario does not pan out, a revolutionary change of government becomes a possibility regardless of the price of oil. But a decrease in the price of oil and gas could spur dissatisfaction with the political leadership. Delays in the choice of a successor and the transfer of power and disappointment with the weak efforts to modernize the regime from within through constitutional self-limitation would increase the size of the protest movement. Because of the demand for 'fairness' described above, the regime that would result from such a scenario would likely be on the 'left' of the political spectrum.

In this scenario, it would take several years to restructure the foundations of government according to democratic principles, to fight corruption, and to remove the 'USSR-style' from various aspects of public life. The 'left' would probably have to increase spending on education, health care, and the construction of infrastructure and, as a result, would have to raise taxes. It seems likely that a progressive taxation system would be implemented. Pensions would be raised, causing the pension budget to become even more unbalanced. We should also expect attempts to nationalize 'unfairly privatized companies'. Only this time it will not primarily concern the winners of loans-for-shares auctions. Instead, the focus will be on the companies of Putin's friends, who were able to grow their businesses by purchasing pieces of Gazprom, Rostechnology, and other state corporations. The 'left' will attempt to improve conditions for small business, lower interest rates, and, when possible, support investment in projects to protect the environment.

3. **Stagnation.** High prices of oil and other natural resources, together with astute and manipulative policies, could theoretically make possible the preservation (stagnation) of the current socio-economic regime until the early 2020s. But this scenario is less likely than a transition to scenarios 1 or 2 by the end of this decade. In any case, this transition is simply a matter of time. Even if high oil prices allow the regime to hold on for another 5–7 years, it will still have to give way to either the evolutionary (1) or revolutionary (2) scenario.

4. **Police state.** The only way the regime could protect itself from modernization for a longer period of time and keep power in the hands of the current elite would be to create a police state. In this scenario, the government would have to substantially suppress political, civil, and even (as a last resort) economic freedoms in order to maintain control of the situation. Many different factors make this scenario seem unlikely, including the integration of the Russian economy into the global economy. However, we cannot completely eliminate the possibility of such a scenario. After that, following a delay of several years, the country's eventual development would still follow either scenario 1 or 2.

Conclusion

Potential reform in all of the areas we have examined is being blocked by powerful interest groups and government institutions responsible for this or that particular policy. The government has fallen noticeably behind the urban middle class in terms of development, but this state of affairs is perfectly satisfactory for a large section of the population, as well as various interests. In this context, the modernization of the economy is impossible without modernizing the government, which is becoming more archaic with each passing year. This leads to a loss of trust and the defenselessness of business and the broader population in the face of the government machine. At the same time, the public is not particularly disposed to self-organization.

If the price of oil does not go down, the government could continue to survive for another few years by purchasing the allegiance of the elites and various social groups. Of course, the regime will not last until 2025, but it could certainly maintain its position until the end of this decade. An external shock (economic – resulting from a decrease in the price of natural resources, and/or political – resulting from disappointment in an outmoded government) would initially hurt the economy. But, if it is rebuilt on a new foundation by eliminating excess government interference and liquidating the many public pork barrels, then Russia could see two to three decades of impressive growth. Most importantly, this growth would be productive, as it was in Turkey, Indonesia, Brazil, and other developing countries.

Notes

1. J. Cassidy (2010) *Interview with Eugene Fama*, http://www.newyorker.com/online/blogs/johncassidy/2010/01/interview-with-eugene-fama.html, date accessed 2 April 2013.
2. F. Khan and others (2012) 'North America, the New Middle East? The Fastest Growing Energy Supplier in the World', Citigroup Global Markets, 20 March 2012.
3. The Energy Research Institute of the Russian Academy of Sciences (ERI RAS) in cooperation with Russian Energy Agency (REA) (2012) *Global and Russian Energy Outlook until 2035*, http://www.eriras.ru/data/94/eng, date accessed 2 April 2012.
4. I. Bashmakov (2011) 'Energoeffektivnost v Rossii: politica, dostizhenia, paradoksy', The report in the conference at Institute of World Economy and International Relations (IMEMO) of the Russian Academy of Sciences, October 2011. http://www.cenef.ru/file/Bashm2011.ppt.
5. I. Bashmakov, V. Bashmakov (2012) *Sravnenie mer rossiskoi politiki povyshenia energoeffektivnosti s merami, prinyatymi v razvitykh stranakh*, CENEF, http://www.cenef.ru/file/comparison.pdf, data accessed 2 April 2013.
6. *BP Statistical Review of World Energy* (2012), www.bp.com/statisticalreview.
7. K. Kozlov, K. Yudaeva, and M. Zavyalova (2012) *Prirodniy gaz: kratkii obzor mirovoy otrasli y analiz slantsevogo buma*, Center for Macroeconomic Research of Sberbank, http://www.sbrf.ru/common/img/uploaded/files/pdf/analytics/pg1.pdf.
8. Ernst & Young (2012) *Avtomobilny rynok Rossii y SNG. Obzor otrasli*, February 2012, http://www.ey.com/Publication/vwLUAssets/Automotive-industry-overview-2012-RUS/$FILE/Automotive-industry-overview-2012-RUS.pdf.
9. For example: S. Porshakov, Ch. Gilbert A. Ivakhnik, and E. Chumakova (2010) *Modern Corporate Governance in Russia as Seen by Foreign Business-men and Experts. Findings of Survey Held by National Council on Corporate Governance and Russo-British Chamber of Commerce* (Moscow), http://www.nccg.ru/site.xp/050052048120404905205105l.html, date accessed 3 April 2013.
10. S. Avdasheva, V. Golikova, K. Gonchar, T. Dolgopyatova, B. Kuznetsov, and A. Yakovlev (2010) *Predpriyatia y rynki v 2005–2009 godakh: itogy dvukh raundov obsledovaniya rossiskoy obrabatyvayushey promyshlennosti. The Report of Higher School of Economics – National Research University (HSE)*, (Moscow).

https://www.hse.ru/data/2010/04/07/1218109141/report.pdf, date accessed 4 April 2013.
11. A. Shleifer, D. Treisman (2004) 'A Normal Country', *Foreign Affairs*, March/April 2004.
12. It is sometimes pointed out that Russia has fewer civil servants than other countries. 'Russia has 67 civil servants per 10 thousand, while France has 400', government news agency RIA Novosti writes (RIANovosti (2012) *Slukhi o vysokom urovne burocratizatsii Rossii silno preuvelicheny*, http://ria.ru/research_rating/20120412/623975661.html). Cutting down the number of civil servants, however, is not an end in itself. They are generally associated with elimination of redundant functions (or with outsourcing these functions). The fact that Russia has failed to reduce the number of civil servants indicates that it has, in fact, failed to eliminate the redundant functions of the government apparatus.
13. The World Bank (2012) *The World Bank Worldwide Governance Indicators*, http://info.worldbank.org/governance/wgi/.
14. I. Mikhailovskaya (2012) 'Prostye veschi', Forbes Woman, No 14/2012, http://www.forbes.ru/forbes-woman/issue/2012-11-0/171723-prostye-veshchi
15. 'Koroli goszakaza', Forbes Russia, March 2012, http://www.forbes.ru/sobytiya-slideshow/lyudi/79623-koroli-goszakaza-reiting/slide/1
16. Higher School of Economics – National Research University (HSE), the Center for Strategic Research (CSR), in cooperation with International Monetary Fund (IMF) and the World Bank (WB) (2000) *Investicionniy klimat y economicheskaya situatsiya v Rossii. Materialy dlya obsuzhdeniya*, April 2000.
17. I. Klyamkin, L. Shevtsova (eds) (2008) *Put' v Evropu* (Moscow: Liberalnaya missia).
18. T. Maleva, L. Ovcharova (eds) (2010) *Socialnaya podderzhka: uroki krizisov y vektory modernizatsii* (Moscow).
19. V. Magun, M. Rudnev (2012) *Bazovie tsennosti dvukh pokoleniy rossiyan y dinamika ikh socialnoi determinatsii*, http://www.hse.ru/data/2012/05/31/1252375640/ %D0%9C%D0%B0%D0%B3%D1% 83%D0%BD-%D0%A0%D1%83%D0%B4%D0%BD%D0%B5%D0%B2-%D0%A6%D0%B5%D0%BD%D0%BD %D0%BE%D1%81%D1%82%D0%B8.pdf. Accessed 5 April 2013.

Bibliography

S. Avdasheva, V. Golikova, K. Gonchar, T. Dolgopyatova, B. Kuznetsov, A. and A. Yakovlev (2010) *Predpriyatia y rynki v 2005–2009 godakh: itogy dvukh raundov obsledovaniya rossiskoy obrabatyvayushey promyshlennosti. The Report of Higher School of Economics – National Research University (HSE)* (Moscow). https://www.hse.ru/data/2010/04/07/1218109141/report.pdf, date accessed 4 April 2013.
Avtomobilny rynok Rossii y SNG. Obzor otrasli, February 2012, http://www.ey.com/Publication/vwLUAssets/Automotive-industry-overview-2012-RUS/$FILE/Automotive-industry-overview-2012-RUS.pdf, date accessed 5 April 2013.
BP Statistical Review of World Energy (2012), www.bp.com/statisticalreview.
I. Bashmakov (2011) *Energoeffektivnost v Rossii: politica, dostizhenia, paradoksy*, The report in the conference at Institute of World Economy and International

Relations (IMEMO) of the Russian Academy of Sciences, October 2011. http://www.cenef.ru/file/Bashm2011.ppt

I. Bashmakov, V. Bashmakov (2012) *Sravnenie mer rossiskoi politiki povyshenia energoeffektivnosti s merami, prinyatymi v razvitykh stranakh*, CENEF, http://www.cenef.ru/file/comparison.pdf, date accessed 2 April 2013.

Higher School of Economics – National Research University (HSE), the Center for Strategic Research (CSR), in cooperation with International Monetary Fund (IMF) and the World Bank (WB) (2000) *Investicionniy klimat y economicheskaya situatsiya v Rossii. Materialy dlya obsuzhdeniya*, April.

J. Cassidy (2010) *Interview with Eugene Fama*, http://www.newyorker.com/online/blogs/johncassidy/2010/01/interview-with-eugene-fama.html, date accessed 2 April 2013.

I. Klyamkin, L. Shevtsova (eds) (2008) *Put' v Evropu* (Moscow: Liberalnaya missia). 'Koroli goszakaza. Spetsproect', Forbes Russia, March 2012, http://www.forbes.ru/sobytiya-slideshow/lyudi/79623-koroli-goszakaza-reiting/slide/1

K. Kozlov, K. Yudaeva, and M. Zavyalova (2012) *Prirodniy gaz: kratkii obzor mirovoy otrasli y analiz slantsevogo buma*, Center for Macroeconomic Research of Sberbank, http://www.sbrf.ru/common/img/uploaded/files/pdf/analytics/pg1.pdf.

V. Magun, M. Rudnev (2012) *Bazovie tsennosti dvukh pokoleniy rossiyan y dinamika ikh socialnoi determinatsii*, http://www.hse.ru/data/2012/05/31/1252375640/%D0%9C%D0%B0%D0%B3%D1%83%D0%BD-%D0%A0%D1%83%D0%B4%D0%BD%D0%B5%D0%B2-%D0%A6%D0%B5%D0%BD%D0%BE%D1%81%D1%82%D0%B8.pdf.Accessed April 5, 2013

T. Maleva, L. Ovcharova (eds) (2010) *Socialnaya podderzhka: uroki krizisov y vektory modernizatsii* (Moscow: Delo Publishers).

I. Mikhailovskaya (2012) 'Prostye veschi', Forbes Woman, No 14/2012, http://www.forbes.ru/forbes-woman/issue/2012-11-0/171723-prostye-veshchi

S. Porshakov, Ch. Gilbert, A. Ivakhnik, and E. Chumakova (2010) *Modern Corporate Governance in Russia as Seen by Foreign Businessmen and Experts. Findings of Survey Held by National Council on Corporate Governance and Russo-British Chamber of Commerce* (Moscow), http://www.nccg.ru/ site.xp/050052048124049052051051.html, date accessed 3 April 2013.

RIANovosti (2012) *Slukhi o vysokom urovne burocratizatsii Rossii silno preuvelicheny*, http://ria.ru/research_rating/20120412/623975661.html.

A. Shleifer, D. Treisman (2004) 'A Normal Country', *Foreign Affairs*, March/April.

The Energy Research Institute of the Russian Academy of Sciences (ERI RAS) in cooperation with Russian energy agency (REA) (2012) *Global and Russian Energy Outlook until 2035*, http://www.eriras.ru/data/94/eng, date accessed 2 April 2012.

The World Bank (2012) *The World Bank Worldwide Governance Indicators*, http://info.worldbank.org/governance/wgi/.

6
Russian Regime Dynamics through 2025: Comparative Thinking about the Future

Henry E. Hale

The dramatic Russian winter of 2011–12, featuring the largest street protests Moscow has seen since the 1990s, gave new vigor to speculation on the future of Russia's regime, and the prospect of major democratizing change suddenly came to appear more imminent.[1] The present chapter addresses this question by discussing the internal logic of Russia's political system, branded here as 'micromanaged democracy' (or 'overmanaged democracy'[2]) and exploring likely paths of its future development over the next 12 years in light of comparative experience with regimes in other parts of the world that share some of the Putin system's key traits. It focuses on the importance of conditions creating a broad desire for regime replacement in the population, 'focal points' that can trigger the sudden mass abdication of officials and other regime loyalists, and certain institutional and structural features that would be necessary for any regime breakdown actually to lead to democratization. Ironically, comparative experience suggests that it is the regime's own sense of insecurity and quest for guarantees of stability that have the greatest chance of destabilizing it, making it vulnerable to unpredictable uprisings and collapse. At the same time, actual democratization remains an unlikely outcome by 2025, though it is within the realm of the possible. More likely, however, would seem to be a pattern of regime cycles, whereby a political opening punctuated by the fall of a regime from power is followed by something that turns out to be similar, despite the spread of social media and growing public clamor for change. The continuation of the current leadership and the current micromanaged democracy is possible, but Putin and his leadership have missed major opportunities to anchor the system and their

125

own positions long into the future, most notably through undermining the authority of their own dominant party and undercutting the potential that Medvedev's presidency had to solve the Achilles' heel of non-democratic regimes everywhere: succession.[3]

Micromanaged democracy in Russia

It can be helpful to conceive of Russia's post-Soviet political history as a process whereby a wide variety of political-economic networks emerged through the transition from communism and were gradually coordinated informally around a single dominant 'patron' who for most of this period occupied the formal post of the presidency.[4] Indeed, Russia is widely regarded as a political society in which patron–client relations are central, formal rules and laws are typically overwhelmed by informal ones, and the most important collective actors generally do not correspond to formal institutions like 'parties' or 'the parliament' but to extensive networks of actual acquaintance that permeate a wide range of formal institutions (typically involving both business and politics) and are not limited to, empowered by, or defined by any one of them.[5] Whether such a polity is 'open' (and apparently 'democratic') or 'closed' (and apparently 'authoritarian') depends far less on the design and operation of particular formal institutions than on the extent to which these extended political-economic networks are tightly coordinated around a single patron in a kind of 'single pyramid' of power as opposed to being uncoordinated and openly pretending to the status of patron in a 'competing pyramid' system.[6]

Russia in the 1990s was essentially a competing pyramid system. Clusters of powerful networks used all resources at their disposal against each other in an all-out battle for power, culminating in the 1999–2000 election season.[7] After winning that struggle, Putin perfected the indirect methods of managing opposition in Russia in the 2000s, enticing and forcing major networks to coordinate their activities around his wishes (a prospect helped by the growing economy that made it possible for all together to increase their share of the spoils).[8]

To the extent that individuals and networks in such polities care primarily about their own livelihoods and the well being of their families and friends, one crucial feature is that the system's survival hinges on the *expectation* that the incumbent patron will remain in power long enough into the future to carry out promises of reward and threats of punishment made today. And underpinning this expectation of a leader's enduring potency is that elites must also generally expect that *other* elites will in fact carry out the rewards and punishments dictated by the chief patron. Expecting other elites to carry out presidential orders, each individual elite is likely to do the same, since resisting would be futile and likely mean the expropriation of one's resources by others (or worse).

In this way, then, power in such clientelistic societies tends to be a kind of self-fulfilling prophesy that their leaders are careful to maintain by working hard to divide and conquer elites (so that individual elites would not expect many other elites to back them should they challenge the main patron) and by otherwise erecting barriers to coordinated action that could threaten the effectiveness of their threats and promises. This is much of the 'management' in the concept of 'managed democracy', and Russia is dubbed *micro*managed democracy because this management has become extremely intricate and sophisticated.[9] Seeking to avoid losses and to try to gain in the system, elites generally do not challenge the system as such, but instead coordinate their activities around the will of the patron, though often competing with other elites for better positions within the system and fiercely defending their own place in the system against possible incursions from others. But the art of management is as much about managing expectations as about managing institutional levers of the system, since the key to the successful coordination of elites around the chief patron is sustaining the perception that there are no viable alternatives to the patron and the team that he personally endorses.

Generally speaking, such systems can break down when two conditions come into place that can undermine the coordination of elites around the incumbent patron. First, a strong desire for replacement of the leadership among the masses and elites provides a key (if not absolutely necessary) precondition. Elites are more likely to initiate a regime change when they sense that they would get public support in the process, because public support can be a key resource in battle, especially where generating an official election result is still the formal means by which top office is assumed. Second, the key to this dissatisfaction translating into a breakdown or fundamental change of the single-pyramid system is the emergence of some kind of *focal point* for coordinated elite defection from the incumbent patron. For an event to serve as such a focal point, it must generally do two things: communicate an *expectation* that the end of the regime is inevitable and provide a single point in time when this is expected to occur, or, more precisely and crucially, a *single point in time when elites expect other elites to be defecting* from the regime and thus rendering it unable to mete out rewards and punishments. Elections have proven to be one such critical focal point for elite defection and mass unrest in non-democratic regimes that nevertheless continue to allow at least some opposition to compete in elections.[10] Particularly potent are elections in which the incumbent leader is expected to leave the presidency (that is, presidential *succession elections*) because such elections provide a single moment in time (the election) when masses and elites interested in regime change expect that others potentially sharing their sentiments will act in concert. Thus, each president ousted in the color revolutions was not only unpopular, but was already in his constitutionally final term or had decided not to seek reelection.[11] Even in Russia, where Putin's popularity has enabled him to manage multiple formal presidential successions, each such instance has involved great tensions within the elite, with the 2011–12 election season generating massive protests and a great deal of uncertainty as to the future of the regime.

Elections as focal points have the feature of being fairly predictable sources of instability, which at least gives incumbents a chance to prepare and compete for a chance to stay in power or organize their own exit in a way that works to their advantage.[12] Comparative experience also shows, however, that where regimes increasingly gut elections of any uncertainty at all, so blatantly filtering candidates and stacking the deck that public opinion (even as it exists in a controlled media environment) obviously has little bearing on the outcome, the kind of focal points that spark mass elite defection and regime collapse do become fewer and farther between. Moreover, the emergence of such focal points becomes increasingly unpredictable, possible at seemingly any moment. One hypothesis is that, if hybrid regimes (even micromanaged democracies) tend to feature elite defections creating opportunities for protest to grow to regime-threatening scale (that is, elite-led revolution), then 'pure authoritarian' countries tend to feature something like the opposite, with the rise of unexpectedly large protests suddenly provoking regime-breaking splits within the elite (mass-led revolution). That is, the sudden rise of protests can simultaneously give elites incentive to defect so as to ride the protest wave to power and create a sense that the regime is doomed, thereby facilitating its collapse in a kind of self-fulfilling prophesy. And protests in such environments can break out very suddenly for unexpected reasons, as events somehow capture the imagination and inspire emotion, thereby resulting in a cascade of people revealing their dissatisfaction and thereby inspiring others to do the same.

Fascinating research by Timur Kuran finds that such cascading protest outbreaks are surprising by their very nature, virtually impossible to foresee yet potentially overwhelming in their demonstrative power once they occur.[13] Thus, in Africa, it was largely the outbreak of mass protests in the wake of Eastern Europe's democratic revolutions at the end of the Cold War that prompted elite splits within Africa's authoritarian and seemingly eternal 'neo-patrimonial' regimes, resulting in a wave of liberalization in the first half of the 1990s.[14] Similarly, in the Arab world in 2011, an event as random as a provincial fruit vendor setting himself on fire somehow caught the imagination of the public, sparking an upswell of protest in Tunisia that led its military to oust its president, an event that then inspired far larger protests in Egypt, which in turn led its military to believe longtime leader Hosni Mubarak's time had come and to turn against him, taking power for itself and arranging new elections. And these events inspired related ones across the Arab world, long regarded as a bastion of authoritarianism and with hardly any warning for the regimes themselves.[15] In 1848, the downfall of France's Louis Philippe suddenly sparked a 'wildfire' of protest that unexpectedly swept across much of Europe and even to Latin America in just a single month and toppled many leaders along the way – and without the help of any means of communication or networking more modern than the telegraph.[16]

Some of these other 'waves' of revolution, as well as the post-Soviet color revolutions, also illustrate that the simple downfall of a leader does not necessarily (or even usually) lead to an actual, enduring change in the political system. If the chief factors that cause the old political system to be the way it is are not somehow changed leading into or during the leader's downfall, there is a strong likelihood that something like the old system could reemerge. Additional changes necessary for a regime change in Russia might include economic development, constitutional change, or a new responsiveness to Western influence.

Looking to 2025: Public opinion, focal points, and democracy-consolidating conditions

Are any of the various change-promoting conditions in place now in Russia, and, if not, what chance is there for them to materialize in the dozen years now remaining before 2025?

The desire for regime replacement

First, let us consider the extent of desire for regime replacement among the population. The survival of the Putin system has arguably been underpinned over the last 12 years by the ability of Putin and his closest subordinates to sustain high levels of popular approval.[17] Tellingly, it was only after a noted drop in his ratings over the course of 2011 that the massive protests occurred at the end of that year.[18] It remains to be seen whether this drop will ultimately continue to the point where Putin will be regarded as broadly unpopular, but what one can say now is that major urban centers of Moscow and St Petersburg have become increasingly alienated from the regime, leading Putin and company to increasingly emphasize support among a 'real Russia' outside the most Westernized cities.[19] This effort is likely to be unsuccessful if the years ahead bring economic decline.[20] Such an effect would not be instant or direct, however, since the regime also draws on many other bases of public support (as its weathering of the 2008–09 world financial crisis demonstrates) and has ways of retaining the support of the large share of the population outside the largest cities, should it properly employ them.[21]

Yet, over the dozen years until 2025, it may become not only actual economic growth that matters, but also whether growth occurs that meets or exceeds popular expectations. The growth achieved in the 2000s brought public support not only because it was rapid by global standards, but also because it came against the backdrop of one of the most horrendous economic depressions ever to have befallen a society in peacetime. The success of the 2000s may ultimately have laid a trap of expectations for the regime's staying in power for a long time by setting the bar above what can likely be sustained beyond the initial recovery from the 1990s. The regime could try to pave the way for higher growth by adopting unpopular radical economic reforms, but many of those that economists have been calling for could be unpopular, with only an uncertain chance of success. As the history of massive grassroots protests against the cash-for-benefits reforms of 2005 indicates, the potential for mass protests originating from unpopular policies is significant, and to date Putin's team has not shown willingness to tough it out to see them through. An anti-corruption campaign could conceivably stem a decline in popular support, but this would also be risky, since a genuine one would undermine the regime's own power pyramid and might be understood by the population as insincere, representing political motives while confirming for them that the regime is corrupt.

Not all possible sources of popularity decline come from the economy; some stem in some way from the very possibility of the Putin regime's endurance for 25 years following his rise to the presidency in 2000. For one thing, the system of micromanaged democracy itself requires constant creativity and dynamism on the part of the leadership, anticipating new challenges effectively and finding ways to dispose of solutions that were once effective after they have outlived their usefulness and are becoming a drag on the system.[22] So far, Putin and his chief associates have proven remarkably skilled at sustaining dynamic system management through a variety of initiatives over a dozen years. But it is far from clear that the same team could keep this up for another dozen years, and the regime is less likely to be fortunate enough that any new people brought on board will share the same talent. This could be tested fairly soon, with longtime regime strategist Vladislav Surkov having left the presidential administration after the 2011 protests. One might already question the political wisdom of sentencing the young women of the punk rock group Pussy Riot to two years in prison, though the long-run implications of this and other very recent events will become evident only in the years to come.[23]

Related to this, one of the biggest challenges could be sustaining the general perception that the regime is responsive to people. Polls have consistently shown that Russian citizens tend to prefer strong leadership, yet, in light of what they widely see as inevitable norms of corruption, are willing to satisfice by giving their leaders considerable leeway to enrich themselves and engage in other inappropriate activity in the process. At the same time, it is critical to note that large majorities also want those same leaders to respect their rights and respond to their most basic needs.[24] One of the ironies of micromanaged democracy is, thus, that the more the regime fears instability and therefore centralizes control in a single person, the more likely it is to make individual gaffes and the more likely it is that a single political misstep could spark a major protest cascade, destabilizing the regime. This is unlikely in any given year, but, over 13 years, the odds grow substantially of at least one major mistake.

Such systemic problems are magnified by the prospect of an aging leadership. Putin turned 60 in October 2012, which means that by 2025 he will be 73, about the same age as Konstantin Chernenko was when he came to power in the USSR and older than Yury Andropov. His associates will obviously age with him, risking the growing sense over the next decade of the emergence of a gerontocracy unless some way can be found for renewal. This prospect should be worrisome for the Putin administration, as a leader's aging also risks turning him or her into a 'lame duck' expected to depart the political scene due to the end of his natural active life cycle, making elite splits increasingly likely to happen when a focal point unexpectedly emerges, as was the case in the Arab spring. Indeed, some have linked the Egyptian military's decision to defect to the protesters and remove Mubarak from power with its opposition to Mubarak's evident plans to usher in his son Gamal as successor in what was then an anticipated 2012 presidential election, and influencing the succession was also a driving motivation behind the youth and other popular mobilization in that country.[25]

In this light, the political evisceration of Dmitry Medvedev that was accomplished by forcing him to yield the presidency back to Putin in 2011–12 can be considered a major blow to the regime's long-term survivability prospects, since he for a time potentially represented a younger, more 'modern' step in the evolution of the regime that would have made an Egyptian scenario less likely. He also represented a natural 'focal point' that could have preserved elite unity should the unthinkable unexpectedly have happened to Putin himself. Instead, Medvedev's potential to become regarded as a strong and independent politician was badly damaged among the elite (though less so among the broader population) by Putin's easily strong-arming him from the presidency. These developments reflect a deeper problem for micromanaged democracies: the leader can become seen not only by the leader himself but also by key elites as irreplaceable, and the desire to avoid becoming a lame duck and/or to prevent the triggering of inter-network wars can generate a tendency to avoid grooming promising young stars who could become seen as natural successors, and even to sabotage those that might seem to be emerging anyway.

Of course, it is also possible that the regime will find a way to sustain its popular support much as it has done to this point, though the odds would seem to be more against this possibility than in favor of it unless Putin does in 2018 what he did not do before: orchestrate the actual handover of power to a younger generation, if it is not too late at that point. As long as the regime can sustain at least a credible claim to be the most popular force in the country, however, its survival is likely.

Focal points for mass protest and coordinated defection from the regime

If popular support does seriously erode to the point at which opposition political activity starts to look inviting to a critical mass of ambitious political and economic elites, what could be the most likely focal points between today and 2025 for catalyzing their cascading defection to something or someone new? The most likely, judging from past post-Soviet experience, could be elections, so long as they are maintained with at least some opposition allowed to contest them. If the drop in popularity happens after 2018, the next scheduled presidential election, then the regime is likely to survive the 2018 test: Putin would almost surely secure reelection or have the ability, as he did in 2008, to make his hand-picked candidate the most likely successor by virtue of his very endorsement so long as the person comes with reasonable talents and without a very negative reputation. The best option for the regime would be for Putin to usher in someone new and younger, thereby giving it a chance to regain dynamism and retain support for years to come. Should Putin stay on, however, he risks a popularity drop over the six years beyond 2018 that could undermine his effort to choose a successor then.

If the drop in popularity occurs before 2018, however, much will depend on whether Putin decides to run again or endorse a successor. In this latter case, any succession is unlikely to go as smoothly as in 2008, and, if anticipated by elites, it could set up the 2016 parliamentary election (and even nationwide regional elections prior to that) as critical battlegrounds, as elite groups considering a challenge to Putin test their ability to tap into mass dissatisfaction and probe their ability to induce elite defections. And fractures in the regime would likely become visible well before 2016, since operational elite preparation for elections begins long in advance.[26] If Putin decides to run in 2018 despite being unpopular, the presidential election will still likely serve as a focal point for mass and elite coordination against him, though post-Soviet history suggests his odds of winning will be good as long as he makes absolutely clear he intends to do so. But this, of course, would set up what could be a calamity for the regime in anticipation of the 2024 presidential elections, a calamity that could have as its focal point the 2021 'elite primary' of the parliamentary elections, with associated ruptures in the regime occurring beforehand as elites prepare for battle.[27]

Of course, if Putin's leadership continues to crack down on opposition to the point of effectively eliminating it from any official opportunities to contest the ruling authorities, the regime will become increasingly vulnerable to more random focal points that could trigger sudden, surprising mass protests that could in turn cause officials in the regime to lose confidence in its continuation and to abdicate en masse in a much more unpredictable fashion than if elections remained contested. But the randomness of such focal points means that they could be a long time in coming. Mubarak and his Tunisian neighbor Ben Ali ruled for some 30 years before succumbing to sudden massive protests sparked by (unexpected by all) a self-immolating fruit vendor, so if Putin and company are equally lucky their regime could conceivably hang on even beyond 2025. But, whenever such an outcome should happen, it would likely involve far more dire consequences for the incumbents and society than would ouster by election. And the fact that the regime has so far weathered Moscow protests numbering over 100,000 also means that protests of similar scale are unlikely to give officials sufficient and sufficiently uniform fright to trigger mass defection from the regime. The bar has been raised, suggesting something much larger would be necessary.

We must also, however, consider the possibility that the leadership will 'get wise' and recognize the risks of either staying the present course or cracking down, and will consequently react by liberalizing, perhaps taking Vladislav Inozemtsev's advice in adopting 'preventive democracy' as a path to actual democracy.[28] But the events of 2011–12 suggest that it is unlikely to do so unless it faces a much larger and sustained protest than before, or its position is weakened (and they perceive it as weakened) through a substantial drop in popular support.

Factors promoting the consolidation of democracy after a leadership ouster

Finally, as was noted above, simple change of leadership does not regime change make, but democratization becomes more likely if the new leaders declare support for it and if key factors found in comparative analysis to be supportive of democratic transition have come into place. Are such factors likely to emerge in Russia by 2025? We can probably rule out dense ties with and vulnerability to the exertion of Western leverage, factors that much research has found have underpinned many successful transitions to democracy in Europe and Latin America, a possibility few expect in Russia.[29] More promising would seem to be sustained economic growth. One also cannot entirely rule out the possibility of constitutional change away from presidentialism, though the presidentialist model generally remains attractive to the set of politicians who might be in a position to influence the constitution in the next dozen years. Nevertheless, unpopular presidents can have incentive to weaken a strong presidency, for instance when: a president who is declining in popularity or otherwise planning to leave office decides to disperse power so that his successor will be less likely to amass enough concentrated power to harm his interests after he has left office (a Georgian scenario); a stalemate in the streets between regime and opposition leads to dispersion of executive power as a compromise (a Ukrainian scenario); or an opposition coalition rises to power without a dominant leader and pledges to distribute executive power relatively evenly among the various parties as a way of sealing the coalitional deal (a Kyrgyzstan scenario). Of course, the outcome of such formal constitutional change is far from certain, and not all non-presidentialist distributions of power are workable, as Ukraine may have taught us after the Orange Revolution. But it could give democracy a chance in Russia, especially if time were taken to design the reform well.

Scenarios

The preceding analysis leads us to several 'scenario clusters': concentrations of myriad detailed scenarios that have similar outcomes in terms of the broad nature of the political system, which is this chapter's focus of analysis. As the focus of the volume is on the prospects for a true change in political regime type, the main clusters discussed below are the inertial scenarios and two scenarios representing major change: successful full autocracy and democratization.[30]

Inertial scenarios

There are two primary inertial scenarios, with public support for Putin and his top associates being the crucial factor determining which version comes into being. We will dub the first *Putinism Prolonged*: Putin keeps in place the current micromanaged democracy with himself or a hand-picked successor in place straight through 2025. Given the heavy centralization of decision-making under micromanaged democracy, this scenario would require the kind of extraordinarily skilled and nimble leadership witnessed only seldom in recent history, for example with Lee Kwan Yew's remarkable personal stewardship of Singapore. And it would have to happen in one of the largest and most complex countries of the world, very different from Singapore.

An alternative version of Putinism Prolonged, one that would spare Putin some of the *personal* burden of having to sustain remarkably skilled micromanagement of the entire country, would be for Putin to use his popularity (while it still exists) to put in place a strong ruling party that could provide a regular, predictable, and widely accepted mechanism for managing succession. Crucially, the anchor would need to be not just the institutional apparatus of such a party but also its reputation in the population, something that stands for something beyond Putin himself – like an ideology or successful style – and could thus survive him and anchor the system even should he personally lose his 'Teflon' coating. The endorsement of such a party could be decisive in moments of succession and thereby undermine incentives for other elites to mount a serious challenge. Mexico's Institutional Revolutionary Party (PRI), which remained in power for decades in something like a micromanaged democracy, is perhaps the iconic example, a system that also worked by limiting presidents to only one six-year term, which meant that rivals to a given president could hope to have their own turn in the office after just a few years.

But here Putin appears to have missed a major chance to add stability to Russia's political system: instead of endowing the United Russia Party with his unreserved personal authority and possibly anchoring its position in the political system long into the future (as Kemal Ataturk did with the Republican People's Party in Turkey) during the major economic boom of the early–mid-2000s, Putin has consistently refused to call himself a party 'member' – even when formally occupying the position of party chairman! This distancing, combined with his sniping at it during critical junctures and his refusal to govern through it, has weakened United Russia's ability to serve a true stabilizing function in Russia. Its pronounced dip in popularity in 2011, and the way that the moniker 'Party of Swindlers and Thieves' gained currency around that same time, suggests that it may not become a truly stabilizing dominant party like the PRI, though it has been found to have a substantial core of support that is distinct from Putin and thus can provide some limited support into the future.[31] Putin has exacerbated his regime's problem of succession by returning to the presidency in 2012, reinforcing the sense of his own indispensability, which will increasingly cause problems as he ages, even though in the short run his remaining in office reduces uncertainty. The party-building version of Putinism Prolonged thus looks increasingly more difficult to pull off, and thus less likely to occur.

Another inertial scenario, dubbed here *Regime Cycles*, might develop in the event that Putin's own popularity plummets before 2025. A shorter cycle could complete itself before the 2018 presidential election if his popularity drops significantly before then and he attempts to hand off power to a successor, resulting in a lame duck syndrome and his defeat at the hands of an opposition candidate (likely a defector from Putin's own elite) who would be likely to campaign in the name of democracy. A longer cycle could result if Putin stays in office in 2018 but his popularity drops after that point, setting up an epic succession struggle in anticipation of the 2024 elections that could culminate before the elections themselves, a struggle his chosen successor could lose. This Regime Cycles scenario hinges on two other possible developments not occurring: continued rapid economic development capable of sustaining a democratic transition and the changing of the strongly presidentialist constitution. Barring these developments, the new president would be highly likely to restore a single-pyramid system that might well bear strong features of the early stages of Putin's micromanaged democracy (early, because the new leader would have to rebuild the system from the rubble of the old, depending on the scale of the rupture involved in the power struggle).

Successful full autocracy (Russia becomes Uzbekistan)

According to this scenario, the political system becomes increasingly closed in reaction to the 2011–12 protests or other factors, much as the monarchies of 1848 generally reacted to the revolutions of that era by making tactical concessions and then tightening their political grip.[32] Russia's political system would start to look a lot like Uzbekistan's does today. For such a highly closed system to survive in Russia until 2025, however, would require either a great deal of luck (avoiding the kind of regime-threatening focal points that did in Mubarak) or skill in sustaining economic development and popularity. Regimes like China's feature a strong party apparatus that provides a mechanism for handling succession and can make it less vulnerable to mass protest, but, as discussed above, Putin may have already missed his own historic chance to firmly establish such a party in Russia.

Democratizing regime change

True democratization in Russia is possible through at least three distinct paths: (1) a leadership ouster that is preceded by major economic development; (2) a leadership ouster that is followed by a constitutional change away from presidentialism; or (3) an initiative by the leadership itself to preemptively democratize to ward off protests that would be dangerous to its interests. Paths (2) and (3) cannot be ruled out, but are not very likely for reasons noted above. Russia's best democratizing hope would likely be through robust economic development, though global historical evidence suggests economic growth is not likely to *generate* democratization, instead tending only to strengthen democratizing initiatives that occur for other reasons.

Conclusion: Assessing relative likelihood

One conclusion is that much depends on essentially chance events. First and foremost is the will of Putin himself. Slightly less stochastic is the variable of popular support, which is likely to be very influential in determining: (a) whether an attempt at full autocracy will be successful if tried; and (b) whether the inertial scenario, if realized, takes the form of Regime Cycles or Putinism Prolonged. Popular support does, of course, partly depend on Putin and his team, especially their avoiding major missteps and laying out a vision for Russia that can be supported. But it also depends on factors like economic growth and changes in society, and how society's interests in relations with the regime evolve. Economic development has also been found to bear more directly on prospects for regime change, with higher levels of development making it more likely that any political opening that happens to occur (for example, an unexpected revolution) will actually lead to political liberalization and possibly democracy. The system of micromanaged democracy itself was also argued to be a driver of its own, very difficult to sustain over a long period of time and requiring unusually sensitive, subtle, and nimble leadership.

What can we say about the likelihood that these factors will deviate from current trends? One claim that can be made is that Putin has shown little inclination to usher in democracy. He has also shown reluctance to go all the way to full dictatorship; surely this could have been relatively easily accomplished in 2007–08. In this sense, Putin has been a fairly typical hybrid regime leader, though one who is more easily spooked than most and lacks confidence in his ability to win genuine, open political competition (a confidence Yeltsin possessed in much greater measure). This suggests he is likely to try to stick with micromanaged democracy, constantly tightening the screws in response to threats and loosening them only under extreme duress, with some risk of tightening them too far. Prospects for major economic transformation over the next dozen years are also uncertain. There are also signs that the regime's soft touch in micromanagement is becoming more clumsy, and this ability is likely to deteriorate as Putin himself ages and grows more out of touch.

Probably, then, the inertial scenarios are the most likely by 2025, with the most likely of all some kind of Regime Cycle, though Putin Prolonged remains a possibility if fate smiles kindly on him. If the economy grows robustly and Russia becomes noticeably more prosperous outside Moscow alone, however, there is a good possibility that supporting conditions could be in place for sustaining a democratic opening should one occur around the 2024 presidential election. There is also at least some chance of a democratic opening leading up to 2018, though this chance would be underpinned not only by modest socio-economic change but also by the possibility that a succession-related political opening could produce a changed constitution that would significantly complicate the arrangement of the country's extended political-economic networks in a single-pyramid configuration. We cannot exclude the Uzbekistan scenario by 2025, but a leadership attempt to enact it without accompanying economic growth is likely to render salient the cliché often applied to Russian politics: 'expect the unexpected'. This is because earth-shaking revolutions unseating fully dictatorial regimes become highly unpredictable, as the focal points that enable them to happen can result from essentially random events that just happen to crystallize an emotion, capture the imagination, or generate a breakthrough in consciousness of some kind.[33] Such events can be very long in coming, of course, though they become more likely as the leadership itself ages. But one hopes that the leadership understands this and avoids this most worrisome of scenarios.

say that authoritarian turnover made ...... crises most unlikely

Notes

1. For example, M. Dmitriev, S. Belanovsky (2012) 'Vlast prokhodit period poluraspada', *Vedomosti*, 4 July; L. Shevtsova (2012) 'Putin's Ironic Potential', *Project Syndicate*, 26 June, http://www.project-syndicate.org/commentary/putin-s-ironic-potential, accessed 18 August 2012.
2. N. Petrov, M. Lipman, and H.E. Hale (2010) *Overmanaged Democracy in Russia: Dilemmas of Hybrid Regime Governance*, Carnegie Paper no.106 (Washington, DC: Carnegie Endowment for International Peace).
3. Ch. Tilly (1993) *European Revolutions, 1492–1992* (Oxford: Blackwell), for example, p.18; G. Tullock (1987) *Autocracy* (Springer).
4. H.E. Hale (2010) 'Eurasian Polities as Hybrid Regimes: The Case of Putin's Russia', *Journal of Eurasian Studies*, vol.1, no.1, 33–41.
5. M.N. Afanasiev (1997) *Klientelizm i Rossiiskaia Gosudarstvennost* (Moscow: Moscow Public Science Foundation).
6. V. Gelman (2012) 'Political Opposition in Russia: A Dying Species?', *Post-Soviet Affairs*, vol.21, no.3, 226–46; G. Golosov (2012) *Demokratiia v Rossii: instruktsiia po sborke* (St Petersburg: BKhV-Peterburg); G.B. Robertson (2011) *The Politics of Protest in Hybrid Regimes: Managing Dissent in Post-Communist Russia* (New York: Cambridge University Press).
7. H.E. Hale (2006) *Why Not Parties in Russia? Democracy, Federalism, and the State* (NY: Cambridge University Press).
8. P. Goode (2011) *Boundary Issues: The Decline of Regionalism in Putin's Russia* (New York: Routledge); Hale (2010) 'Eurasian Polities as Hybrid Regimes...'; Robertson (2011) 'The Politics of Protest...'; D. Treisman (2011) *The Return* (New York: Free Press).
9. The term micromanaged democracy does not mean Russia is actually a democracy; see N. Petrov, M. Lipman, and H.E. Hale (2010) *Overmanaged Democracy...* for an explanation as to why 'overmanaged democracy' (by which we mean the same concept) is appropriate despite Russia's status as a non-democracy.

10. J. Tucker (2007) 'Enough! Electoral Fraud, Collective Action Problems, and the "2nd wave" of Post-Communist Democratic Revolutions', *Perspectives on Politics*, vol.5, no.3, September, 537–53.
11. H.E. Hale (2005) 'Regime Cycles: Democracy, Autocracy, and Revolution in Post-Soviet Eurasia', *World Politics*, vol.58, no.1, October, 133–65.
12. Indeed, there is a strong argument to be made that this is why strongmen allow them: Robertson (2011) '*The Politics of Protest . . .*', 12–13.
13. T. Kuran (1995) *Private Truths, Public Lies: The Social Consequences of Preference Falsification* (Cambridge: Harvard University Press).
14. M. Bratton and N. van de Walle (1997) *Democratic Experiments in Africa: Regime Transitions in Comparative Perspective* (New York: Cambridge University Press).
15. M. Lynch (2012) *The Arab Uprising: The Unfinished Revolutions of the New Middle East* (New York: PublicAffairs).
16. K. Weyland (2009) 'The Diffusion of Revolution: "1848" in Europe and Latin America', *International Organization*, vol.63, Summer, 391–423.
17. Treisman (2011) *The Return*.
18. H.E. Hale (2011) 'The Putin Machine Sputters: First Impressions of Russia's 2011 Duma Election', *Russian Analytical Digest*, no.106, 21 December, 2–5.
19. L. Gudkov (2012) 'Sotsialnyi kapital i ideologicheskie orientatsii', *Pro et Contra*, May–June, 6–31. Or at least the loyalty of the 'second Russia', 'third Russia', and 'fourth Russia' (those outside the biggest cities) that remain oriented to clientelistic rule for different reasons, according to N. Zubarevich (2011) 'Chetyre Rossii', *Vedomosti*, 30 December.
20. Treisman (2011) *The Return*.
21. T.J. Colton, H.E. Hale (2009) 'The Putin Vote: Presidential Electorates in a Hybrid Regime', *Slavic Review*, vol.68, no.3, Fall, 473–503; L. Gudkov (2012) 'Sotsialnyi capital . . .'; N. Zubarevich (2011) 'Chetyre Rossii'.
22. N. Petrov, M. Lipman, and H.E. Hale (2010) *Overmanaged Democracy in Russia . . .*
23. M. Dmitriev, S. Belanovsky (2012) 'Vlast prokhodit . . .'; *The New York Times*, 18 August, 1.
24. H.E. Hale (2011) 'The Myth of Mass Russian Support for Autocracy: Public Opinion Foundations of a Hybrid Regime', *Europe-Asia Studies*, vol.63, no.8, October, 1357–75.
25. Z. Barany (2011) 'The Role of the Military', *Journal of Democracy*, vol.22, no.4, October 2011, 24–35; M. Lynch (2012) *The Arab Uprising . . .*
26. M. Dmitriev, S. Belanovsky (2012) 'Vlast prokhodit . . .'. L. Gudkov (see L. Gudkov (2012) 'Sotsialnyi capital . . .', 29) expects that regional elections, which take place every year, will become defining points of struggle for the evolution of the regime.
27. The term elite primary comes from O. Shvetsova (2003) 'Resolving the Problem of Pre-Election Coordination: The 1999 Parliamentary Election as Elite Presidential "Primary"', in V. Hesli and W. Reisinger (eds) *Elections, Parties and the Future of Russia* (New York: Cambridge).
28. V. Inozemtsev (2012) 'Preventivnaia demokratiia', *Vedomosti*, 8 June, 4.
29. S. Levitsky, L.A. Way (2010) *Competitive Authoritarianism: Hybrid Regimes after the Cold War* (New York: Cambridge University Press); M.A. Vachudova

(2005) *Europe Undivided: Democracy, Leverage, and Integration after Communism* (New York: Oxford University Press).
30. These three clusters are clearly not exhaustive, but are the focus here due to the goals of the present book. Other possibilities could include the emergence of nationalist, theocratic, or military regimes, as well as regimes based on ideological principles.
31. H.E. Hale, T.J. Colton (2009) *What Makes Dominant Parties Dominant in Hybrid Regimes? The Unlikely Importance of Ideas in the Case of United Russia,* paper presented at the Annual Meeting of the American Association for the Advancement of Slavic Studies, Boston, 12–15 November.
32. K. Weyland (2010) 'The Diffusion of Regime Contention in European Democratization, 1830–1940', *Comparative Political Studies,* vol.43, nos. 8–9, 1148–76.
33. T. Kuran (1995) *Private Truths, Public Lies...*

Bibliography

M.N. Afanasiev (1997) *Klientelizm i Rossiiskaia Gosudarstvennost* (Moscow: Moscow Public Science Foundation).

Z. Barany (2011) 'The Role of the Military', *Journal of Democracy,* vol.22, no.4, October.

M. Bratton, N. van de Walle (1997) *Democratic Experiments in Africa: Regime Transitions in Comparative Perspective* (New York: Cambridge University Press).

T.J. Colton, H.E. Hale (2009) 'The Putin Vote: Presidential Electorates in a Hybrid Regime', *Slavic Review,* vol.68, no.3, Fall.

M. Dmitriev, S. Belanovsky (2012) 'Vlast prokhodit period poluraspada', *Vedomosti,* 4 July.

V. Gelman (2012) 'Political Opposition in Russia: A Dying Species?', *Post-Soviet Affairs,* vol.21, no.3, 226–46.

G. Golosov (2012) *Demokratiia v Rossii: instruktsiia po sborke* (St Petersburg: BKhV-Peterburg).

P. Goode (2011) *Boundary Issues: The Decline of Regionalism in Putin's Russia* (New York: Routledge).

L. Gudkov (2012) 'Sotsialnyi kapital i ideologicheskie orientatsii', *Pro et Contra,* May–June.

H.E. Hale (2005) 'Regime Cycles: Democracy, Autocracy, and Revolution in Post-Soviet Eurasia', *World Politics,* vol.58, no.1, October.

H.E. Hale (2006) *Why Not Parties in Russia? Democracy, Federalism, and the State* (NY: Cambridge University Press).

H.E. Hale (2010) 'Eurasian Polities as Hybrid Regimes: The Case of Putin's Russia', *Journal of Eurasian Studies,* vol.1, no.1, 33–41.

H.E. Hale (2011) 'The Myth of Mass Russian Support for Autocracy: Public Opinion Foundations of a Hybrid Regime', *Europe-Asia Studies,* vol.63, no.8, October.

H.E. Hale (2011) 'The Putin Machine Sputters: First Impressions of Russia's 2011 Duma Election', *Russian Analytical Digest,* no.106, 21 December.

H.E. Hale, T.J. Colton (2009) *What Makes Dominant Parties Dominant in Hybrid Regimes? The Unlikely Importance of Ideas in the Case of United Russia,* paper presented at the Annual Meeting of the American Association for the Advancement of Slavic Studies, Boston, 12–15 November.

V. Inozemtsev (2012) 'Preventivnaia demokratiia', *Vedomosti*, 8 June.

T. Kuran (1995) *Private Truths, Public Lies: The Social Consequences of Preference Falsification* (Cambridge: Harvard University Press).

S. Levitsky, L.A. Way (2010) *Competitive Authoritarianism: Hybrid Regimes after the Cold War* (New York: Cambridge University Press).

M. Lynch (2012) *The Arab Uprising: The Unfinished Revolutions of the New Middle East* (New York: PublicAffairs).

N. Petrov, M. Lipman, and H.E. Hale (2010) *Overmanaged Democracy in Russia: Dilemmas of Hybrid Regime Governance*, Carnegie Paper no.106 (Washington, DC: Carnegie Endowment for International Peace).

G.B. Robertson (2011) *The Politics of Protest in Hybrid Regimes: Managing Dissent in Post-Communist Russia* (New York: Cambridge University Press).

L. Shevtsova (2012) 'Putin's Ironic Potential', *Project Syndicate*, 26 June, http://www.project-syndicate.org/commentary/putin-s-ironic-potential, accessed 18 August 2012.

O. Shvetsova (2003) 'Resolving the Problem of Pre-Election Coordination: The 1999 Parliamentary Election as Elite Presidential "Primary"', in V. Hesli, W. Reisinger (eds) *Elections, Parties and the Future of Russia* (New York: Cambridge).

The New York Times, 18 August 2012.

Ch. Tilly (1993) *European Revolutions, 1492–1992* (Oxford: Blackwell).

D. Treisman (2011) *The Return* (New York: Free Press).

G. Tullock (1987) *Autocracy* (Springer).

J. Tucker (2007) 'Enough! Electoral Fraud, Collective Action Problems, and the "2nd wave" of Post-Communist Democratic Revolutions', *Perspectives on Politics*, vol.5, no.3, September.

M.A. Vachudova (2005) *Europe Undivided: Democracy, Leverage, and Integration after Communism* (New York: Oxford University Press).

K. Weyland (2009) 'The Diffusion of Revolution: "1848" in Europe and Latin America', *International Organization*, vol.63, Summer.

K. Weyland (2010) 'The Diffusion of Regime Contention in European Democratization, 1830–1940', *Comparative Political Studies*, vol.43, no.8–9.

N. Zubarevich (2011) 'Chetyre Rossii', *Vedomosti*, 30 December.

7
Regime Changes in Russia: Trajectories of Political Evolution[1]

Vladimir Gel'man

For political scientists, there is probably nothing more demanded and at the same time more speculative than the business of political predictions. These so-called 'political experts' actually produce forecasts that are no more precise and substantively grounded than predictions made by an 'average Joe'. Virtually all political forecasts of this sort – whether made by professionals or amateurs – are based on projections of a current state of affairs into the future, with certain corrections and reservations. However, the real world developments often follow another logic, which is not always clearly understood, especially considering 'wild cards' – unexpected and sometimes unpredictable factors that alter possible scenarios.

Nevertheless, it appears that discussing the political future still makes sense, so we can agree with Daniel Treisman, who believes that

> even if one cannot say which of many paths history will go down, it is still useful to think about the layout of the paths, their forks and intersections. If nothing else, this prepares one to interpret rapidly what is happening as events unfold. At the same time, the attempt to think systematically about the future imposes a certain discipline and perspective that are helpful for understanding the present. One is forced to think about how different aspects of current reality fit together.[2]

Using this logic, we will start with assessment of the current state of the Russian political regime (as of September 2012) and analyze the trends and constraints that prevent fundamental changes, thus preserving the status quo. After discussing the prospects for the regime's political stagnation, we will turn to the possible alternatives, such as the rise of a repressive version of authoritarianism ('the iron fist' scenario), the sudden collapse of the regime, and finally the gradual ('creeping') democratization scenario, each with its opportunities and risks. Possible implications for the evolutionary logic of Russia's political development will be presented in the conclusion.

Diagnosis: An 'Institutional Trap'

It appeared that by the summer of 2012 the Russian political equilibrium – the political order typical for the country in the previous decade – had been restored. Putin has returned to the presidency and distributed key posts and sources of rent among his 'ruling coalition' members; the regime's 'fellow travelers', such as 'systemic' opposition parties, business people, and a significant part of the general public, have reconciled themselves to the idea of preserving the status quo – whether willingly or not; after a series of clashes with the police, the mass protests wave has turned into small-scale nuisances for the regime; the economic growth continued, although not so impressively; the concessions that the Kremlin made to the public – such as a return to popular elections of regional governors – were scaled down to a point where they could no longer hurt the regime; finally, though still far from the 'golden age' period of Putin's first presidency, the regime's popular support has increased after its severe decline in December 2011, according to the public opinion polls.[3] In other words, Russian rulers have been able to accomplish their goals of consolidating the major institutions – formal and informal 'rules of the game', a sort of institutional 'core' of the Russian political regime.[4] These rules are the following:

(1) unilateral presidential monopoly on adopting key political decisions (regime's personalism);
(2) a taboo on open electoral competition among elites given unfree and unfair elections (electoral authoritarianism); and
(3) de facto hierarchical subordination of regional and local authorities to the central government ('the power vertical').

These rules are clearly imperfect, since they are inherently and notoriously inefficient given extremely high corruption; interest groups' ('the Kremlin towers') hidden but quite stiff competition for rent access and resource redistribution; and, finally, the ruling groups' inability to conduct reforms that may challenge the current equilibrium, which also explains the ineffective attempts at Russia's authoritarian modernization. Nevertheless, if the 'rules of the game' do not fully 'serve the interests of those with the bargaining power to devise new rules',[5] to use Douglas North's well-known notion, at least they prevent infringement upon these interests today.

However, behind the façade of the restored political equilibrium, bitter disappointment and growing discontent with the current status quo are rising. Besides data on mass attitudes from public opinion polls and focus groups, the research on Russia's elites also reveals this discontent.[6] After the wave of 2011–12 protests, the societal and elite divisions and discontent have only intensified.

At first glance, the growing demand for change among various segments of Russian society, given the regime's claim to supply the previous 'stability', poses a threat of the rise of political tensions and increases risks of regime change. However, such a conclusion would be premature and unfounded. In reality, attractiveness of the status quo is not the only reason for maintaining political equilibrium. The alternatives to the status quo may look even more unattractive or unrealistic; and, more importantly, the costs of transition from the existing political order to something else seem prohibitively high. The business community fears the risks of new property redistribution, while the employees of state-dependent enterprises are afraid of structural reforms and unemployment; the 'systemic' opposition, which, to some extent, remains loyal to the regime, believes that regime change will significantly reduce its influence, and the like. In short, many of those actors, and ordinary people discontented with the status quo, see its continuity as a lesser evil in comparison with major regime change. It is unsurprising that the protest wave of 2011–12 received little support from those social groups who were quite critical of the Russian regime.[7] As long as the costs of the status quo equilibrium do not exceed its current benefits for the ruling groups and society at large, this equilibrium will be endorsed by the major actors: they have little incentive for challenging it. Thus, the institutional trap – a stable but socially ineffective equilibrium that almost no one wants to break – becomes rooted in Russian politics.[8]

Such political equilibrium may well prove self-enforced – not only due to the lack or weakness of serious actors that are capable of challenging the regime, but also because of the inertia created by 'the rules of the game' that were established in the 1990s and especially in the 2000s. To put it simply, the longer the current status quo regime is maintained, the more costly it will be to overcome.

As the regime and the 'stability' it offers are sustained over time, Russia ends up in a 'vicious cycle'; the longer the status quo regime persists, the smaller the chances of successfully overcoming the 'institutional trap' it found itself in. Also, fragmentation of political actors and numerous institutional barriers hinder collective actions aimed at challenging the current status quo. Indeed, the current political equilibrium effectively creates incentives for the ruling groups to preserve the status quo at any cost, becoming the end in itself; at the same time, the notorious inefficiency of political institutions narrows the time horizons for major actors, making them sacrifice long-term goals for the sake of short-term gains here and now. Moreover, as the current Russian leadership learned from Gorbachev's perestroika experience, politicians that launch political liberalization run a risk of losing power – hence, they must put a 'No Entrance' sign along this path.

Is Russia's exit from the 'institutional trap' possible? Can Russia reject inefficient electoral authoritarianism and establish new, more stable and successful 'rules of the game'? If so, how can it be done? The answers to these questions are not clear, at least in the short term. The problem does not only stem from the fact that Russia now lacks conditions for this type of transformation. As the experience of various countries suggests, exit from 'institutional traps' often resulted from the impact of exogenous shocks – wars, ethnic conflicts, revolutions, economic crises, and so on. However, predicting such developments is an impossible task a priori, as is speculating on their possible impact on politics and society in Russia and beyond.

For instance, some specialists believe that the nature of the Russian political regime and its possible changes is a byproduct of economic development.[9] This claim produces expectations that a possible economic decline brought on by the global economic developments may provoke a collapse of the political status quo in Russia and lead to open elite competition and revision of the fundamental 'rules of the game'. While such developments are possible, one has to bear in mind that authoritarian regimes do not always respond to economic crises in such a way: they often demonstrate trends of involution, losing capacity to change for a long period of time. Also, according to some studies, incentives for regime changes depend upon the length of economic recession rather than its depth.[10] Short-term shocks similar to those of 2008–09 are not long enough to affect political regimes, or their impact is insufficient to effect major changes. The same caution might be applied to the assumption that long-term, sustainable, and relatively rapid economic growth in Russia will lead to an increasing demand for democratization among the expanded urban middle class, thus triggering political reforms.[11] Although such a line of reasoning is quite logical and can be endorsed by the experience of numerous countries, there are no guarantees that this demand will play a major role at a certain 'critical juncture' of the Russian history, nor is there any evidence that it will meet an adequate supply from the political class.

Therefore, our analysis will attempt to avoid further discussion on exogenous shocks and their possible impacts; instead, we will focus on the role of internal political factors in the continuity and/or change of the Russian political regime. With this approach in mind, we will consider a number of major alternative paths of the evolution of the Russian political regime, namely:

- preservation of the current political regime in Russia (to use the Soviet-era terminology, a further 'decay' of the Russian regime),
- increasing authoritarian tendencies as a result of the ruling groups' reaction to the challenges to its dominance (the 'iron fist' mechanism),
- wild card scenario – a sudden collapse of the current regime in certain circumstances (not necessarily those caused by powerful external shocks), and
- a gradual and, most probably, inconsistent creeping democratization of the political regime under societal pressure.

In fact, the regime's trajectory may represent a combination of some of these scenarios or consistent or inconsistent alternation of their elements. We will try looking at each of these political development scenarios separately in order to understand their potential constraints and risks.

Institutional decay: Toward a new stagnation?

Many observers of Russian politics assume that dissatisfaction with the status quo regime creates incentives for political change in a certain direction nearly by default. Nothing could be further from the truth: 'staying away from trouble' is the maxim that can explain the logic of political development that posits the preservation of the status quo as an end in itself for the ruling groups and for society at large. Indeed, provided the environment in which the Russian political regime operates does not significantly change in the foreseeable future, given roughly the same constellation of key actors with their rent-seeking capabilities and granted that the opposition and protest movement pressure on the regime is brought back to the pre-late 2011 degree, one should not expect that Russian ruling groups will be likely to revise the rules of the game and change the institutional core of the political regime. An inertia-based scenario that preserves the current political institutions with some insignificant changes looks more desirable for the Russian elites compared with both regime democratization and the turn to more repressive authoritarianism.

However, maintaining the inefficient political equilibrium cannot occur by default; it will require substantial effort on the part of Russian ruling groups. Besides the skillful constellation of use of 'carrots' and 'sticks' that was misbalanced on the eve of 2011–12 elections, the authorities will most certainly be forced to resort to targeted and strictly limited repressions against their radical opponents; they will have to adopt 'divide and rule' tactics toward moderate opposition and correct both formal and informal rules of the game in order to consolidate the institutional core of the political regime rather than simply preserving it in the current form. Some examples of such behavior can be seen in the steps the Kremlin took after the end of the 2011–12 protest wave. Crackdown on some protest activities, increasing fines and sanctions for violations of rules of meetings and rallies, the return of criminal prosecution for defamation, and a number of other frightening actions were accompanied by the partial liberalization of party registration procedures and return to popular elections of regional chief executives. But the partial revision of the rules of the game was intended to entrench and reinforce the status quo, though under a new guise. As Grigorii Golosov noted in this regard, the goal of such political reforms is not democratization but, rather, consolidation of authoritarianism by making it more institutionally viable; in other words, it is a correction of mistakes and a rectification of certain excesses of the previous stage of authoritarian regime building in Russia.[12]

A path to 'institutional decay' that involves further regime consolidation and rearrangements will not be able to solve the problems of the current political order in Russia, but will most probably exacerbate them. In this case one should expect further deterioration of the principal–agent problems in central–regional relations as well as an increase in corruption at all levels and permanent conflicts over rent redistribution among interest groups. The 'decay' will also lead to sharp increases in the costs of maintaining the political equilibrium due to the rising payoffs which authorities will have to offer to the political and economic rent-seekers as a side payment for their loyalty.

And what about society at large? The demand for change, which was so vividly demonstrated to the authorities during the 2011–12 protest wave, can be satisfied to a certain extent through some concessions on second-order issues through the effective co-optation of some moderate regime opponents, and through the relatively successful resolution of certain issues, or in some instances it may simply remain at the level of latent discontent and local 'rebellions', which do not pose major threats to a regime. In other words, a significant part of society may react to 'institutional decay' through passive individual 'exit' rather than through collective and open 'voice', as Albert Hirschman termed it.[13] The 'exit' can take different forms, but it will pose no danger to the authorities, since not only does it not challenge the status quo as such, but it also increases the protesters' costs for overcoming the institutional trap. One should not expect major changes without cumulative and relatively prolonged societal pressure on the regime. If so, this will mean that the 'institutional decay' may last until the costs of maintaining the status quo become prohibitively high or until the current generation of Russian leaders simply become extinct, akin to the generation of the Soviet leaders of the Brezhnev period.

Although the 'decay' scenario should be presently treated as baseline, there are two important constraints to its implementation in Russia. First, in order to maintain the political equilibrium, Russian ruling groups will require a constant and substantial rent inflow that will support the loyalty of all the important actors and society at large. Second, the regime's manipulative strategy may become less efficient over time, resembling Lincoln's quote that one can fool some of the people all of the time, and all of the people some of the time, but cannot fool all of the people all of the time. Thus, attempts to preserve the status quo regime through an 'institutional decay' are not necessarily bound to be successful.

'Iron Fist': A dictator's solution?

An alternative scenario of Russian political developments assumes that the ruling groups will face an increase in actual and potential challenges to its domination, which may take a vast variety of forms. Protest activism in Moscow and other cities might grow in scope and scale and take new, possibly violent, forms. Risks of 'rebellions' of some of the regime's current loyalists might increase, and the potential for their co-optation and/or use of other tools for maintaining loyalty might be exhausted. The experiences of some other authoritarian regimes in different parts of the world (ranging from the South Korean regime's massacre of the student uprising in Gwangju in 1980 to the installation of martial law in Poland in 1981) suggest that under such circumstances their leaders tend to pick up a 'stick' and use it in a full-fledged manner. Although this authoritarian regime strategy rarely proves to be successful in the long term (especially if the regimes do not enjoy mass support, and the protests increase), in the short term such a reaction to crises may postpone negative consequences for the regime despite the resulting increase in violence and conflicts for the future. Thus, in order to maintain their domination, the Russian authorities can possibly opt for an 'iron fist' response, which means they will have to partially or completely dismantle the democratic façade of some of the current institutions and replace them by openly authoritarian rules of the game while still retaining the regime's institutional core. Even if the 'iron fist' option looks suicidal, the delayed suicide and its possible consequences also merit some consideration.

It is hard to predict the Kremlin's steps along this path; they may involve various restrictions on political parties (including those loyal to the government), a radical overhaul of legislation and practice that expands the powers of law enforcement agencies and security services and further restrictions of individual rights and liberties, vicious attacks on independent media, greater pressure on civil society organizations, and so on. Finally, moving along this path may logically result in adopting a new constitution that would be stripped of declarations of individual rights and liberties and denied the supremacy of Russia's international obligations over domestic legislation and other liberal statements. Possible design of new rules of the game, as well as the scale and scope of repression, will depend upon *perceptions* of threats or challenges and associated risks by the ruling groups rather than upon the actual danger of these challenges and risks. 'Tightening the screws', even in the version which will be most favorable to the authorities, allows them to cope with symptoms of the regime's pathologies but not their underlying causes. One should not expect these measures to increase regime performance: corruption, 'Kremlin towers" struggle for rent redistribution, and the aggravating principal–agent problems will not disappear but will take other forms. On the contrary, one might expect that the turn toward the 'iron fist' will lead to a sharp increase in costs of maintaining the political equilibrium in the country. The ruling groups will not just have to significantly increase agency costs but will also need to raise the payoffs to the coercive apparatus to reward its loyalty. Risks of becoming a hostage to the coercive apparatus might be a problem for any repressive regime, and, in the case of Russia, law enforcement agencies and security services do not enjoy large support in Russian society. However, one should not expect that the turn toward the 'iron fist' scenario as such will provoke political disequilibrium, even if the rise of repression poses a threat to a large number of previously loyal actors or other dissidents. At least, as long as the 'advanced' segment of Russian society considers 'exit', that is, leaving the country, a more viable alternative to the anti-status quo protests, public resistance risks will not be excessively high for the ruling groups.

In the case of Russia, there are other risks for the ruling groups if they opt for an 'iron fist' authoritarian turn. First, international experience suggests that authoritarian regimes that initially refrain from repression quite rarely become far more repressive. Using a 'stick' is quite a difficult task after a long and successful distribution of 'carrots'. Second, the international consequences of the turn to repressive authoritarianism will most probably be clearly negative, while international legitimacy is of utmost importance to the Russian elites, primarily due to the need to legalize their money and status in the West, where they and their families live and spend considerable periods of time. This phenomenon, once called 'offshore aristocracy' by Vladislav Surkov,[14] provides another incentive for various segments of the elites – rather than 'tightening the screws', they may find it more advantageous to relocate and legalize their assets overseas in response to threats to their current benefits. Finally, repressive authoritarianism threatens to open the door to conflicts within the ruling groups, and may reveal the poor performance of the coercive apparatus. The unsuccessful use of repression may in turn bring about the collapse of the authoritarian regime, as happened after the August 1991 coup in the Soviet Union. Given the unpredictable consequences of such developments, the 'iron fist' may prove to be one of the possible causes of regime collapse – far from being a 'dictator's solution'.

The regime collapse: A horrible end vs. endless horror?

At first glance, political regime collapse appears unlikely in contemporary Russia. Such collapse implies a regime's sudden and relatively rapid breakdown as a result of mass protests or other internal conflicts accompanied by a virtually complete turnover of the ruling elite and a total rejection of the previous rules of the game. Such a scenario is hindered by the conspicuous lack of a 'revolutionary situation' in Russia, at least as of yet. The scale of anti-system mobilization and the opposition potential are clearly insufficient to overthrow the regime; at the same time, the degree of consolidation of the ruling groups and their allies is still quite high. Moreover, even the emergence of a revolution-ary situation does not necessarily lead to the revolutionary outcomes of a political process. But, quite frequently, such developments result in spontaneous, sometimes even mostly accidental, constellations of events at a given 'critical juncture' in history. Neither the February rev-olution of 1917 that ended the monarchy in Russia, nor the fall of the authoritarian regime in Tunisia in early 2011 that launched the 'Arab Spring', was inevitable and predetermined. Therefore, one cannot completely rule out the possibility of regime collapse, especially given the ever-increasing difficulty of the authorities in maintaining political equilibrium.

A horrible end is sometimes better than endless horror, as conven-tional wisdom goes. However, this notion is questionable when it comes to the collapse of political regimes. Both the 1917 collapse of the monar-chy and the 1991 collapse of Soviet Communism led to replacement of one authoritarian regime by another, which may become even more repressive. If, after the collapse of the current authoritarian regime, Vladimir Putin were just replaced by a new authoritarian leader, it would probably not bring about the country's democratization, but would, rather, signal regime change from bad to worse.

Yet, it is also plausible that Russia may successfully capitalize on a chance of democratization if and when such a chance appears upon the regime's collapse. However, such a situation will hardly emerge by default and be followed by successful democratization without special efforts by political actors and society at large; thus, relying on such a scenario is as reasonable as relying on a winning lottery ticket. While the risks of a sudden Russian regime political collapse are quite high, its positive consequences are not so obvious.

'Creeping democratization': Opportunities and risks

'Creeping democratization'[15] is a complex, incremental, and sometimes quite lengthy process of transition from authoritarianism to democracy through a series of strategic interactions of the ruling groups and the opposition, who adjust their strategies in response to each other's respective moves. Ruling groups may agree to partial regime liberaliza-tion under pressure from the opposition, and then – given increasing pressure and the regime's inability to eliminate liberalization – accept the extension of the room for political participation, which, in turn, leads to increasing divisions within ruling groups and involvement of the opposition in the political process. Further developments may involve different options, among which are a compromise between the reform-minded part of the ruling groups and the moderate segments of the opposition ('elite settlements', like the Polish roundtable in 1989),[16] as well as the ruling groups' initial steps for regime democratization, which allows it to maintain power upon competitive elections (as in South Korea in 1987). Finally, the process may develop into a series of electoral competitions with a more equal level playing field over time, guaranteeing a peaceful transfer of power to the opposition (as in Mexico in 1997–2000).[17] Such trajectories resulted in democratization 'success stories' in some countries, and there is no reason to rule them out in the case of contemporary Russia. Bearing these prospects in mind, we can consider the 2011–12 protest wave to be the first – necessary yet insufficient – step of the country's 'creeping democratization'. Of course, turning away from democratization and restoration of the status quo and/or other forms of authoritarianism are as likely as the possibility of a 'success story': 'creeping democratization' often turns out to be inconsistent and may involve numerous attempts.

The ruling groups' strategy of maintaining electoral authoritarianism may change only due to simultaneous and cumulative pressure from the opposition and society at large – in other words, only if various social groups and political actors are able to consolidate and mobilize a large number of their supporters on the basis of negative consensus against the status quo. At the moment, the Russian opposition has limited potential, resulting not only from its organizational weakness but also from the fact that a large part of Russian society does not perceive the opposition as an attractive and realistic alternative to the current political order – at least, for now. Yet, this situation is not forever: a lot will depend upon the opposition itself. The experience of 'creeping democratization' in a number of countries suggests the crucial importance of organizational consolidation in the struggle against a common enemy personified by the ruling groups; in order to reach their goal, the regime opponents require a cooperation of different opposition segments and mutual support of potential allies. As an important element for such cooperation, various opposition segments would have to seek support of different cross-sections of the citizens; they would also have to refrain from publicly attacking one another to accomplish their principal goal; in addition, they would have to demonstrate their ability to reach tactical compromise and their willingness to be ideologically flexible.

Besides different forms of mass protest activism, elections serve as an extremely important element capable of undermining the current authoritarian equilibrium in Russia. This does not mean that Russia's transition to democracy – if and when it happens – will come as a result of the opposition's election victory over the ruling groups while the electoral authoritarianism is preserved. It will not just go away by itself, but the 'stunning elections' effect[18] observed in the December 2011 voting and later at some mayoral elections suggests that electoral cooperation among the opposition, nomination of common candidates and party lists, and even support of anyone but the regime nominees may deal the Kremlin the most serious blow. If regional and local elections prompt a cascade of 'stunning' effects, one might expect that, in the run-up to the 2016 parliamentary and 2018 presidential elections, the ruling groups will be forced to opt for far more serious and swift regime liberalization by changing formal and informal rules of the elections, thus opening political opportunities for the opposition. It can then be expected that in a number of regions regime loyalists will quite frequently end up under opposition banners and will even rely on the opposition support in their appeal to voters' protest moods. With these trends spreading across space and time, the national elections may become a key challenge to preservation of the status quo, especially under highly uncertain conditions.

However, successful democratization does not happen by default as the authoritarian regime is overthrown. It becomes possible, but is not guaranteed, if and when the key political actors are able to accept the new rules of the game and, more importantly, ensure they are successfully implemented – in other words, these rules have to work both to prevent power monopoly and to guarantee efficient governance. Such rules are not always accepted and implemented (Ukraine after the 'Orange Revolution' is a classic example of failures in democratic institution building).[19] That is why politicians concerned about democratization in Russia will have to learn lessons from these failures, including those of Russia's own experience of the 1990s and 2000s. These risks are inevitable, but they can and must be minimized.

The new rules of the game are most likely to emerge because of a change in balance of different actors' resources and interests. Nevertheless, a minimal consensus among the elites and society at large is necessary to avoid the abuse of power by the executive branch, establish a workable system of checks and balances, ensure political accountability, and prevent power monopolization by both federal and regional authorities. It is still too early to name the specific institutional solutions that will be sought in the wake of the democratization process in Russia, but one should be ready for a possible revision of the rules of the game; meanwhile, a chance to consolidate democratic changes should not be missed, as it was in the early 1990s. However, it will only be possible to accept these rules of the game in the process of dismantling an authoritarian regime or immediately after its collapse – until then, choosing the new democratic institutions in Russia as being the first priority resembles putting the carriage before the horse.

What we don't know and why it's important

Political forecasting is faced with the unavoidable of multiple unknown variables, which at times cannot be measured even at the given moment, let alone reasonable estimations of their changes in the future. Therefore, evaluation of the probability of each of the four scenarios outlined above – 'decay', 'iron fist', 'regime collapse', and 'creeping democratization' – looks nearly useless. None of them can be ruled out, as well as their combination or succession, and this makes an analysis even more difficult.

The list of unknown variables that might lead to a particular scenario or to their interchange or combination is too long and not country-specific. Thus, there is no need to list all the factors whose impact is known to be unpredictable. However, there are at least three unknown variables, which are especially important in the context of contemporary Russia. The direction of possible changes, inter alia, is highly contingent upon their dynamics.

First of all, there are possible changes in the public opinion of Russians – both at the level of the elites and in society at large – and in the political behavior of citizens. There is no need to explain the ultimate role of these changes as such, but their evaluation and prediction under authoritarian regimes are a particular challenge, since the data are often systematically distorted due to 'preference falsification effect'[20] – in other words, instead of being truthful, the public provides responses that are socially acceptable in the eyes of the regime. To use a colloquial description, people 'give the authorities the finger' behind their backs. Sometimes people decide to give the authorities the finger out in the open at the most unexpected 'critical juncture'. At times, sudden preference changes may lead to the collapse of the authoritarian regime, but very often the finger may remain behind the back for quite a while, and the true public preferences are unknown until new challenges to the status quo emerge seemingly out of the blue. Since an ostensibly stable authoritarian regime may be toppled at any 'critical juncture', the actual behavior of all political actors at these points is certainly unpredictable.

Second, the key question for the survival of any authoritarian regime is how ready the ruling groups are to use violence and repression against their challengers, and also what the consequences of such actions will be. In case of Russia, this issue is particularly salient. Indeed, repressive regimes habitually use violence in the case of even the most minor threats to their survival, and sometimes even killing their fellow citizens is just a routine affair for them. However, non-repressive authoritarian regimes may face the tough choice of a forced turn from 'carrot' to 'stick'. Even if turning this way does not cause immediate political consequences for the regime, it determines ruling groups' strategy for many years to come (as was the case with the Novocherkassk massacre of 1962 in the Soviet Union). Actually, the key question 'to beat or not to beat?', referring to the choice between the use of violence against anti-regime protests or refraining from it, is often answered based on the past experience of using mass violence. The 1989 China example demonstrates that the use of force against the protesters on the Tiananmen Square became possible because the veterans of revolution, accustomed to killing their fellow citizens since the time of the Communist Party's struggle for power, prevailed over their less harsh rivals in Chinese leadership.[21] Russia is a special case in this respect, not only due to the low repressiveness of the regime but also because the means of mass repression are unreliable. In fact, the security apparatus is largely lacking authority and too heavily involved in rent-seeking. But it would probably be incorrect to reduce this issue to one of merely technical constraints in repressive capabilities that can be overcome if and when protests reach a certain scope and scale.[22] Rather, the questions should be posed in a different sequence: (1) will the Russian leaders resolve to order mass-scale use of violence against the citizens in the case of real or imaginary threat to their political survival? (2) if so, will the order be successfully carried out, and will the violence be able to eliminate the threat? and (3) if so, will the Russian leaders end up being hostages to the executors of this order? The answers to all of these questions are unclear, and one may only hope that they will not become part of the country's political agenda.

Third, we still do not know to what extent the country is manageable (or, rather, unmanageable) by the ruling groups. Under a highly corrupt authoritarian regime the 'power vertical' hierarchy simply cannot handle even relatively small overloads and emergency situations. For example, when it comes to natural disasters, the federal government has to deal with local issues in 'manual control', while the lower links of the 'power vertical' consistently misinform the higher authorities.[23]

We cannot predict the possible consequences of such management crises in contemporary Russia, but, given the preservation of the current political regime and the attempts at maintaining the status quo at any cost, the inefficiency of the entire hierarchical chain of command and the rising principal–agent problems will most probably only be aggravated. This means that certain challenges may arise at any moment and suddenly turn into a new 'critical juncture' in Russia's history.

Even a short list of unknown variables, which includes (1) 'preference falsification' and unpredictability of the political behavior of Russians; (2) a degree of ruling groups' willingness and capability to suppress mass protests; (3) degradation of governance and inability to implement anti-crisis policies, looks rather impressive. However, we are more focused on the overall logic of political evolution, which will allow seeing the 'forest' of evolutionary trends of the Russian politics beyond the 'trees' of the current events.

In lieu of conclusion: Russia will be free

The collapse of the Communist regime and the breakup of the Soviet Union occurred in 1991, when many observers believed that the world-wide process of ultimate transition to democracy would also affect the post-Soviet states, which were doomed to become democratic nearly by default. These naïve expectations proved to be wrong. What was being considered as an emergence of a new post-Soviet democracy in Russia over 20 years ago has actually turned into the rise of a new post-Soviet authoritarianism. This process of proliferation of electoral authoritarian regimes has been a part of the global trend that affects many countries and regions of the world.[24]

However, the failure of Russia's first post-Communist democratization attempt after 1991 by no means indicates that democracy is doomed to fail in this country, and that the second democratization attempt – if and when it takes place – will inevitably result in a new cycle of flight from democracy to authoritarianism, or, say, a vicious cycle of conflicts, crises, and violence (although these possibilities cannot be ruled out). At first glance, it seems that after two decades of authoritarian regime building the ruling groups were able to shut the 'window of opportunities' for democratization. However, the situation in Russia is gradually changing over time due to learning effects of the recent past and also due to effects of generational changes. The stunning elections of 2011 and the protest wave of 2011–12 slightly opened the window of opportunity for Russia's democratization. Today there is an increasing understanding of needs for democratic institutions and rising demands for political changes among different segments of Russian society.[25] The trial-and-error political experience of the post-Soviet development was not in vain: two decades after the Soviet collapse, the country is probably better prepared for a conscious and consistent transition to democracy than it was in the early 1990s, despite the fact that the political conditions for such a transition are less favorable today than immediately after the fall of the Communist regime. The public demand for democratization is likely to grow over time, and this trend offers some basis for hope that Russia will not jump out of the frying pan into the fire, as happened in the 1990s and especially in the 2000s. Therefore, the major slogan of opposition rallies – 'Russia will be free!' – may be perceived not just as a call for action but also as a key item of our country's political agenda in the foreseeable future. Russia will indeed become a free country. The question is exactly when and how this will happen, as well as what the costs of Russia's path to freedom will be.

Notes

1. The article was written as a part of the MODNORTH project funded by the Research Council of Norway and of the project 'Choices of Russian Modernization' funded by the Academy of Finland.
2. D. Treisman (2011) 'Russia's Political Economy: The Next Decade', in Maria Lipman, Nikolay Petrov (eds) *Russia in 2020: Scenarios for the Future* (Washington, DC: Carnegie Endowment for International Peace), 150.
3. According to the Levada Center nation-wide polls, Putin's job approval rating (the difference between respondents' positive and negative assessments of him) fell to 27 per cent in December 2011 but returned to the 35 per cent mark in July 2012 (similarly to his rating in October 2011); Levada Center (2012) All indexes, www.levada.ru/indeksy, date accessed 31 August 2013.
4. The Soviet 1977 Constitution provided the Communist Party of the Soviet Union with the official status of the 'core of political system of the USSR'; in a similar vein, one can also speak of an institutional core of the current political regime in Russia.
5. D. North (1990) *Institutions, Institutional Changes, and Economic Performance* (Cambridge: Cambridge University Press), 16.
6. Back in 2008, the survey of the Russian elites conducted by Mikhail Afanas'ev indicated that the majority of the Russian ruling class supported democratization, free elections, party competition, and checks and balances of the presidential powers, although a significant number of those with a background in the coercive apparatus among the Russian elites unequivocally opposed any democratic changes. See M. Afanas'ev (2009) *Rossiiskie elity razvitiya: zapros na novyi kurs* (Moscow: Liberal'naya missiya Foundation).
7. See 'Obshchestvo' (2012) *Obshchestvo i vlast' v usloviyakh politicheskogo krizisa: Doklad ekspertov Tsentra strategicheskikh razrabotok*, An Expert Report of the

Center for Strategic Research, http://www.echo.msk.ru/doc/891815-echo. html, date accessed 31 August 2013.
8. V. Polterovich (2008) 'Institutional Trap', in *New Palgrave Dictionary of Economics Online* (New York: Palgrave Macmillan), http://dictionary ofeconomics.com/article?id=pde2008_I000262, date accessed 31 August 2013.
9. D. Treisman (2011) 'Russia's Political Economy...'
10. B. Magaloni (2006) *Voting for Autocracy: Hegemonic Party Survival and Its Demise in Mexico* (Cambridge: Cambridge University Press).
11. See, for instance: M. Gaidar, M. Snegovaya (2012) 'Dremlet pritikhshii severnyi gorod', *Vedomosti*, 3 February http://www.vedomosti.ru/opinion/news/1493008/dremlet_pritihshij_severnyj_gorod, date accessed 31 August 2013.
12. G.V. Golosov (2012) *Demokratiya v Rossii: instruktsiya po sborke* (St Petersburg: BHV-Peterburg).
13. A.O. Hirschman (1970) *Exit, Voice, and Loyalty: Response to Decline in Firms, Organizations, and States* (Cambridge, MA: Harvard University Press).
14. V. Surkov (2006) *Suverenitet – eto politicheskii sinonim konkurentosposobnosti*, 7 February. http://www.intelros.org/lib/doklady/surkov1.htm, date accessed 29 August 2013.
15. A. Przeworski (1991) *Democracy and the Market: Political and Economic Reforms in Eastern Europe and Latin America* (Cambridge: Cambridge University Press), 69–72.
16. A. Przeworski (1991) '*Democracy and the Market...*', 54–66.
17. K. Greene (2007) *Why Dominant Parties Lose* (Cambridge: Cambridge University Press).
18. S.P. Huntington (1991) *The Third Wave: Democratization in the Late Twentieth Century* (Norman, OK: University of Oklahoma Press), 174–80.
19. O. Haran (2011) 'From Victor to Victor: Democracy and Authoritarianism in Ukraine', *Demokratizatsiya: The Journal of Post-Soviet Democratization*, vol.19, no. 2, 93–110.
20. See T. Kuran (1991) 'Now out of Never: The Element of Surprise in East European Revolution of 1989', *World Politics*, vol.44, no.1, 7–48.
21. For a detailed analysis, see, for instance: D. McAdam, S. Tarrow, and Ch. Tilly (2001) *Dynamics of Contention* (Cambridge: Cambridge University Press), 307–22.
22. A. Przeworski (1991) '*Democracy and the Market...*', 64.
23. The disasters after proliferation of wildfires in various regions of Russia in summer 2010 or the flood in Krymsk (Kransodar Krai) in summer 2012 are vivid examples of such local issues.
24. See Y.L. Morse (2012) 'The Era of Electoral Authoritarianism', *World Politics*, vol.64, no.1, 161–98.
25. See, for instance: H.E. Hale (2011) 'The Myth of Mass Russian Support for Autocracy: The Public Opinion Foundations of a Hybrid Regime', *Europe-Asia Studies*, vol.63, no. 8, 1357–75; see also Kirill Rogov's chapter in this volume.

Bibliography

M. Afanas'ev (2009) *Rossiiskie elity razvitiya: zapros na novyi kurs* (Moscow: Liberal'naya missiya Foundation).

M. Gaidar, M. Snegovaya (2012) 'Dremlet pritikhshii severnyi gorod', *Vedomosti*, 3 February, http://www.vedomosti.ru/opinion/news/1493008/dremlet_pritihshij_severnyj_gorod, date accessed 31 August 2013.

G.V. Golosov (2012) *Demokratiya v Rossii: instruktsiya po sborke* (St Petersburg: BHV-Peterburg).

K. Greene (2007) *Why Dominant Parties Lose* (Cambridge: Cambridge University Press).

H.E. Hale (2011) 'The Myth of Mass Russian Support for Autocracy: The Public Opinion Foundations of a Hybrid Regime', *Europe-Asia Studies*, vol.63, no.8.

O. Haran (2011) 'From Victor to Victor: Democracy and Authoritarianism in Ukraine', *Demokratizatsiya: The Journal of Post-Soviet Democratization*, vol.19, no.2.

A.O. Hirschman (1970) *Exit, Voice, and Loyalty: Response to Decline in Firms, Organizations, and States* (Cambridge, MA: Harvard University Press).

S.P. Huntington (1991) *The Third Wave: Democratization in the Late Twentieth Century*, (Norman, OK: University of Oklahoma Press).

T. Kuran (1991) 'Now out of Never: The Element of Surprise in East European Revolution of 1989', *World Politics*, vol.44, no.1.

Levada Center (2012) All indexes, www.levada.ru/indeksy, date accessed 29 August 2013.

B. Magaloni (2006) *Voting for Autocracy: Hegemonic Party Survival and Its Demise in Mexico* (Cambridge: Cambridge University Press).

D. McAdam, S. Tarrow, and Ch. Tilly (2001) *Dynamics of Contention* (Cambridge: Cambridge University Press).

Y.L. Morse (2012) 'The Era of Electoral Authoritarianism', *World Politics*, vol.64, no.1.

D. North (1990) *Institutions, Institutional Changes, and Economic Performance* (Cambridge: Cambridge University Press).

'Obshchestvo' (2012) *Obshchestvo i vlast' v usloviyakh politicheskogo krizisa: Doklad ekspertov Tsentra strategicheskikh razrabotok*, An Expert Report of the Center for Strategic Research, http://www.echo.msk.ru/doc/891815-echo.html, date accessed 31 August 2013.

V. Polterovich (2008) 'Institutional Trap', in *New Palgrave Dictionary of Economics Online* (New York: Palgrave Macmillan), http://dictionaryofeconomics.com/article?id=pde2008_I000262, date accessed 31 August 2013.

A.Przeworski (1991) *Democracy and the Market: Political and Economic Reforms in Eastern Europe and Latin America* (Cambridge: Cambridge University Press).

V. Surkov (2006) *Suverenitet – eto politicheskii sinonim konkurentosposobnosti*, 7 February, http://www.intelros.org/lib/doklady/surkov1.htm, date accessed 31 August 2013.

D. Treisman (2011) 'Russia's Political Economy: the Next Decade', in Maria Lipman, Nikolay Petrov (eds) *Russia in 2020: Scenarios for the Future* (Washington, DC: Carnegie Endowment for International Peace).

8
Frameworks of Political System Development

Boris Makarenko

Making predictions about Russian politics based on comparative political analysis is akin to 'measuring Russia's build unique with a common yardstick', which Fyodor Tyutchev once warned against. Russia's 'build unique' is usually associated with defining it as a 'country stuck in transition' or 'a nation at crossroads'. To use an *ex contrario* argument, the unique aspects of Russian political development can be formulated by analyzing political decisions that differ from the decisions of other states that find themselves at a comparable stage of political development.

Such analytical frameworks appear after the 'third wave' of democratization and the incorporation of post-communist political experience into the body of comparative politics' knowledge of political systems and their evolutions. Post-communist transition significantly differs from the classical models. The main distinction is completely non-market economy at the start of these countries' 'triple transition' (from totalitarianism, from command economy, from provincial status in the Communist empire). By the end of 1980s, these societies had to varying degrees solved the classical modernization problems of transitioning from agrarian to industrial societies and increasing urbanization and education levels. At the same time, they completely lacked the institutes of both economic and political competition. The most important corollary of this condition was a substantially greater role played by agency factors of political development in comparison with structural ones. If the latter set of factors is relatively favorable (as it was in most post-communist countries), then the development scenario is contingent upon the behavior of political elites and society.[1]

The 'European vector' consistently implemented by political elites with society's support helped the countries of Central and Southeast

Europe to overcome structural weaknesses: a lower level of development (in Southeast Europe, Moldova, and Mongolia) or the aftermath of ethnic conflict (in the former Yugoslav republics). According to all generally accepted rankings and other criteria, most of these countries are now considered at a minimum electoral democracies,[2] which, of course, does not diminish fair skepticism about the quality of these democracies and certain cases of their backslide.

Where actors were deliberately 'crafting democracy',[3] the choice of political and electoral systems' model was also deliberate. All 16 states to the west of the Soviet 1939 borders have established a parliamentary (seven cases) or premier–presidential regime (nine cases).[4] Perfectly consistent with comparative policy postulates,[5] such institutes checked authoritarian tendencies and facilitated the formation of party systems and the political class, thus eventually consolidating democracy. In the Commonwealth of Independent States (CIS) countries whose regimes are closer to electoral democracy than authoritarianism (Moldova, Ukraine, Kyrgyzstan), the political system has changed numerous times, but it never took the shape of a super-presidential regime. The direction of the cause-and-effect relationship in this analysis is the following: both the choice of a political system and the acceptance of the 'rules of the game' that it imposes can be either a consequence of the political will to democratize or the political elites' reluctant acceptance of a model that would allow for power sharing. East of the 1939 borders, the elites choose the regime that strengthens presidential powers to the greatest extent possible.

The casus Russia: Bureaucratic authoritarianism 'upside down'

How does Russia look on this spectrum? A presidential–parliamentary republic appeared to be the optimal system under such a regime: a stronger opposition parliament would have blocked the reforms, while an even stronger presidency would have fixed Russia on a course similar to that of Belarus. The pluralism in Russian politics in 1990s did not amount to democracy, but it helped to overcome the antagonism between 'new' and 'old regime' elites and lay the foundations of a market economy.

However, the high economic growth rates of the next decade, as well as the restored state capacity, were accompanied by clear stagnation or even degradation of the quality of political institutions. This trend had been monotonously developing until the end of 2012, and its change vector for the last few months and the nearest future is not completely clear.

For a comparative politics framework for this analysis, we may apply certain elements of Latin American experience, although with an important substantive caveat. Political development in these countries was a function of 'classical' transition from an agrarian to an industrial society. In such transitions, the political process is focused on managing conflicts and disproportions between the urban and rural 'top' and 'bottom'. As in the case of Russia, the power ends up in the hands of a bureaucracy, and, at a certain point, the 'bureaucratic authoritarianism' phenomenon emerges. Guillermo O'Donnell, who coined this term, describes it as a political system that 'attempts exclusion of the already activated urban popular sector... by coercion and/or closing electoral channels... electoral arena no longer exists... only government-sponsored parties can participate'.[6]

As modernization processes develop, the relationship between the cost of suppression (O'Donnell assumes it grows linearly) and the cost of toleration undergoes changes.[7] The latter initially diminishes, which creates a possibility of democratization. However, if conflicts aggravated by developmental processes start to intensify, the ruling class senses a threat, which dramatically increases its 'cost of toleration'. This is exactly what brings forth 'bureaucratic authoritarianism'.[8]

The Russian regime of the last decade is reminiscent of precisely such bureaucratic authoritarianism, with an essential difference: its support base is 'turned upside down'. In Latin America, 'the active urban segment' reflects 'the bottom' – the poor, the workers' unions, and the left-wing political forces; whereas the upper and middle classes and entrepreneurs form the political base of the regime that safeguards their property and political interests from pressure from 'the bottom'. Contrariwise, in the Russian case, authoritarianism serves to stem fears associated with competition for power and property in a country that has undergone an extremely controversial privatization of enormous economic assets. Therefore, in Russia it was the part of the elite and middle class dissatisfied with the effective monopolization of economic and political resources by the 'ruling class' and bureaucracy that underwent exclusion.

The exclusion manifested itself through marginalizing potential political leaders from this part of society and applying administrative pressure to liberal political parties, weak anyway. In addition, there was an effective ban on establishing new political parties and a mass anti-liberal propaganda effort culminating in accusing liberals of serving external forces hostile to Russia. We can also mention the Soviet era legacy of law enforcement and justice system bias against entrepreneurial activity.[9] Among the consequences of this bias are not only administrative pressure and property divestment in different forms but, effectively, mass persecution of businessmen, a social stratum that normally supports a state's modernization efforts.[10]

As for the regime support base, it stems from the 'resource curse', a factor well known in comparative politics. Not only does it vest rulers with resources to maintain a repressive apparatus, but it also provides them with an opportunity to anchor themselves, build narrow distributive coalitions, disregard the need for effective governing, and support the sustainability of outmoded political practices. Consequently, elites in these countries are focused on consolidating power and maximizing their economic and political rent. Not a single oil-rich post-communist country had a successful democratization experience.

Dramatic increases in hydrocarbon export and extraction revenues made the solution of numerous socio-economic problems possible. At the same time, the revenues had a twofold negative impact on political development. On the one hand, they raised the costs of maintaining power and controlling key economic assets for the ruling bureaucracy and the business interests associated with it. On the other hand, they allowed implementation of a robust redistributive policy that benefited the paternalistically inclined 'bottom'. To adopt Natalya Zubarevich's 'Three Russias' classification, supporters of the regime come from the depressed 'third Russia', for whom paternalistic support is critical, and the 'second Russia' – small and midsize industrial cities – since the state had the resources to support inefficient industrial sites. Applied to Russia, the variation of O'Donnell's scheme indicates that, starting around 2003, the regime deemed the 'cost of toleration' to be too high; as a result, pluralism was restricted, while the 'suppression cost' still remained low (Figure 8.1).

The reforms of the political system (abolishing gubernatorial elections, switching to proportional representation system in Duma elections, and so on), as well as strengthening of the 'administrative resource' during the election period, did not only limit active participation and the role of opposition parties and politicians, but – even more importantly – made the 'regime party' itself completely dependent on the 'bureaucratic vertical'. Institutional development slowed down, and the regime was becoming more personalistic.[11] The business community was 'equidistant', that is, made completely dependent on the bureaucracy. The 'bottom' segment that was not inclined to support the

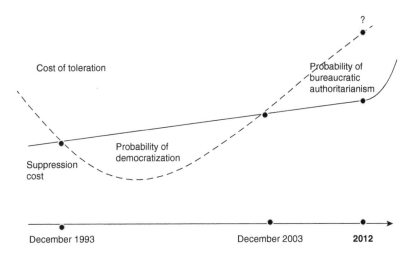

Figure 8.1 The evolution of bureaucratic authoritarianism in Russia (Variation of G. O'Donnell Scheme)

regime could turn to the 'system opposition' – the parties whose presence in parliaments was not considered a threat to the regime, namely, Communist, Liberal Democratic and "Just Russia" parties.[12]

High export revenues implied that inefficient state management and lack of modernization solutions in economic and social policies were compensated by the ever-growing oil export revenues. The 'paternalistic bottom' felt that redistribution handouts were growing; the middle class still had some opportunities for development. There were no powerful motives for anti-regime social mobilization.

Herein lies one more difference of the Russian case from that of the 'classical' bureaucratic authoritarianism: the latter appeared during an economic crisis and served as a mechanism that facilitated implementing unpopular social policies – reducing public expenditures and curbing inflation.[13] On the contrary, in Russia, state revenues continued to grow; thus, clamping down on political pluralism had fundamentally different underpinnings – the regime sought to reduce competition for the distribution of a growing resource base.

The cause of this system's inevitable disintegration has been repeatedly described in comparative political research. It is a decrease in state effectiveness, which the public feels more and more strongly.[14] Under the Russian conditions, society's reaction happened to be delayed. At the height of the socio-economic crisis of 2008–09, trust in the political system was practically unshaken, while the socio-economic expectations radically declined.[15] However, by 2011, the stunted economic growth and stagnant living standards had weakened social optimism and given way to a crisis of confidence. This crisis was dramatically exacerbated by Vladimir Putin's presidential nomination, which came with a victory guarantee, thus signifying the unchangeability of the Russian regime; meanwhile, obvious electoral fraud during the parliamentary elections had led to the eruption of street protests. Even Putin's convincing victory in the presidential election three months later did not help in overcoming the crisis.

In both parliamentary and presidential elections, the regime suffered a serious setback with 'first Russia', Russia of the middle class – the same modernist segment of society that was being excluded. However, the 'second' and 'third' Russias voted differently: in the parliamentary elections their support of the 'regime party' had decreased substantially, although not as much as that of 'first Russia', while, in the presidential election, the numbers of Putin voters had practically not changed since the last decade. The fact of the matter is that, in political systems with a strong executive and weak legislature, motivation for voting in parliamentary elections indicates emotional attitude toward the regime; in our case, it reveals significant loss of confidence. Presidential elections, on the other hand, reflect a rational, almost existential preference for the unchangeable political course, and, as we can see, the paternalistic Russia still has not exhausted its faith in the regime.

Claiming that society has generally 'outgrown' the current regime would be an overstatement, although this is exactly what Putin claimed in one of his election campaign articles.[16] However, one can certainly talk of an emerged community that does not accept the bureaucratic and authoritarian model of power and its neo-corporate imitational institutions and practices.

The new bifurcations and the political system development scenarios

The societal shifts that surfaced at the end of 2011–12 make the preservation of the old political model virtually impossible.

- The protest is not limited to massive street rallies, but also includes the electoral behavior of society's modernized segment and approval of the protests, which still remains quite high (above 40 per cent) nine months later.[17] The question is whether the regime will interpret this signal as an increase of 'cost of toleration' or its decrease, and whether it will consequently resort to liberalization or greater authoritarianism. In the first year of his third presidency, Putin has apparently demonstrated more signs of authoritarianism.

- It is evident that the preservation of the old political model is impossible, and political reforms have already begun. The question is whether they will resemble institutional 'landscaping' or 'gardening', as Andreas Schedler quipped.[18] In other words, does the regime intend to preserve the high degree of control and ability to manipulate the political field or will it strive for quality in developing political competition institutes?

- How will society evaluate regime efficiency (which includes, but is not limited to, socio-economic indicators); in this light, how will the modernized segment's attitude toward the regime evolve (will the crisis of confidence intensify or become less intense); how will the 'paternalistic Russia' feel, given its ambivalence, highlighted by the 2011–12 elections?

The initial scenario: 'neo-Bonapartism' rather than inertia

The first steps taken by the 'post-crisis regime' after the mass protests led us to believe that it had decided to undertake reforms dismantling the key elements of the power vertical built a decade ago. However, when Putin successfully put the presidential elections behind him, the changes were reduced to a minimum.

Evidently, the regime also numbers some supporters of harsh authoritarianism, who seek to 'keep the middle class home' through repressive measures directed at protesters. However, the mainstream ruling elite apparently understands the harm of such behavior, and leans toward a strategy that can be tentatively referred to as 'neo-Bonapartism'.[19] The term describes a regime that preserves the dominant role of the executive without an administrative clampdown of the opposition but, rather, by diffusing the opposition forces, 'dividing and ruling'. In addition, the 'neo-Bonapartist scenario' assumes the following measures:

- Moderate expansion of political competition framework. The increasingly active societal segment is not the only factor that forces the regime to move in this direction. It is equally important that the elections of 2011–12 made the rulers of the country realize that clamping down on opposition and constructing a 'power vertical' in a matter of only a few years had led to the loss of public feedback and a sharp decline in effective state management.

- A more competitive atmosphere would call for a renewal of the 'regime party'. It would require more active personnel selection, attracting individuals capable of public politics, consideration of public moods.
- The improvement of neo-corporate mechanisms. The regime largely interprets pluralism deficit as lack of feedback, and, to correct the situation, creates new neo-corporate structures: 'All-Russia People's Front', 'The Open government', and so on. Not only do they imitate the communication between the regime and society, they essentially expand the mode of non-binding consultations and discussions, but do not provide real power sharing.
- The given scenario also involves 'bureaucratic optimization'. Under the new conditions, resignations of government officials implicated in high-profile scandals and disciplinary action against them should become more frequent; the personnel rotation should some-what accelerate; there will also be technocratic managerial decisions ('e-Government', regulatory impact assessment) and singular concessions to public opinion.

However, the cumulative effect of such measures cannot be high: this is not 'landscaping' but 'gardening', which does not eliminate any of the causes and manifestations of crisis.

The 'neo-Bonapartist' scenario is essentially being implemented already and is apparently viewed as a strategic course by the regime. The regime lacks a holistic political development strategy (nor does it have a socio-economic one); the haste in adopting new legislation and clear ignorance of the consequences of even its nearest steps testify to the lack of strategy. However, it will face serious challenges even in the short term.

The first challenge is the low regime efficiency, which does not allow a way out of the dead-end socio-economic model. Virtually none of the economists doubt that the midterm projections of economic growth will not exceed 4 per cent a year, and the resource revenue dependency will not be eliminated. Archaic social policy model and the growth of irrevocable social obligations have been a heavy budget burden even with the current oil prices, whose possible fall will sharply increase social tensions. The entire governance model remains archaic – from managing state investments and corporations to reacting to public protests, which have only been exacerbated by the new draconian laws on public rallies and non-governmental organizations, and so on.

It is obvious that different societal strata will react to different elements of this ineffectiveness. 'First Russia's' actively forming social protest may be complemented by 'second Russia's' socio-economic protest, and it will seriously challenge the 'neo-Bonapartist scenario'.

These developments will reveal the 'Achilles' heel' of the current regime – the problem of succession, which is characteristic of all personalized regimes. If the ruling elite loses confidence in its leader's reelection, it will be forced to either strengthen the grip of 'bureaucratic authoritarianism' or liberalize the regime, thus effectively dismantling it. As time runs out for the 2018 presidential elections, the regime and all the political and administrative elite will have to change their behavior. The year 2016 will become an important 'interim finish' when Duma elections will demonstrate the scale of changes in the party system. Under these circumstances, the elites are more likely to split, or at least 'fissure'; today we can only speculate about these 'fissures' by observing their indirect symptoms, but they are practically inevitable, especially as a result of the ambiguous power succession scenario of 2018.[20]

Prospective vector: Authoritarianism or liberalization

In the 'O'Donnell scheme' 'cost of suppression' rises in the described conditions both because of the sheer mass of the protest and due to the protestors' high social status. In fact, the lower the effectiveness of governance and the state's capacity to satisfy society's diverse demands, the steeper is the curve (in the case of a large-scale crisis, it will grow exponentially). The political reform has an indirect effect on 'cost of suppression': even in today's half-hearted format, it expands the realm of public politics; it requires 'neo-Bonapartist manipulation' rather than direct injunctions.

However, comparative political analysis suggests that at least a few factors will also increase the 'cost of toleration'.

- Close ties between the regime and property interests will increase fears of the ruling bureaucratic apparatus and its cronies that the loss of its monopoly on power will bring about the loss of economic privileges.[21]
- The configuration of power in both elite and opposition is extremely unfavorable to democratization. In classical liberalization contexts, it was supported by the right-of-center elite and wealthy classes, who were ready to cooperate with the democratizing regime; whereas, in Russia, specifically the liberal business elite and the middle class were

excluded. The 'systemic opposition' is conditioned to conform, and the 'non-systemic' opposition is marginalized and fractured in terms of both its political ideology and its degree of radicalism. The liberal status figures and the 'street protest' communicate intermittently, but they do not comprise a coalition. This makes extremely complicated the creation of a classical democratization algorithm, according to which the regime and the opposition moderates establish the framework for compromises and guarantee compliance, thus isolating the hardliners in both camps.

- Both internal and external fears of the ruling elite further complicate the situation. Internally, it fears losing control of society if the protest sentiment intensifies. Externally, the proverbial security obsession related to the opening of the economy and deep-seated mistrust of the West play their role. These very fears are taken advantage of by *siloviki*, the force structure elite, who oppose liberalization of the political system. Meanwhile, the neutrality of the influential security establishment means as much for Russia's liberalization as did the army's neutrality at the early stages of the Latin American or Korean democratization.

All these factors ostensibly make the growth of authoritarianism more likely than the development of liberalization. However, significant factors also work in the opposite direction:

- Social development level (education, urbanization) and a relatively high 'social profile' of the protesters imply that the 'cost of suppression' rises steeply. Consequences of using force to quell the protests are unpredictable, especially if there is bloodshed.
- Besides, a sharp lurch to authoritarianism guarantees the ruling class pariah status internationally. Unlike the Belarusian rulers, who have achieved this status already, the Russian ruling elite will suffer far greater losses in this case (they will be deprived of their bank accounts and other assets in the West).
- The regime has already passed the peak of its legitimacy, sustained some damage to its image as a result of elections, and made a few steps toward liberalization; there was clear lack of acceptance by a segment of society, that is, the neo-corporate 'unity of the regime and people'[22] is essentially destroyed. Under such conditions, it is much harder to turn to authoritarianism.[23] Besides, opposition is mobilized through the Internet and social networks, a factor unknown to the classical scholarship of transitions.

- Most importantly, growing authoritarianism will not solve a single socio-economic problem. The political system freeze in the second half of the previous decade resulted in an incredibly fast and dramatic decrease of state effectiveness despite a relatively stable socio-economic situation. The middle-class demands for human dignity and quality of life will be increasing even more drastically.

'Neo-Bonapartism' might persist for years. But it will inevitably bring the regime to a crisis – either when power is transferred or due to a sharp increase in street protests. The crisis may be outlined in the following way:

- failure to reform the 'regime party';
- complete offset of liberalization efforts; for instance, not allowing any real competition during gubernatorial elections by applying 'municipal filter'; opposition to developing parties that are close to mainstream;
- refusal to return to direct mayoral elections;
- active application of repressive legislative norms against street protests and non-governmental organizations;
- prohibiting and dispersing rallies; maximizing the administrative resource during elections.

All of this will trigger middle-class response (civil protests), while the socio-economic situation will determine the reaction of 'second Russia'. The likelihood of an 'explosion' will be rising even during the inter-election period, while during the Duma elections in 2016 and the presidential elections in 2018 it will be at its peak (especially if the ruling elite and the president's fears induce him to run for one more term in office). In April 2012, 43 per cent wanted Putin to be replaced by someone else, and Putin's or Medvedev's new term was supported by merely 23 per cent.[24] Cracking down on the protests would lead to a 'spiral effect': the fall of the regime's legitimacy inside the country and its complete breakdown in the eyes of the West will prompt the regime to declare Russia a 'besieged fortress' and consider the opposition outlaws and traitors. However, even according to earlier studies,[25] such scenarios are unacceptable for the vast majority of Russians. The destruction of the 'social peace' inside the country and drastic decline in its relations with the West will be perceived as loss of stability, which has been the key value associated with Putin's rule.

An attempt to suppress the opponents will be a throwback to the 1991 coup events: dictatorship will not be able to provide effective state management in today's Russia. The unpredictability of the 'dictatorship exit' scenario notwithstanding, it will likely lead to a significant elite renewal, and its creators will try to reduce the power concentration risks by seeking a form of premier–presidential model with a stronger parliament. This may open the door to democratization.

The contours of democratization scenario

This scenario constitutes 'thoughtful wishing' rather than reality: the regime's behavior in 2012 clearly reveals 'neo-Bonapartist' choices, stripping timid attempts at political system liberalization of their reform rationale. The points outlined below are more like signposts on the road based on the wisdom of comparative politics, provided the regime and society will choose to avail themselves of it.

The critical parameter of abandoning bureaucratic authoritarianism is changing the nature of the regime and its socio-economic agenda, which would make it more acceptable to the 'modernized class' and business elite and also more flexible, thus allowing power sharing and, ultimately, the transfer of power. Let us reiterate: such definition of purpose may come only out of a sense that the next handover of power carries significant risk and/or that it will not be able to prevent substantial deterioration of social crisis.

The launch of this scenario requires drawing up a Magna Carta of sorts: the elites remain loyal to the supreme power in exchange for creating universalist institutes of political and economic competition (which would guarantee their own security) and apparently in exchange for Putin's exit in 2018. Thus, we once again state that now, even more than in the last two decades, the choice of scenario is contingent upon agency factors.

As was mentioned above, Russia lacks experience and mechanisms for conflict resolution and interest coordination, while the opposition is weak and fractured. However, on the other hand, some disengagement, if not schism, within the elites and the political class is emerging. The lines of this disengagement are drawn between the 'modernist elite', the majority of whom are radically distanced from power now, and the 'resource-curse addicts' and 'rental distribution' elites; part of the regional elite, whose status will rise as a result of the first shifts in the political system, may soon join forces with the 'modernists'.

At the same time, society's cleavages became visible, as reflected in the 'Three Russias' model or the model of modern, pre-modern and anti-modern segments of society.[26]

The process will be stimulated by the effects of political reforms that are already underway: the effects are inevitable, although the pace and scale of the developments listed below depend on the force of resistance on the part of 'guarding tendencies'. The expansion of the political competition framework makes room for new political figures and a more adequate interest representation. There will be new parties and public politicians (mayoral, gubernatorial, and parliamentary candidates).

Further steps to correct the political system should follow these changes. They would include the return to the mixed electoral system at the federal parliamentary level and the permission of electoral blocks to stimulate consolidation of the newly founded parties.

The question of legislative power expansion remains open. According to various measurements made in the middle of the last decade, the Russian parliament appears to be on the same institutionally weak level as the imitation assemblies of the Central Asian or Belarusian authoritarian regimes.[27] After 2003, the real impact of the Federal Assembly has declined even further as a result of the absolute domination of the pro-presidential party, which, in turn, is completely accountable to the bureaucratic vertical. Under such conditions, perfunctory power expansion would prove ineffective; rather, some corrective process is in order – the parliamentary powers that are currently at the parliament's disposal should be put to work. The correction should include turning the presentation of annual government reports into a genuine deliberation, substantive parliamentary investigations, and restoring the parliament's right to nominate candidates for the auditors of the Accounts Chamber. Another change that would contribute to the parliament's self-sufficiency would be the return of single-member district deputies, who have closer ties with voters and their regions and are less dependent on party bureaucracies. Only the parliament that considers itself an institute will be ready for greater pluralism, which is imminent after the next Duma elections and replacement of the Federation Council carpetbaggers with senators who are truly connected with their regions. Otherwise, Russia's exit from the bureaucratic authoritarianism mode will be even more complicated.

A more fragmented parliament does not imply a less efficient governance: a presidential republic with an institutionally weak parliament offers the executive branch a broad spectrum of opportunities for advancing its agenda. However, its implementation would require restoring the skills of coalition building and bargaining that existed between 1994 and 2003. Further strengthening of the parliament – generally desirable for democratic consolidation – is only possible after a more mature and authoritative party system takes shape. Even in their limited role, parties are capable of drawing lines on the field of political competition, setting the rules, and forcing the executive branch to consider the presence of alternative interests in the political space.

The party system greatly depends on the 'United Russia's' ability to adequately respond to the increased electoral and parliamentary competition; public politics, parliamentary work, and opposition negotiation skills also have to be developed. Comparative political research suggests that the pro-regime party actually becomes the 'weak link' for a liberalizing regime that is developing political competition.[28] In the 'United Russia's' case, the additional essential factor is the regime's deliberate opposition to the UR's becoming an independent political force.

Creating alternatives in the party political space is a lengthy process. The newly formed parties will, for the most part, be stillborn. The competition will be joined by a host of anti-regime parties that will go after the 'United Russia's' peripheral electorate and the regime-supported spoiler projects devised to erode the support base of the opposition parties. Another inevitability is the emergence of franchise formations like pensioners' or women's parties, created for the benefit of regional businesspeople bent on having a personal political career. Given the important role of the Internet and the mistrust of traditional party structures, the appearance of some Russian variety of the 'pirate party' cannot be ruled out.

Despite common predictions, strong left-wing or nationalist parties are unlikely to appear in the near future. New nationalists will not be able to compete with Vladimir Zhirinovsky's successful nationalist/populist project – at least while he is politically active – because of their ideological factionalism and feuds between leaders, as well as their inability to reconcile nationalism and left or right-wing populism. Persistent notions of 'turn to the left' notwithstanding, there is a rather narrow niche for a new left-wing party in Russia. The Russian left is not different from European social democracies in its demand for the greater redistributive state, but in Russia this demand is more socially conservative than leftist. Therefore, different shades of leftist views are already expressed by the United Russia, the Just Russia, or the communist parties – though different, all these parties are united by their archaic social conservatism. The only empty niche on the left is the intellectual youth movement of Marcuse rather than Marxist type, but it is unlikely to rise to the level of a serious electoral participant.

The question of creating the 'party of middle class' is more complex. The name is tentative; the program is hard to predict; the potential leadership figures are yet unclear. Nevertheless, the median estimate of the electoral demand for such a party ranges from 8 to 15 per cent of the voters. It will strive for evolutionary, not revolutionary, development and advocate the 'accumulated status' of the middle class – both material and socially symbolic – by protecting its own interests from the populist pressure of lower social segments.

The development of a multi-party system is what will determine the evolutionary vector of the Russian political system. Its first stage is creating pluralistic political representation and reducing the 'United Russia' vote share. The second stage becomes critical: the rise of one or two mainstream political parties whose electoral strength will compare to the 'regime party' (roughly speaking, 15 per cent to 20 per cent of the electorate). The 'Just Russia' and an even more hypothetical 'Prokhorov-Ryzhkov-Kudrin space' on the right may become the nuclei of such parties. 'Yabloko' may join any of these coalitions. The described parties can either be coalition partners to the 'regime party' and work against more radical left or right-wing opposition forces or act as a counterbalance to the 'regime party', serving as the centers of moderate opposition blocks. At the same time, the Communist and the Liberal Democratic Parties, apparently shrunk to their core electorate, will remain at the party system periphery.

If at least one influential mainstream party appears by the end of the electoral cycle that started in 2012, it will lay a foundation for genuine pluralism with the possibility of a multi-level regime change and a firm two or three-party center interested in maintaining a stable system. Even if the president manages to remain above the fray, he will lose his power-proprietary monopoly – consequently the 'cost of toleration' will sharply decrease, which is tantamount to the departure from the 'bureaucratic authoritarianism' and turn to democracy.

In conclusion, we will reiterate that the optimistic liberalization and subsequent democratization scenario is presently seen as far more hypothetical than the neo-Bonapartist or authoritarian ones. However, other scenarios will also be unstable, even in the relatively short run. The life expectancy of the 'neo-Bonapartist' scenario is in direct proportion to favorable socio-economic development parameters, and, as shown above, the current state of affairs does not portend its long life. For the same reason, the authoritarian tendency is unlikely to prevail in

Table 8.1 Interrelation of political development scenarios and socio-economic tendencies

Political Development Scenarios	Socio-economic development trends		
	Positive	Stable	Negative
Liberalization	More problematic launch, simpler implementation: 'cost of toleration' decreases	Role of agency factor increases: liberalization becomes dependent on 'political will'	Risk of failure: 'cost of toleration' increases
'Neo-Bonapartism'	Extends over longer term	Slow 'regime sinking'	Risk of failure: fast 'regime sinking'
Stronger authoritarianism	Probability increases	Social and political tensions accumulate	Social explosion

the long term – although it is clearly discernible in the presently implemented 'neo-Bonapartist' scenario.

The hypotheses on the interrelation of political development scenarios and socio-economic tendencies are summarized in Table 8.1.

These assumptions imply that Russia may remain undemocratic only given the increased effectiveness of the current regime, which seems to be impossible a priori. Last decade's oil abundance allowed the regime to create a 'power-proprietary vertical' monopoly that objectively contradicted both the development of the market economy and the maturation of the socio-political order; however, this strategy is now exhausted. The regime is unlikely to cope with a negative socio-economic scenario by either liberal or authoritarian methods. The bifurcation in political development is about 'direct democratization' or 'democratization after authoritarianism's collapse'.

Notes

1. The correlational analysis of 29 cases in the post-communist world reveals greater significance of procedural factors, especially for explaining transition success under less favorable structural factors. A. Melville, D. Stukal (2011) 'Democratic Conditions and Democracy Limits. Regime Change Factors in Post-Communist Countries. Comparative and Multivariate Statistical Analysis', *Polis*, no.3, 178–80.
2. Albania, Bosnia Herzegovina, and Kosovo are the exceptions.

3. Giuseppe Di Palma's famous though controversial term. G. Di Palma (1991) *To Craft Democracies. An Essay on Democratic Transitions* (Los Angeles: University of California Press).
4. Author's calculations are cited in full in B. Makarenko, A. Melville (2012) *How and Why Do the Democratic Transitions get Stuck?* (M.: MGIMO (U)).
5. For instance, in M.S. Fish (2006) 'Stronger Legislatures, Stronger Democracies', *Journal of Democracy*, vol.17, no.1, January; M.S. Fish (2005) *Democracy Derailed in Russia: The Failure of Open Politics* (Cambridge, UK: Cambridge University Press).
6. G.A. O'Donnell (1973) *Modernization and Bureaucratic-Authoritarianism* (University of California Press), 51–52. Initially, the model had been developed for Brazil and Argentina, but was subsequently used to analyze the situation in other Latin American countries, and also in South Korea and the Philippines.
7. This model traces its origins from Robert Dahl's concept of polyarchy. R.A. Dahl (1971) *Polyarchy: Participation and Opposition*. (New Haven, CT: Yale University Press).
8. G.A. O'Donnell (1973) *Modernization...*, 87.
9. It is effectively acknowledged even by the regime leadership. V. Putin (2012) 'On Our Economic Goals', *Vedomosti*, 3 January.
10. According to the data provided by Boris Titov's 'Right Turn' movement, in the last ten years, more than 39 per cent of business enterprises were subjected to criminal persecution (three million out of 7.5 million businesspeople). S. Bocharova, *Business Russia Asks for Amnesty for the Economic Crimes*, http://www.gazeta.ru/politics/2012/06/14_kz_4626557.shtml.
11. On the subject of 'United Russia's' similarities to and differences from the classical dominant parties, refer to V. Gelman (2006) 'Dominant Party Prospects in Russia', *Pro et Contra*, vol.10, no.4, July–August, 62–71; B. Makarenko (2011) 'Post-Soviet Regime Party: The United Russia in Comparative Context', *Polis*, no. 1, 42–65.
12. Actually, even the appearance of a few mainstream figures in the 'Just Russia' greatly unnerved the power bureaucracy. For instance, see Aleksei Chesnakov's interview 'The Just Russia That We Have Lost', *Izvestiia*, 1 September 2011.
13. G. O'Donnell (1988) *Argentina 1966–1973, In Comparative Perspective* (University of California Press).
14. For instance, in L. Pye (1990) 'Political Science and the Crisis of Authoritarianism', *American Political Science Review*, vol.84, no.1, March; L. Diamond (2003) 'Can the Whole World Become Democratic? Democracy, Development and International Policies' (CSD Working Papers. Center for the Study of Democracy, UC Irvine).
15. WCIOM (2012) Indeksy socialnogo samochustvia, http://wciom.ru/178/, date accessed 21 February 2013.
16. 'Today the quality of our state lags behind civil society's readiness to participate in it'. V. Putin (2012) 'Democracy and State Quality', *Kommersant*, 6 February.
17. Levada Center (2012) *Protest Sentiment Growth*, 1 August, http://www.levada.ru/01-08-2012/rost-protestnykh-nastroenii.

18. A. Schedler (2009) *The New Institutionalism in the Study of Authoritarian Regimes* (Mexico).
19. We interpret 'neo-Bonapartism' as a political regime featuring strong elements of authoritarianism, which are decorated with plebiscite procedures, and virtually complete state control over expression of popular will. This is a precise description of the Napoleon III regime in France. For instance, in Th. Zeldin (1958) *The Political System of Napoleon III* (NY: W.W. Norton).
20. One of such indirect symptoms is the VTB Bank's President Andrei Kostin's frank interview, in which he discusses the inevitability of the Putin team's serious renewal and the desirability of Putin's declaring that he will not seek another term: 'For Fair Elections of Vladimir Putin' (2012), *Kommersant*, 13 February 2012. One more symptom of such breaks is the events surrounding the Internet-released film 'The Lost Day'. The film sharply criticized Commander-in-Chief Dmitri Medvedev for the war in Georgia and sparked an indirect polemical exchange between the president and the prime minister.
21. For more details, see G. Marks (1992) 'Rational Sources of Chaos in Democratic Transition', *American Behavioral Scientist*, vol.35, no.4/5, March/June, 401.
22. As described by Vladimir Gelman, who cites Andrew Wilson. V. Gelman (2012) 'Cracks in the Wall', *Pro et Contra*, vol.16, no.1–2, January–April, 99.
23. G. Marks (1992) 'Rational sources...', 412.
24. Levada Center (2012) *Putin's Third Term. What Will His Policies Be? Will He Deliver On His Promises?*, 3 April, http://www.levada.ru/03-04-2012/tretii-srok-vladimira-putina-kakim-budet-politika-prezidenta-vypolnit-li-obeshchaniya.
25. M. Melville, I. Timofeyev (2008) 'Russia-2020: Alternative Scenarios and Public Preferences', *Polis*, no.6; G. Satarov, Y. Blagoveshchensky (2008) 'What Will Happen to Russia? Political Scenarios of 2008–2009', *Analytical Report* (M.).
26. I. Gudkov (2012) 'Social Capital and Ideological Orientation', *Pro et Contra*, vol.16, no.3, May–June, 6–31.
27. For instance, in M.S. Fish (2007) *Stronger Legislatures...*; O. Zaznayev (2007) 'Index Analysis of Semi-presidential States', *Polis*, no.2, 146–65.
28. S. Mainwaring (1989) *Transitions to Democracy and Democratic Consolidation: Theoretical and Comparative Issues*, no.130, 9 November (Kellogg Institute. Working Paper).

Bibliography

S. Bocharova (2012) *Business Russia Asks for Amnesty for the Economic Crimes*, http://www.gazeta.ru/politics/2012/06/14_kz_4626557.shtml. Accessed on 14 August 2012.

A. Chesnakov (1988) 'The Just Russia That We Have Lost', *Izvestiia*, 1 September 2011.

R.A. Dahl (1971) *Polyarchy: Participation and Opposition* (New Haven, CT: Yale University Press).

L. Diamond (2003) *Can the Whole World Become Democratic? Democracy, Development and International Policies* (CSD Working Papers. Center for the Study of Democracy, UC Irvine).

G. Di Palma (1991) *To Craft Democracies. An Essay on Democratic Transitions* (Los Angeles: University of California Press).

M.S. Fish (2005) *Democracy Derailed in Russia: The Failure of Open Politics* (Cambridge, UK: Cambridge University Press).

M.S. Fish (2006) 'Stronger Legislatures, Stronger Democracies', *Journal of Democracy*, vol.17, no.1, January, 5–20

'For Fair Elections of Vladimir Putin' (2012), *Kommersant*, 13 February 2012.

V. Gelman (2006) 'Dominant party Prospects in Russia', *Pro et Contra*, vol.10, no.4, July–August, 62–71; B. Makarenko (2011) 'Post-Soviet Regime Party: The United Russia in Comparative Context', *Polis*, no.1.(121), 42–65.

V. Gelman (2012) 'Cracks in the Wall', *Pro et Contra*, vol.16, no.1–2, January–April; 94–115.

I. Gudkov (2012) 'Social Capital and Ideological Orientation', *Pro et Contra*, vol.16, no.3, May–June, 6–31.

Levada Center (2012) *Protest Sentiment Growth*, 1 August, http://www.levada.ru/01-08-2012/rost-protestnykh-nastroenii. Accessed on 14 August 2012.

Levada Center (2012) *Putin's Third Term. What Will His Policies Be? Will He Deliver On His Promises?*, 3 April, http://www.levada.ru/03-04-2012/tretii-srok-vladimira-putina-kakim-budet-politika-prezidenta-vypolnit-li-obeshchaniya. Accessed on 14 August 2012.

S. Mainwairing (1989) *Transitions to Democracy and Democratic Consolidation: Theoretical and Comparative Issues*, November, no.130 (Kellogg Institute. Working Paper).

B. Makarenko, A. Melville (2013) *How and Why Do the Democratic Transitions Get Stuck?*, in *Democracy in a Russian Mirror*, A. Migranyan and A. Przeworski (eds.) (M: MGIMO (U)), 429–476.

Marks, G. (1992) 'Rational sources of chaos in democratic transitions', in *Reexamining Democracy*, G. Marks & L. Diamond (eds.) (Sage, London), pp. 47–69.

A. Melville, D. Stukal (2011) 'Democratic Conditions and Democracy Limits. Regime Change Factors in Post-Communist Countries. Comparative and Multivariate Statistical Analysis', *Polis*, no.3 (123), 164–184.

M. Melville, I. Timofeyev (2008) 'Russia-2020: Alternative Scenarios and Public Preferences', *Polis*, no.4 (106), 66–86; G. Satarov, Y. Blagoveshchensky (2008) 'What Will Happen to Russia? Political Scenarios of 2008–2009', *Analytical Report* (M).

G.A. O'Donnell (1973) *Modernization and Bureaucratic-Authoritarianism: Studies in South American Politics* (Berkeley: University of California Press, 1973), pp. 1–165.

G. O'Donnell (1988) 'Bureacratic-Authoritarianism: Argentina, 1966–1973' in Comparative Perspective (Berkeley: University of California Press, 1973), pp. 1–165.

V. Putin (2012) 'Democracy and State Quality', *Kommersant*, 6 February.

V. Putin (2012) 'On Our Economic Goals', *Vedomosti*, 3 January.

L. Pye (1990) 'Political Science and the Crisis of Authoritarianism', *American Political Science Review*, vol.84, no.1, March.

A. Schedler (2009) *The New Institutionalism in the Study of Authoritarian Regimes* (Mexico).

WCIOM (2012) Indeksy socialnogo samochustvia, http://wciom.ru/178/, date accessed 21 February 2013.

O. Zaznayev (2007) 'Index Analysis of Semi-presidential States', *Polis*, no.2(98), 146–164.

Th. Zeldin (1958) *The Political System of Napoleon III* (NY: W.W. Norton).

9
From a Federation of Corporations to a Federation of Regions

Nikolay Petrov

The basic premise of this chapter is that in its essence the current state organization is primitive and therefore is often extremely complicated in form. The deepening rift between the system's potential and the challenges of rapidly changing socio-economic conditions make the transformation of the state apparatus a matter of the nearest future; while, barring a radical overhaul, its preservation until 2025 is virtually impossible.

Two major trends and resulting changes in administrative organization will determine Russia's political development processes in the coming years: reformatting relations between the authorities and society and reconfiguring arrangements between the federal center and regions. The former may be the case of democratization, and the latter is a matter of federalization. These are not predetermined developmental vectors, although they appear more likely than moving in the opposite direction.

Relations between the authorities and society described in other chapters are more widely known and visible; there is also an expanding discussion on the country's socio-economic and political development strategy. The center–regions format has more to do with various inter-elite pacts and modifications, as well as changes in internal system mechanisms, so it is reflected upon far less frequently. Meanwhile, this aspect is of extreme importance to Russia given its enormous territory and diversity.

Russia as a corporation of corporations

Russia is often described as a state-corporation.[1] This is not entirely correct: Russia is a corporation of corporations; it is both a corporation and a holding consisting of a multitude of different corporations whose interrelations essentially resemble those of confederation: each corporation has its own territory, administrative and frequently force resources, hierarchy, honorable distinctions, and leaders. Corporation membership is based on class or profession; the '*Chekist*' corporation is one of such examples.[2]

There are myriad such corporations if a corporation is defined as an association on any basis, including economic. They may intersect, and their corporate loyalties may overlap. For instance, Vladimir Putin's career can be viewed through the prism of different corporate network structures: those of Leningrad State University Department of Law, Putin's judo sparring partners, his Leningrad KGB colleagues, his Dresden foreign intelligence colleagues, St Petersburg mayor's office employees, 'Ozero' cooperative co-founders,[3] as well as an All-Russian *Chekist* network. The elements of all these networks can be easily found in Putin's inner circle.[4] Naturally, the exaggerated role of these networks is particular to the situation in Russia, where institutions are extremely weak.

Corporation is a complex organism which to varying degrees combines both individual and population system traits. Each of the Russian corporations possesses its own resource, quite often through a simplified access to resources thanks to ties with other corporate members. The corporations also have their own elements of internal organization that include large private and state enterprises and agencies.

Corporations can be territorial (a region may act as a corporation) or 'territorialized', that is, featuring a significant territorial component (Gazprom, for instance); they can also be aterritorial, such as an ever-present *Chekist* corporation. As a rule, administrative corporations are aterritorial, while business corporations, regardless of their assets, are territorial or territorialized.

Wherever their business interests lie, business corporations enter into contractual relations with regional authorities through the so-called social partnership agreements. These are annually signed agreements that usually stipulate a fixed amount of monetary transfers into the region's consolidated budget; the agreements also outline the corporation's regional production development plans and its charity projects, which primarily include education, health care, and sports. In exchange for tax breaks provided by regional authorities, corporations agree to invest part of their tax savings in social, image, and other projects of regional and local authorities.[5]

Networks serve as a personal corporate dimension, while Russia as a state of corporations can be described as a network state.[6] A large number of multi-level corporations produce complex hierarchies and network intersections. The intersection of *Chekist* network, Sechin group, 'Rosneft', 'Rosneftegas', and 'oil industry' is an example in which various overlapping corporations form networks of different territorial reach, density, and interconnectedness. People who play a key role in a few of these networks act as their hubs; in the example above, this role is played by Igor Sechin, executive chairman of state oil company Rosneft'. These multi-network players co-opt multiple loyalties and identities.

The relative political power of large corporations can be gauged by their representation in the upper power echelons. Evgeni Minchenko describes the uppermost segment of Russia's modern political elite as 'Putin's Politburo',[7] alluding to the Politburo of the Communist Party's Central Committee where all the power and decision-making was concentrated during the Soviet era.[8]

Putin's 2012 Politburo

'Putin's 2012 Politburo', according to Minchenko, includes business corporation heads close to the president, as well as the prime minister, the president's political deputy, and the Moscow mayor; the mayor has joined this exclusive group due to his personal influence rather than simply by virtue of being Russia's capital chief executive. Out of 44 candidates to become the 'Putin's Politburo' members, the most numerous cluster is represented by the CEOs of private and state business corporations (13 candidates). The key managers of the president's team came in second (ten candidates), followed by the chiefs of power agencies and law-enforcement bodies (eight candidates) and politicians (nine candidates that include the patriarch of the Russian Orthodox Church and two major administrative executives). There are only four regional leaders in the candidate cohort, and two of them, the current heads of Saint Petersburg and the Moscow Region, had previously served on Putin's managerial team, having been appointed governors relatively recently.

Treating the country as a corporation is evidenced by the appointments of regional leaders who are shuffled from one region to another as if they were department heads. The same can be said of appointing the top managers of industrial enterprises to regional political posts.

The current Russian administrative elite can be envisioned as a matrix with vertical and horizontal lines. In the early 2000s, horizontal lines represented regions, and the vertical lines were the corporations present in these regions. In the last decade, the matrix has been transposed, and the industry-specific corporations are arrayed horizontally, while the regions where they are present are positioned vertically. The regional political machines had been formed in the 1990s and were fully dismantled in 2010 as the remaining influential regional leaders departed from the political scene. At the same time, corporate political machinery has been strengthened. However, as it turned out, corporate political machinery cannot completely replace the regional apparatus – unlike the regional apparatus, the corporate one does not extend to all of the citizens and is intended for other purposes: it is there to monitor corporate accountability and internal order. Herein lies the reason for the United Russia's weaker performance in the 2011 Duma elections, which was more palpable in the post-industrial cities where the political machinery of mostly industrial corporations has limited reach.

Stable leadership is important for the effective functioning of the political machine. Therefore, the length of time corporate heads have been in power provides some initial insight into the corporation's stability and its 'leadership' political machine.

The entire judicial system is probably a record in this respect. The chairman of the Supreme Court, Vyacheslav Lebedev, has held his position since 1989; the Constitutional Court's chief justice Valeri Zorkin has continuously served in this capacity since 2003 and held the same post from 1991 to 1993. Incidentally, the regional heads of judiciary also boast the longest tenures among federal officials.

The regularly published *Nezavisimaya Gazeta* rating of 100 most influential Russian politicians cited in Table 9.1 allows the dynamics of the Russian political elite's macro-corporate structure to be evaluated. For instance, it can be seen that the ratio of official, business, and regional corporations for this group of 100 most influential politicians amounts to 50:20–25:5–10 and is quite stable over time. The length of the executives' tenures is far more dynamic. In 2002, the regional and business corporation executives had held their posts for approximately equal periods of time, while by 2012 the length of tenure for the most influential regional executives has almost halved, and the tenure of business corporations' executives has increased more than twice, making for an almost threefold gap between them.

Corporations in the parliament's upper house

The Federation Council (FC) – the upper house of the Russian parliament – provides an illustration of the numerical balance of the industrial and government agencies' corporations, on the one hand, and the regional ones, on the other hand. From 1993 to 1995, the FC was an

Table 9.1 Shifts in the macro-corporate structure of the Russian political elite, 2002–12 (according to the *Nezavisimaya Gazeta* rating of 100 leading politicians)

Elite groups	2002			2012		
	Number	Average length of tenure, in years	Average rating	Number	Average length of tenure, in years	Average rating
Heads of administrative corporations	25	2.4	4.1 (8.5–2.8)	19	6.7	4.7 (9.3–3.4)
Members of administrative corporations' leadership	29	2.2	3.8 (5.6–2.7)	35	2.2	4.1 (6.7–3.0)
Heads of business corporations	21	4.7	4.0 (5.8–2.8)	26	10.9	4.3 (7.0–3.0)
Heads of regions	6	5.2	3.4 (5.0–2.8)	8	3.1	4.1 (6.3–3.0)
Heads of parties/Federal Assembly	13	4.1	3.4 (4.5–2.8)	10	6.3	4.0 (5.3–3.0)
Others	6	8.7	3.8 (5.3–2.9)	2	1.5	4.8 (5.5–4.1)

Source: http://www.ng.ru/ideas/2002-05-31/1_top_polit.html; http://www.ng.ru/ideas/2012-04-27/8_top100.html. Accessed 5 April 2013.

elective body, its members elected directly in their regions. Beginning in 1995, the chamber was an ex-officio body formed of regional administration chiefs and the speakers of regional parliaments. Since Putin's federal reform, the regional executive and legislative authorities have delegated their representatives to the FC.

Two snapshots of the FC are most telling – one from early 2002, when it was completely renewed, and the other from early 2012, when another reform of the upper house was announced.

The Federation Council in 2002 and 2012

The Federation Council – 2002

This was the first time when the FC was filled with lobbyists and not public politicians, as had been the case previously. They came directly from the government or business. Sixty-seven out of 166 Federation Council members were civil servants (33 of them were federal officials, 10 represented federal agencies in the regions, 22 worked for the regional governments, and 2 for municipalities); 45 members represented the business community. Twenty out of 33 federal officials – most of them former heads of ministries and their deputies (13), FC and Duma administration employees (8), and presidential administration employees (3) – had no connection to the regions that they were slated to represent.

Only half of the seats in the new council were occupied by the regional political and business elites – 87 out of 166. One fourth of the senators (37) had a remote connection to the region they represented; another fourth (42) had no previous connection with the region whatsoever. Among these representatives from outside the region, government officials outnumbered businessmen 23 to 14. The government officials came mostly from the FC administration and the federal government (they were former ministers and their deputies); there were also five high-ranking generals in this cohort.

Regional interests were quite substantially represented in the 2002 Federation Council. There were 16 former speakers of regional legislatures as well as 6 former regional heads.

Business corporations were represented by Gazprom (four members), Lukoil (two members), Yukos, Sibneft, TNK, and Slavneft (one representative each). Norilsk Nickel and Sibal/Gorki Avtozavod/Oleg Deripaska had two members each. All of these companies have clear territorial interests in the regions where their enterprises are located. Regionally diversified Russian Railways, RAO UES of Russia, Alfa-Eko, and Russian Credit had one representative each.

If corporations are to be defined broadly, besides the oil industry (seven members), other significant corporate representation in the FC included Army and Navy (14), Komitet gosudarstvennoi bezopasnosti (Committee of state security, Soviet secret service) – Federalnaya sluzhba bezopasnosti (federal security service, Russian secret service) KGB-FSB (ten), other power agencies and law enforcement officials (ten), agribusiness (three), and energy companies (three).

Federation Council – 2012

This is the last 'pre-crisis' makeup of the FC (before the new elections and the mass replacements of regional leaders that occurred in January–October 2012). Only about 13 per cent of the 2002 FC members remained in the 2012 body.

Fifty-eight out of 164 seats in the FC were now occupied by government officials (35 of them were federal employees, 7 represented federal agencies in the regions and 16 were regional government officials). Power agencies' representatives accounted for more than a third of the officials (20 people), and, if only federal officials are taken into account, two out of five come from power agencies. The business share remained practically unchanged in comparison with 2002 – every third FC member represents business (47 members in total). The ratio of federal to regional business is 27 to 20; banking, insurance, and media are the industries with the largest representation. Large property owners have also joined the Upper House: five of them are billionaires, and four are multi-millionaires (it is hard to compare these numbers with 2002 since there was no solid system of assessing net worth at that time, but there were no billionaires in the 2002 FC).

There have been sharp shifts in the upper tier regional elite representation: there are only five former speakers of regional parliaments (and two deputy speakers) and 16 former regional leaders in the FC now. These changes can be explained by the fact that, after the switch to appointing regional leaders in 2005, a senate seat was frequently part of the 'retirement package' of the governor who was invited to resign. The new Federation Council also includes a few mayors of large regional capitals, for instance, Yekaterinburg, Perm, and Irkutsk, which had not been the case in the past.

The number of members directly representing business corporations has declined. This especially applies to corporate giants such as Gazprom, which apparently no longer considers the Upper House an important instrument of political influence. ALROSA has two FC representatives; Lukoil, Norilsk Nickel, Severstal, Ilim, Stroigas, and a number of large regional companies have one.

The professional corporations cluster has seen a sharp increase in the numbers of members representing the Ministries of Internal Affairs (MVD) and Emergency Situations (ten and three members respectively). The number of the armed forces representatives has declined significantly (down to five members), while the number of FSB officials has remained virtually the same (eight members). There are still other power agencies' officials as well as representatives of the legal profession in the FC.

Another new phenomenon is the 'politicization' of the FC, since the United Russia's regional party bureaucracy is represented there now (four members). There is also a large slew of young activists from the United Russia's 'Youth Guard' and other young political hopefuls (seven members).

Russian Railways (RZhD)

Russian Railways, the state company abbreviated RZhD in Russian, is not simply a giant corporation, the largest employer in the world (one million employees), and the world's largest corporation in both size and density of its territorial network. It is a state within a state. It boasts its own armed force (30,000 strong militarized guard), its own infrastructural, technical, and medical systems, as well as enormous financial and political resources. RZhD is the country's bloodline that provides approximately one-third of all cargo shipments (1.2 billion tons) and passenger traffic (1.1 billion people). The former ensures access to practically all of the large businesses, while the latter connects RZhD to almost all of the country's citizens who occasionally use its services.

In the 79 regions of its presence, RZhD enters into agreements with regional authorities. At different times, the company had its 'own' governors: Aleksandr Tishanin[9] in the Irkutsk Region and Aleksandr Misharin[10] in Sverdlovsk; one of the longest-serving governors, Kemerovo's Aman Tuleyev, also has a railway background. The RZhD head Vladimir Yakunin is a friend of Putin and, according to some reports, his KGB colleague as well. He was also another 'Ozero' cooperative member.

Oligarchs, bankers, presidential envoys in federal districts, governors, and Russian Academy of Sciences functionaries serve on the board of directors of the 'Governance and Problem Analysis Center' headed by

Yakunin. The Center positions itself as a 'Russian RAND' (its web address is rusrand.ru). Another Yakunin-run center, the 'St Andrew the first-called Fund', engages in publishing and even has its own movie studio; it organizes conferences, one of which is the 'Dialogue of Civilizations' world forum on the Rhodes. Every year Yakunin brings Jerusalem Holy Fire and Christian relics to Russia (one of the relics is the Cincture of the Blessed Virgin Mary, which in 2011 attracted over three million pilgrims in the 14 cities to which it was brought). He is also the founder of the Center of Russian National Glory.

RZhD's political machine displayed its full strength in forming teams for the 'railway' governors Tishanin and Misharin in Irkutsk and Sverdlovsk Regions, as well as in collecting signatures for another Irkutsk governor, Dmitri Mezentzev, during the 2012 presidential elections. If public politics starts playing a greater role in Russia, RZhD's political clout, especially that of its media holding, may also substantially increase, as happened with 'Ukrzaliznitsya' in the neighboring Ukraine at the time of its 2004 presidential elections.

Region as a territorial corporation

As democratic institutions weaken, power inevitably shifts to corporations – both administrative and territorial; power is simply being fractured instead of being institutionally divided. A strengthening of administrative corporations implies only relative weakening of their territorial counterparts; however, territorial corporations did not disappear, as many administrative decisions can only be made at a territorial level.

The central government actually views regions as territorial corporations, and not simply as a stage for industry-specific corporations.

'Regional political machine' with the governor as the political boss conjures up images of classical urban political machines prevalent in the US in the early 20th century and Southern Italy after World War II. Michael Brie once pointed to the similarity of the patron–client relationship system in Luzhkov's Moscow to the urban political machine.[11]

Clear hierarchical organization, discipline, and clientele's dependence on a strong stable patron lead to desired outcomes in local and federal elections. By delegating virtually full powers to the regional leader, the Center receives order and stability in the region in return. The region also displays its loyalty to the Center by delivering it favorable results in federal elections.

If the regional machine is dismantled or replaced with another (corporate) model, it is likely to result in malfunctions. The ousters of the Moscow mayor and Bashkortostan's president in 2010 may serve as an illustration of this. By removing Yuri Luzhkov and Murtaza Rakhimov, who had been in power for 17 and 20 years respectively, the Kremlin also dismantled the political machines they created. In addition to the United Russia's poor showing in the elections, these changes caused numerous scandals at the polls, which in many respects contributed to the emergence of the first protest wave in Moscow.

The sense of belonging to a corporation and corporate loyalty, which are important for business corporations, matter even more to the regional corporations that have almost no entry tickets or intensive personnel rotation. For regional corporations, regional identity is the main factor that ensures citizens' loyalty (expatriate communities help to maintain the identities outside the region). Material incentives are provided in the form of various compensations and benefits, such as free public transportation for senior citizens or 'Luzhkov's' pension supplements. Non-material incentives are created through regional brands and myths, as well as forcefully propagated regional patriotism.

Because of low spatial mobility, exacerbated by the absence of a unified housing market and high housing prices, people develop long-term, oftentimes lifelong, ties to regional corporations. As a result, social lifts that enable individuals to break out of this cycle of dependency are almost exclusively corporate. The situation resembles that of the 1950s and 1960s when military service was the only opportunity for a young man from the countryside to free himself from the confines of his province.

Until recently, the regional elites had also been extremely limited in their ability to change one territorial corporation for another. Nowadays, another extreme occasionally replaces the former regional autarchy – some high-ranking officials spend only a short time in one place before they migrate to another region. Another approach of the last few years has been delegating a corporate team to a region. Proxies of a business corporation fill the positions of power in the region while primarily securing the interests of the business that sent them there. The president's internal politics apparatus may also provide executive cadres for the regional administration's political bloc.

Such practices create sharp conflicts between the newly arrived political elite with the governor as its head and the local political and business elites; besides, new officials are not familiar with regional specifics and are often simply unable to delve into the life of the region.

Power agencies (*Siloviki*) as the backbone of the administrative system

The power vertical, or, rather, a bundle of power verticals, serves as the foundation of the system and ensures its coordination on all levels.

In the last 30–40 years of the Soviet era, the vertical was maintained through a stiff competition of the KGB and the Ministry of Internal Affairs (MVD), as well as the ubiquitous vertical of the Communist Party apparatus. The demise of the Communist Party and the regionalization of the MVD in post-Soviet Russia made the Moscow-controlled FSB, the KGB successor, the only vertically organized structure at the local level.

Given the extreme lack or total absence of public accountability, weak internal controls and lack of internal competition facilitated the rapid degradation of the entire administrative system. Internal corporate rules and norms previously limited to the power agencies operations started applying to the entire state political machine. These rules consist of strict subordination and absolute authority of the higher tier in the hierarchy over the lower one; the regime's deliberate lack of transparency and accountability; absence of public discourse at policy-making stages; and policy implementation in 'special operation' mode.

Under Putin, the FSB has subsumed all the other force and law-enforcement structures by planting its 'commissars' there. Since the early stage of Russian capitalism, the ties between business and the FSB functionaries have grown increasingly closer and have reached a point of symbiosis. Vadim Volkov, who coined the term 'violent entrepreneurs',[12] describes the change from the 'gangster' stage of the 1990s to the 'state-making' stage under Putin, which is where the country is now. 'Bandits' fell behind at the historical turn of 1999–2003 and 'as the process of forming large vertically-integrated industry-specific holdings was underway, it was done by more qualified people from other walks of life armed with a glut of lawyers and seasoned security services staffed with the former and current FSB operatives'. But the problem is that the power agency resource is not used to advance state interests; instead, it serves the interests of one of the corporations, which pockets the extracted profits.

In 2007–08, during Medvedev–Putin dual rule, when the new president Dmitri Medvedev acquired at least formal control over the power agencies and law-enforcement bodies, the power bloc's architectonics changed significantly.[13]

The main thing has remained unchanged, though: during Putin's reign, power agencies have become the dominant corporation, in terms of both weight and the ability to set its own rules and control other corporations. Putin recentralized the system under FSB control but without restoring the Communist Party vs. KGB rivalry; hence the system's framework appeared to be slanted – with its overly developed vertical and underdeveloped horizontal lines. As a result, *siloviki* act first as an independent interest group, then as an instrument for serving other elites, while working for the common good becomes their last priority.

Siloviki's influence penetrates all of the 'civilian' affairs of the state. Not only do their current or former operatives assume leadership roles in the state, state-like, and formally private structures, but they also introduce their own corporate rules and norms into all institutions that they enter.

The situation has started changing slightly with Putin's return to the presidency in 2012, when the MVD and the Justice Ministry were relieved of the FSB 'commissars'' watchful presence. The FSB's super-institutional positions have weakened, while the MVD has strengthened its position as the largest power agency.

State administration dynamics: Foucault pendulum

Even during the Soviet era, researchers had been pointing to the alternating phases of administrative and territorial governance. Territorial phases included waves of regional enlargement of the mid-1930s and late 1950s–early 1960s, when a number of enterprises that used to be under institutional control were moved under regional control, and the idea of *sovnarkhoz* was revived.

From the late 1980s until the very end of the 1990s, the Soviet Union and, later, Russia had gone through a regionalization phase that effectively ended when Putin came to power. There is a widely accepted idea that the center became stronger and the state centralized under Putin. It is actually not entirely true. While the power balance between the regions and the center has indeed significantly shifted toward the center (it should be noted that the regional authorities have partially made up for their losses by taking some powers away from the municipal administrations), it would be wrong to talk of a consolidated center. The notorious 'vertical construction' under Putin really means that administrative corporations encroach on territorial ones on all levels, including the center. The territorial quasi-federation was replaced by the corporate one.

Thus, besides the pendulum-like cyclical transition phases, we are also witnessing the evolution of the central level of governance. This type of dynamics is analogous to the movements of a Foucault pendulum, which consist of the actual oscillations and the shift in the plane where they happen.

In 2000, the pendulum swung back toward centralization and unitarization, while the center started its active transition from the territorial to the corporate mode of governance. Initially, the changes seemed positive, since they restored the balance between the central and regional levels, which had greatly shifted toward the regions in the 1990s. However, the pendulum did not stop at the imaginary equilibrium point, but kept moving toward excessive centralization and unitarization. The movement continued up until the middle of 2011, when the pendulum's vector changed once again, marking a shift toward regions.

Figure 9.1 details this centralization–unitarization process, which was also described in numerous publications.[14] We will note just a few points that illustrate the dynamics of this process.

- processes occurring at a given moment may have different directions; their final vector is important;
- wide range of the pendulum's oscillations caused by weak institutionalization presents a serious problem: for instance, at the last check it passed the equilibrium point and continued to move toward excessive centralization;
- centralization in the 2000s could have been both a curse and a blessing depending on the region and the sphere. In some instances, unitarization could bring it up to the national average, while in others the system was simplified;
- deregionalization, especially at the outset, brought about some positive changes, such as breaking into the cocoon of the regional elite and curbing the excessive power of local, often authoritarian, leadership;
- both positive and negative experience accumulated over the last decade, as well as an institutional memory of sorts, will have a substantial impact on the pendulum's return.

The situation as of fall 2012 is peculiar since the 'centralization–unitarization' pendulum swung back, while there is still 'corporatization' at all levels. The last decade's dynamics has generally been characterized by the decline of regional corporations and the growth of power agencies (FSB, FSB-2 in the guise of State Drug Control, and others). Business corporations have grown as well, particularly the

194

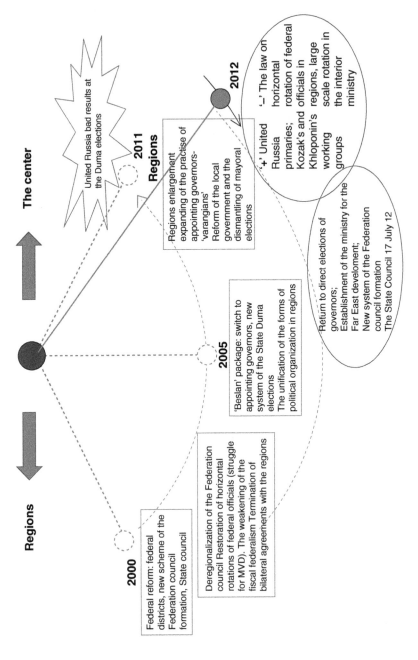

Figure 9.1 Center–regions relationship dynamics, 2000s

raw-material corporations (Gazprom, Rosneft, and others) and the infrastructural ones (RZhD, Transneft, and others). Besides administrative centralization, pulling regional business into the fold of international, national, and transregional corporations greatly contributed to eliminating regional autarky. Tatarstan, where the republican authorities tightly control both political and business spheres, is perhaps the only exception among the large regions.

All these years, the reinforcement of existing administrative verticals and the development of new ones went on. So did the acquisition of one vertical by another and their split-ups. While the number of regions has decreased as a result of some mergers, the number of power agencies and business corporations has grown. The federal districts formed in 2000 can be viewed as a kind of state corporate super-structure over the regional corporations. The same description can be applied to the newer process of forming region development corporations and special state structures responsible for the problematic regions (the Caucasus and Far East); both structures are the elements of the institutional–territorial administration.

Corporatization: Major milestones

2000

- regional FSB heads are appointed to the posts of acting presidential regional representatives;
- federal reform: military and police officers are appointed to the posts of presidential envoys in the federal districts; subsequently, the representatives of these institutions also become governors; the Federation Council is corporatized;
- institutional power verticals are built; the institutions' regional representatives' dual loyalty later transforms into a purely institutional one.
- The 'governors' party 'Fatherland – All Russia' is incorporated into the regime party; the governors' bloc is eroded and total federal control is established.

  2003 – fiscal federalism is consistently weakened; project and institutional–corporate components of budget allocations are expanded.

  2004 – regions and governors are drastically weakened on the federal level after the adoption of 'Beslan' political reform that included the elimination of direct gubernatorial elections and a ban on regional political parties;

2005–2012

- corporate package deals for governors' appointments;
- regular rotation system is consistently phased in for the appointments of federal structures' regional representatives;

2007 – numerous powerful state corporations are created (RosTechnologies, RosNano, and others);

2010 – regional parliament speakers are incorporated in the United Russia party vertical;

2011 – MVD reform is conducted; practically all federal and regional MVD executives are replaced;

2012 – FSB is relieved of controlling and monitoring the rest of force structures; more police personnel are appointed to government positions; MVD assumes the role of regime's main pillar of support.

The question of the pendulum's return trajectory is really important. The Foucault model underscores the fact that the initial and return trajectories will not be identical. For instance, the return to regional autarky in the business sphere is hardly possible, although business conditions will most probably be more differentiated than they are now. In the sphere of politics, the emergence/return of regional parties is to be expected. A much greater diversity in the forms of regional political organization, which might include bicameral legislatures in large regions with complex territorial configurations, is also quite possible. Given the strengthened regional parliaments, the return to personalized power regimes appears unlikely – the spread of leader–parliamentary regimes becomes a more likely scenario.

Business–political elites: The matrix transposed

The current system lacks the 'general assembly' format, in which the heads of major elite groups and clans could discuss their interests and work out compromises. Instead, Putin, playing the role of the supreme arbiter who maintains inter-clan balance, communicates to each of his 'Politburo' members directly. This makes him more powerful but slows down the complex decision-making process, making it less effective.

It appears that such a cumbersome system of inter-elite communication cannot exist for too long, especially in the times of crisis that call for fast decision-making. It is just a matter of time before the elites abandon the system. The problem is that the elites are splintered and perceive unsanctioned consolidation as excessively risky. However, decline in Putin's legitimacy – given that his popularity has so far guaranteed political stability – along with his inability to adjust in response to change in external circumstances may leave the elite with a choice of either unconditional loyalty to the leader, which entails the risk of political collapse, or replacing the leader out of self-preservation.

The elite consolidation may be prompted by both the Kremlin's actions and serious system upheavals brought on by the economic crisis, mass socio-economic and political protests, or the crisis of governance resulting from large-scale terrorist attacks and man-made as well as natural disasters.

The elites cannot replace Putin in his current supreme arbiter role, since a representative of one clan will certainly be unacceptable to the others. Dividing enormous leadership authority among major players can possibly break the stalemate. However, it is also presently impossible, since no one can guarantee the compliance with inter-elite agreements in a personalized deinstitutionalized system. There is a need for political modernization that will result in stronger political institutions. It is the only way to stabilize the position of both individual elite clans and the system as a whole. Thus, a situation emerges in which at least some in the political elites have an interest in stronger institutions. The elites are also concerned with protecting their property and are therefore interested in strengthening their respective rights.

Scenarios for the future

The system has already embarked on its return voyage from the corporate federation to the regional one, and it may take much less time than the initial 20-year trip to its corporate destination. A lot will depend on the state's fiscal solvency and the elite consolidation in the center.

There are many scenarios that may allow different developmental vectors, but, when it comes to relations between the center and the regions, the vector is quite certain, since the highest possible degree of unitarization has already been reached; nevertheless, the return to regionalization may differ in character.

Three scenarios are possible here:

(1) *managed regionalization*, if the regime is savvy enough to follow and adjust to the general trend.
(2) *contained regionalization*, if the regime attempts to reverse the flow of natural development.
(3) *spontaneous regionalization*, if it is not contained at all or the containment is unsuccessful.

In the first case, federal elements will be restored and strengthened. There will be a substantial redistribution of federal, regional, and municipal authorities, favoring the lower tiers in accordance with the subsidiary principle – that is, the higher tier will receive powers to make only those decisions which cannot be effectively implemented at the lower levels. There will also be genuine regional representation in both houses of the fully functional parliament. Genuine fiscal federalism will provide regions and municipalities with independent revenues commensurate with their greater authorities. Additionally, the center will reject unification and will not impose its organizational model and mechanisms on the region. Finally, autonomous local government institutions will be developed.

In the second case, the center that opposes regionalization may lose control over the process partially or completely (the third scenario). This may produce various negative effects, ranging from the loss of time for development to the country's disintegration, provoked by the center that is trying to manage the vast and diverse territory as if it were an army platoon.

Unfortunately, the events that occurred in the second half of 2012 clearly demonstrate the regime's attempts to oppose regionalization, which is strategically wrong and counterproductive. These tactics do not pose particular danger when there is political competition – in this case between the government levels – that takes place according to clear-cut rules monitored by a relatively independent arbiter. However, given the absence of such competition, the attempts to oppose regionalization increase the risks of a breakdown and unilateral rule change.

Finally, the business–political elite should brace for serious changes after Putin's exit. The solar planetary system whose sun is virtually irreplaceable is in for a radical overhaul, if not complete demolition. We can only hope that the demolition of the planetary system of business–political elites will be offset by the elite institutionalization in 'the Politburo'-like fashion.

Greater inter-elite frictions can also be expected while the corporate organization is being transformed into the territorial one. The system's corporate partitions are to be dismantled just as the regional partitions had been in the past, while the upper tier of state organization is to be institutionalized. The regional development corporations can be seen as a makeshift solution.

On its path toward eliminating the network state path-dependence, Russia will have to create and strengthen its institutions and, most importantly, establish the mechanisms under which elite interests will be coordinated and decisions will be made. Such a radical system overhaul will be painful and lead to a number of serious crises, but there appear to be no other alternatives.

Notes

1. Not to be confused with corporate state. The business–corporate state substantially differs from the corporate one.
2. The *Chekists*, from Ch.K. – the Russian abbreviation that stood for the 'Extraordinary Commission', an early Soviet precursor for the KGB-FSB. The Federal Security Service (FSB) operatives are called *chekists*, but the word is also broadly applied to the personnel of any security service.
3. Summer cottage cooperative in St Petersburg suburbs founded by Vladimir Putin in 1996 along with his seven shareholder friends: Yuri Kovalchuk, Vladimir Yakunin, Fursenko brothers, Nikolai Shamalov, and others. All of them later became the pillars of Putin's new elite.
4. Leningrad State University Department of Law (Aleksandr Bastrykin), Higher School of KGB (Sergei Naryshkin), Leningrad KGB-FSB (Sergei Ivanov, Viktor Ivanov, Nikolai Patrushev, Viktor Cherkesov), Judo training (Arkadij Rotenberg), 'Dresden' (Evgeni Shkolov, Sergei Chemezov, Nikolai Tokarev), Sobchak liberals (Dmitri Medvedev), St Petersburg municipality (Aleksei Kudrin, Dmitri Kozak, Igor Sechin), 'Ozero' summer cottage cooperative (Sergei Fursenko, Gennadi Timchenko, Yuri Kovalchuk, Vladimir Yakunin). It should be noted that many individuals on this list also belonged to the KGB-FSB mega-corporation.
5. For more details on social partnership agreements, see N. Petrov, A. Titkov (eds) (2010) *Power, Business, and Society in the Regions: The Irregular Triangle* (in Russian) (Moscow: Carnegie Moscow Center, ROSSPEN), 157–159.
6. V. Kononenko, A. Moshes (eds) (2011) *Russia as a Network State* (L: Palgrave Macmillan).
7. Minchenko Consulting (2011) *Putin's Big Government and Politburo 2.0*, http://www.stratagema.org/netcat_files/2–2.pdf .
8. The Soviet Politburo, as a board of directors of sorts, featured both the heads of the largest regions (Moscow, Leningrad, and some Soviet republics) and the 'corporate' heads (army, KGB, military industry enterprises). The heads of the most important corporate-like ministries, giant state enterprises, and

regions were represented at the level of the Communist Party's Central Committee. There were no 'candidate' positions in the last Politburo of 1990–91, but all of the regional party chiefs were represented. The pantheon of the Soviet leadership had two features that distinguished it from the current 'Politburo': it was far more institutionalized in terms of both the Communist leadership official status and regular meetings that suggested 'collective leadership'; it was the apex of the power pyramid that was being served by the party apparatus.

9. He served as the head of one of the 17 RZhD regional branches – Eastern Siberian Railways' large regional divisions – before being appointed governor in 2005. He was removed after a scandal two and a half years later and in 2008–2012 served the RZhD's vice president.

10. Misharin, the former head of Sverdlovsk Railways and later a federal transportation agency official, also made a rather unsuccessful foray into the regional politics – he was replaced by the Kremlin on the eve of return to direct gubernatorial elections in May 2012, and now serves the RZhD first vice-president.

11. For instance, in M. Brie (1997) *The Political Regime of Moscow – Creation of a new Urban Machine?* (Berlin: Wissenschaftszentrum Berlin fur Sozialforschung).

12. V. Volkov (2002) *Violent Entrepreneurs: The Use of Force in the Making of Russian Capitalism* (Cornell University Press).

13. The essence of changes in the force bloc is largely encapsulated in the maxim 'separation of political and force resource'. Viktor Ivanov and Igor Sechin, who were *siloviki*'s unofficial leaders in Putin's inner circle, now have independent positions: one works for the Federal Drug Control Service (FSKN) and the other for the government. Nikolai Patrushev, the FSB's influential director, got the prestigious job of the Security Council secretary. He was replaced by an inconspicuous technocrat, Alexander Bortnikov. Prior to that, in June 2006, the influential Attorney General Vladimir Ustinov was removed. A year later, the investigative apparatus of the State Prosecutors' office became partially and then fully independent; the prosecutors then lost their rights to supervise the legality of investigative process. The changes were intended to stem the excessive growth of the power bloc as a whole as well as its particular constituent units and their leaders, since, in the absence of effective controls on the part of other state institutions and society, power agencies' structures tend to self-segregate and impose their corporate interests on others.

14. N. Petrov (2000) 'Federalism Russian-style', *Pro et Contra*, vol.5, no.1, 7–33; N. Petrov (2010) 'Regional Governors under the Dual Power of Medvedev and Putin', *The Journal of Communist Studies and Transition Politics*, vol.26, no.2, June, 276–305.

Bibliography

M. Brie (1997) *The Political Regime of Moscow – Creation of a new Urban Machine?* (Berlin: Wissenschaftszentrum Berlin fur Sozialforschung).

V. Kononenko, A. Moshes (eds) (2011) *Russia as a Network State* (London: Palgrave Macmillan).

Minchenko Consulting (2011) *Putin's Big Government and Politburo 2.0*, http://www.stratagema.org/netcat_files/2-2.pdf. Accessed 5 April 2013.

N. Petrov (2000) 'Federalism Russian-style', *Pro et Contra*, vol.5, no.1, 7–33; N. Petrov (2010) 'Regional Governors under the Dual Power of Medvedev and Putin', *The Journal of Communist Studies and Transition Politics*, vol.26, no.2, June, 276–305.

N. Petrov, A. Titkov (eds) (2010) *Power, Business, and Society in the Regions: the Irregular Triangle* (Moscow: Carnegie Moscow Center, ROSSPEN), 157–159.

V. Volkov (2002) *Violent Entrepreneurs: The Use of Force in the Making of Russian Capitalism* (Ithaca, NY: Cornell University Press).

10
Becoming Modern Russian Style
Richard Sakwa

Russia finds itself in a situation of stalemate, where social and political interests and epistemic communities are locked in balance, allowing the 'Bonapartist' political regime extreme freedom of action. The power system (*vlast'*), indeed, draws its authority by balancing between factions and the two pillars of the dual state, the administrative regime and the constitutional state. This is a classic 'stability regime', permanently engaged in the manual manipulation of political processes to ensure pre-eminence. In this context, the 'transition' will end when there is a shift from the stalemate of the stability regime to equilibrium, based on a more or less organic balance of interests and ideas that reflects the dominant consensus in society. The idea of equilibrium is drawn from neo-classical economics and suggests a 'normalization' after a period of turbulence. It is precisely this sort of equilibrium that suggests that a transition is over and society has achieved a degree of normality, until the next period of breakdown and transition to a new equilibrium. 'Normality' in Russia will take distinctive forms, but will ultimately be recognizably modern, in that the institutions and practices of governance will be rooted in the tradition born in Western Europe in the passage from medievalism but now endowed with a certain universal stature.

For over 20 years Russia has been engaged in a classic period of catch-up modernization. In 1991 Russia gave up the attempt to create an alternative modernity, yet a new equilibrium in which the component parts of a modern society work together relatively effectively has still not been achieved. Competing political imperatives, geopolitical orientations, and developmental paths interact to ensure an extremely high degree of epistemic pluralism. Contrasting views of Russia's identity and destiny are locked in tension, creating systemic and developmental stalemate. Equally, there are numerous recipes about how to overcome this stalemate. This lack of an attractive vision of the future and the means to attain it was one of the factors provoking the sharp reaction following the announcement of the 'castling' move on 24 September 2011. Even many of his erstwhile supporters looked at six more years of Putinite stability with dread. Vladimir Putin's personalistic virtuoso performance as leader, however, only reflected the deeper systemic stalemate. Intense activity without movement was, indeed, reminiscent of the period of stagnation and the stability regime of the late Brezhnev years, and reflects the stalemate of the Soviet system in its terminal phase.

A few things that we know

Russia's past is difficult enough to predict, while its future remains shrouded in the mists of incomprehensibility and littered with the rocks of contingency. However, there are a few things that we can predict with a degree of certainty. First, even in the most benign of circumstances, given the country's enormous size and diversity, even if Russia were to become more of a functioning democracy there would remain pockets, and possibly some big ones, not only of authoritarianism but even of barbarism. Equally, if the country's trajectory were to take a malign path, with the consolidation of an authoritarian regime accompanied by widespread and generalized coercion, there would remain islands of relative toleration. Comparisons with the other great continent states, such as America and India, suggest that political development will always be uneven and multiplicity is inherent in such vast agglomerations of peoples and traditions. This is not to suggest that the state and political elites, the focus of this chapter, are shaped by geographical determinism, but to stress a factor that is perhaps not given enough prominence when we endeavor to anticipate patterns of change. Government reach and the intensity of governance will remain uneven. This was clearly in evidence in the post-Stalin years, allowing a rich variety of political practices across the Soviet Union's republics, and even between Russia's regions, by the late Soviet period.

Second, in state-nations (to use Juan Linz's term to describe social formations where the territory takes priority over the nation) the concept of multiculturalism is inadequate, since it suggests toleration by a hegemonic nation of the values of other, more recent, additions to the community. Instead, the notion of *pluriculturalism*, in which the community is comprised of a number of autochthonous peoples, each of whom can be considered native to the country and with equal rights to be counted as the founding people of the state, forces us to think more positively of diversity and multiplicity, rather than of modernist integrative state-building strategies. This certainly would be the view of the Tatars, who have lived on the middle Volga for as long as Russians have inhabited their principalities on the Moscow and upper Volga rivers, or of the Chechens, more recent additions to the Russian state yet with profound roots in their territory. It is right to focus on Moscow elites, but we should not forget the fundamental part played by regional elites, above all those representing Russia's autochthonous nations. In a context where historical and territorial narratives are contested, it is not surprising to find that Russian national identity is fluid and multi-layered.[1] This should act as a salutary warning when we undertake the onerous task of thinking about the future. In other words, at the societal level Russia will not have one future but many. The pluriculturalism of the nation will be reflected in a plurality of futures.

Third, broadening our horizons, it is extremely unlikely that Russia will challenge the reigning neo-liberal orthodoxies, often summed up in the concept of globalization. Identities are forged in struggle with others, and in part Russia's search for self-affirmation in the two decades since the fall of communism has been hampered by the lack of clearly identifiable enemies, quite apart from the lack of self-evident friends. Russia has been pursuing conventional neo-classical macro-economic policies, although their implementation has been mediated by elite concerns. While it would be simplistic merely to state that Russia is a peripheral and resource-dependent economy in the global division of labor, as an 'emerging economy' it is undoubtedly less than central.[2] The grandiose ambition to establish Moscow as a world financial center, while not misplaced in general terms, sounds hollow when faced with Russia's massive governance and regulatory deficiencies.

Fourth, Russian development since 1991 can be characterized as not only dual, in that the constitutional state and the administrative regime are balanced against each other, but also stalemated. The political stalemate is part of the broader developmental crisis, in which the entrepreneurial class inspired by liberal ideas is stymied and perse-cuted by officialdom and corrupt security and judicial agencies, giving rise to the mass phenomenon of 'raiding'. By the time Putin reentered the Kremlin in 2012 Russia was suffering all of the classical symptoms of blocked modernization. Its case may not be as severe as in sev-eral North African and Middle Eastern states up to the 'Arab Spring' in 2011, yet there are enough commonalities (above all in the practices of political exclusion and depoliticized centrism) to make the comparison valid. In broad terms, the stalemate between rent-seeking elites and profit-seeking groups is characteristic of both regions.[3] The protests from December 2011 represented the single greatest challenge to the entrenched powers of the administrative regime since the disintegration of the Soviet Union exactly 20 years earlier, and suggested one way of transcending the stalemate. Political liberalization and the return to genuine constitutionalism may occur in this round of political struggle, or it may be suppressed (at high reputational and possible physical cost); but the unfinished business of 1991 (see below) will one way or another return to the surface until it is given substantive political form.

Two paths from communism

The Soviet Union collapsed as a result of its own contradictions, but the nature of these contradictions is still debated. The contradictions that led to '1989' (taken as the symbolic date for the collapse of the Soviet 'empire' in Eastern Europe) differed from those that precipitated 1991 (the combined dissolution of the communist system and the disintegration of the Soviet state). The 'meaning' of 1989 is very different from that of '1991', and many of the misperceptions and outright mistakes in analyzing Russia and its future derive from the attempt to impose the logic of 1989, whereas the country is in fact pursuing a different transition path to modernity based on the concerns of 1991.

The 'revolutions' in 1989 in Eastern Europe shrugged off Soviet power and the structures of communist rule (even though by then the Soviet Union was reforming itself out of existence), and reoriented the countries to the path of Western integration. The 'return to Europe' represented a powerful ideal, but this was a spatial rather than a philosophical program.[4] The meaning of 1991 is far less clear. The former Soviet republics could not share the spatial (geopolitical) orientation of 1989, except for the Baltic republics and possibly Moldova, and it was precisely the attempt of some other countries to shift from the problematic of 1991 to that of 1989 which in the end provoked conflict, notably the Russo-Georgian war of 2008. Russia always considered itself to be a distinct geopolitical pole of its own, and later perpetuated '1991' as a separate project. This included attempts to maintain some sort of post-Soviet integrative momentum, whose latest manifestation is the plan to establish a Eurasian Economic Union by 2015. The countries in the 'new Eastern Europe' along the Soviet Union's Western borders remain trapped between 1989 and 1991.

The 'project of 1991' included a number of not necessarily compatible elements: national revival, polity development, state building, the capitalist market, international integration, and, far from least, democracy in the generally accepted definition of the term. What 1991 did not embrace was the 'back to Europe' theme, although the idea of joining European international society was certainly present. At various points in the last two decades one or another theme has been emphasized at the expense of the others. The popular mobilization in response to the flawed elections of 2011/12 once again brought the democratization theme to the fore. At no point in the first two decades of Russian post-communism have any of the elements of '1991' been repudiated, however flawed their implementation. We are dealing with a single developmental ('transitional') trajectory, although with several distinctive sub-periods. The whole era is defined by Russia's attempt to find a new geopolitical role, accompanied by stress on the necessity of finding its own form of modernity.

Encompassing the whole period is the idea of modernization and development. Few of the modernization tasks facing Putin when he came to power in 2000 have been resolved. Indeed, it could be argued that the challenges facing the country after Stalin's death in 1953 still remain on the agenda. These include the country's assimilation into the international system and international economy, the integration of the various national communities, the creation of a set of authoritative and universal political institutions of the state, the creation of an equal and free citizenry defended by an impartial and independent judiciary, the thriving of modern representative, participatory, and legislative institutions, the development of a diverse and competitive modern economy, an inclusive and sustainable welfare state, and the attainment of standards of living matching those in advanced societies. Instead, certain patterns have become established in the post-Stalin era, perpetuated across the great divide of 1991. These include the marginalization of the autonomous participation of society in the management of public affairs, a continuing dependence on energy rents, lack of diversity and dynamism in the economy, above all in the small and medium sector, and the repeated failure to integrate into the international community as 'one of us'. In domestic affairs a 'regime' type entity (typically known as *vlast'*) remains external to the operation of the constitutional order, while internationally Russia remains not so much a 'constitutive other' as something alien and indigestible.

Two approaches to comparative democratization

Assessment of Russia's future necessarily requires an examination of its present, and this in turn raises some fundamental methodological issues. How can we define and measure the extent of democratization in a country? I have long argued in favor of an evolutionary approach to democratization. This draws on the insights of the field of comparative democratization, and looks again at the whole problem of 'transitology' in the context of countries grappling with 'the civilization of modernity'.[5]

We should distinguish between two distinct approaches to theories of democratization. The first is the *typological/teleological* form of comparative democratization, which can be located within the framework of critical neo-modernization theory. The typological component refers to the practice whereby a concept is devised that tries to encompass the features of the hybrid political systems that have emerged, for example, in post-Soviet Eurasia. This is accompanied by shades of the *teleological*, the belief that the end point of a transition is knowable in advance. Although very few scholars studying the region actually employed teleological transitology,[6] a degree of teleology is inherent in typological approaches – otherwise it really does become little more than a mechanical exercise in classification. The typological approach is a normative–evaluative exercise in which a whole bestiary of terms has been devised in an attempt to capture the hybrid nature of Russian reality, including 'managed democracy', 'managed pluralism', 'liberal authoritarianism', 'elecoral authoritarianism', 'competitive authoritarianism', 'semi-authoritarianism', 'soft authoritarianism', and many more.[7]

Following the 'orange revolution' in Ukraine in late 2004 the Kremlin advanced the term 'sovereign democracy', to indicate that Russia would find its own path to democracy, and that democracy in the country would have Russian characteristics.[8] The battle of concepts reflects a broader struggle for hegemony. Putin's anti-revolutionism and ideology of decisional gradualism condemned revolutionary change, but shares with radical ideologies a belief in displaced temporality, the view that the present is a preparatory phase for a 'great tomorrow' (a form of allochronic temporality typical of emergency situations). Typological approaches tend to become little more than exercises in taxonomy and mechanical box-ticking, and thus obscure the rich dynamics of a country such as Russia; while the element of embedded teleologism is falsified by the whole course of Russian history. It would take a brave soul to claim that the end point of the country's evolution can be substantively predicted. Nevertheless, this paper argues that Russia's fundamental challenge is to 'become modern' within the parameters of the project of 1991, and that success in this endeavor is not precluded, although it will remain uneven and contradictory.

We label the second approach to comparative democratization *evolutionary*, drawing on the insights of civilizational neo-modernization and open to the diversity of outcomes, accompanied by the methodologies of evolutionary theory in political science (punctuated evolution and the like). Here the emphasis shifts from normative evaluations of the fundamental character of a regime to examining the factors that shape a particular system, how that system operates in a particular environment, and the distinctive forms of engagement with the 'civilization of modernity'. This historical–structural approach helps frame a number of specific questions, in our case on the factors shaping the development of the Russian polity as it engages with modernity. It also gives due consideration to the role of leadership as an independent variable, yet constrained by historical legacies and contextual factors. The evolutionary approach also encourages a shift away from the discourse of transition and consolidation towards a greater emphasis on the 'quality of democracy', and thus reprises debates about substantive notions of democracy.[9] The new concern entails a move away from a focus on institutions and regime types towards the quality of democratic citizenship, emphasizing in particular a bundle of individual rights, including effective access to justice, social, and human rights. Thus, the extension of political rights from this perspective has to be complemented by civil and social rights within the framework of a stable state structure.[10] Democracy cannot function without a state, yet the 'stateness' factor has too often been occluded by technical discussions over crafting institutions or a romantic appreciation of an idealized Tocquevillean characterization of the role of civil society. An evolutionary approach to democratization thus favors *scalar* – more or less democracy accompanied by analysis of the dynamics of change – rather than *sortal* approaches, in which great effort is made to devise a label that can be pinned on a society.

The promise of the new wave of revolutionary activism, characterized as 'color revolutions', was precisely to achieve the 'democratization of democracy', but in the event the exhaustion of the orange revolution in Ukraine and the other color revolutions demonstrates that popular mobilization of this sort was susceptible to manipulation by elites.[11] The 'white revolution' of December 2011–2012 reprised color-style political activism, although with a greater degree of reflexive awareness of

the paradoxical and contradictory nature of this sort of political movement. Perhaps even more debilitating for color revolution as a form
of social and political renewal was its lack of substantive attempts to
achieve endogenous engagement with the civilization of modernity in
an evolutionary way; instead, it sought simply to emulate advanced
modernity in a typological/teleological manner. Here methodology of
analysis shapes ontological categories. In other words, it is not clear that
an effective adaptive strategy was devised that would be appropriate for
a self-imposed '1991' style pattern of social development; rather, it fell
into the category mistake of assuming that a 1989 'necessary' pattern of
political development is appropriate.

Sartori's view of political systems as 'bounded wholes', in other words
as discrete and clearly delineated types of regimes that can be placed
in a single category, is an inadequate way of trying to come to terms
with complex systems.[12] Equally, it is for this reason that the notion
of 'hybrid regimes' is also inadequate, since it too ultimately relies
on a sortal approach to analysis, relying typically on a combination
of terms, the adjectival democracy identified long ago.[13] One of the
most successful hybrid terms, reflecting hybrid regimes, is 'competitive
authoritarianism', yet it too fails to grasp the underlying dynamics.[14]
Instead, the scalar view seeks to identify precisely the dynamics and
complexity of specific historical situations.

The dynamics of politics

Three models of post-communist change were identified in my earlier
paper: imposed, necessary, and self-imposed.[15] East Germany is an
example of the first model; while the second and third correspond to
the models of '1989' and '1991'. The literature tends to confuse these
three very distinct models, leading to false expectations and misleading
analysis. In the Russian case, the attempt to pursue the '1989' model
encourages the development of mimetic practices, in which a social
form is copied but lacks inner dynamism, hence becoming lifeless and
false. The problem is particularly intense in parts of the 'developing
world': 'Under the current "liberal hegemony", democratic elections are
sometimes grafted onto states that are close to legal fictions and the
rudimentary state apparatuses of which are thoroughly illiberal, illegit-
imate, and ineffective.'[16] In the Russian case there was a rather more
robust polity onto which the electoral system was imposed, although
traditional practices continue to subvert the free play of electoral
competition. In keeping with our dual state model, the electoral process

can only be given free rein when the constitutional state is predominant. When the administrative system refuses to subordinate itself to the vagaries of the electoral process, elections become demonstrative affairs. They cannot be entirely repudiated, otherwise the authoritarian inclinations of the administrative system will be exposed, and thus vulnerable to countermovements; but neither can they be fully endorsed, in which case the constitutional order would triumph and the administrative elites would lose their unique position as rulers and economic beneficiaries.

The necessity of electoral legitimation places semi-authoritarian rulers in a bind. How can the electorate be mobilized but not empowered? The longer a regime remains in power, the more reluctant it is to submit itself to democratic outcomes, since it becomes the hub of a dense network of political and economic relations. In Africa rulers are reluctant to relinquish power because 'political office remains the surest path to accumulation – the struggle for control becomes a fight to the death'.[17] However, the Russian case is more complex, and, although the concept of politics as warfare became at various points salient in Putin's thinking not only power maximization and wealth enhancement strategies are at play. Ideational factors are also important, drawing on the view that Russia's leaders not only defend the country from foreign threats, but are also, in broad terms, leading a modernization strategy (although there is no consensus over what this means in practice).

At the heart of a successful transition is the appropriate adaptation strategy. This operates at three levels: the constitutional, the systemic, and the practical (the arena of practices). The mismatch of these various elements (or, perhaps better, their simultaneous operation) has given rise to a distinctive hybrid social form: the society of transition. In the Russian case this has deep historical roots, but after 1985 was once again reproduced in a particularly powerful and durable form. The central characteristic of the society of transition is the prevalence of 'emergency' forms of rule, and of political behavior in general. The political regime seeks to ensure its ability to decide on what is the exception (in Schmittean terms), and this is one of the factors that give rise to the dual state (the administrative regime, operating overwhelmingly in the realm of practices; countered by attempts to regularize the situation through the consolidation of the constitutional state).

Paradoxically, the 'emergency' as a political practice is not limited to the regime, but is also prevalent among the opposition. This was much in evidence during the 2011/12 protest movement. Like the regime against which it protested, the resistance movement suffered from the endemic duality of Russian politics. One wing sought to reduce the element of emergency by restoring the primacy of constitutional politics; but perhaps a larger part effectively perpetuated the arbitrariness against which it protested by calling for extra-constitutional measures (such as pre-term parliamentary elections or a 'Russia without Putin'). Undoubtedly, the events of this period represented a major 'crack in the wall' of electoral authoritarianism,[18] but they also revealed the absence of structured systemic alternatives.

The fundamental cleavage between the regime and opposition, so vividly in evidence in the outburst of political activity in the winter of 2011/12, is mediated by an endlessly recurring set of divisions between the two. Within the regime there are identifiable hard and soft-liners, with this division reflected to some extent in a relatively liberal cabinet under Prime Minister Medvedev and a more conservative presidential administration headed by Putin. As for the 'opposition', it is barely possible to use the singular. Eduard Limonov and his National Bolshevik Party are one of the most irreconcilable groups, but there are a range of other views encompassing nationalists and liberals, all the way to the official 'systemic' opposition such as the Communist Party of the Russian Federation (CPRF). The social liberal Yabloko Party finds itself challenged by the more social populist Just Russia. The heterogeneity of the non-regime forces means that they are unlikely to be able to take structured political form. With the onset of a new era of party formation inaugurated by the 2011/12 protests, the opposition will remain fragmented, and it is unlikely that a new party will emerge capable of challenging United Russia's predominance. Instead, political life will remain structured by the opposition between generalities, notably the regime and its opponents, and, more broadly, between the bureaucracy and the people. This means that elites will remain free-floating, and only a few will devote their political careers to the patient art of party and institution building.

The actuality of democracy?

Vladimir Lenin's political genius lay in his unwavering belief in the actuality of revolution, and this belief in the end allowed him to make a revolution when all others wavered.[19] In looking at Russia's future, the question of the actuality of the democratic revolution is a necessary preliminary. Is democracy the wave of the future, or do the 'great recession' and other changes in the relationship between liberalism and democracy in the post-war era have such profound consequences that democracy, as Inozemtsev suggests, may be unable to resolve its own cultural contradictions?[20] For some, this suggests that some sort of model of authoritarian modernization would be a viable alternative.[21] Inozemtsev himself calls for more elitism,[22] an appeal that is unlikely to fall on deaf ears in Russia. The model of reform applied in the 1990s was a top-down state-driven affair, which in the end threatened the viability of the state itself. In the 2000s Putin restored authority to the governing order, but instead of strengthening the state (constitution-based rule of law, independent courts, defensible property rights, and the like), he reinforced the powers of the administrative regime; precisely that part of the polity on which Yeltsin had come to rely to push through privatization and other reforms. Without the normative support of the constitutional state, accompanied by its infrastructural power based on consent and the authority derived from the ballot box, the 'power vertical' (what we call the administrative regime) will in due course be faced with the stark choice of either legitimating its authority by embedding its rule in constitutional institutions and practices, or being forced to rely on ever more arduous manual management or, ultimately, outright coercion.

The problem, as Inozemtsev notes, is far from unique to Russia. In a moving discussion of the future of the left – or, more precisely, its lack of a future – T.J. Clark argues that the present period is comparable to that following the defeat of Napoleon:

> This is the way Castlereagh's Europe resembles our own: in its sense that a previous language and set of presuppositions for emancipation have run into the sand, and its realistic uncertainty as to whether the elements of a different language are to be found at all in the general spectacle of frozen politics, ruthless economy and enthusiasm (as always) for the latest dim gadgets.[23]

In this context, where reform can be defined as an attempt for the more backward to achieve an approximation of the modernity practiced in the more advanced regions, the hegemonic model is undergoing the most profound crisis since the Second World War, thus throwing models of reform into crisis.

Most current models of Russian reform are exhausted, yet, as Clark notes, 'Reform, it transpires, is a revolutionary demand.'[24] Reformism is back on the agenda, since all revolutionary projects for the transformation of society – from the radical left to the radical liberal and the right – are discredited. It was Putin's genius to recognize this, but at some point in around 2003–04 he lost sight of the dynamic of reformist change, and his leadership thereafter lurched from one crisis to another, reduced to a reactive mode of governance that allowed his own elite group to enrich itself in a period of drift. In other words, he failed to give genuine political form to his radical evolutionary policy, thus locking the country in stalemate. The events of 2011/12 gave new impetus to the reform effort, but once again they were partial and were not negotiated with society.

On his appointment as minister of education in May 2010, for example, Dmitry Livanov immediately spoke of halving the number of students who receive state support for higher education. Dmitry Babich notes that '20 years of reform have taught an average Russian: if a boss speaks about making a certain sphere more "competitive", he means slashing jobs, introducing payment for previously publicly accessible services – in short, about making life harder and more expensive.'[25] Livanov cannot be easily categorized politically, but he had absorbed the neo-liberal spirit of the age and advanced policies against which the majority of Russians had voted in the 2011/12 electoral cycle. As Babich argues, there is a 'strange coexistence in Russia of a leftist voter and a center-right elite'. Putin had been able to connect to leftist sentiments by pursuing various anti-oligarch campaigns and by making populist promises in the election that gained him a third term, but the broader problem could not so easily be resolved.

The classic 'democracy paradox', where newly liberated voters support forces that undermine democracy, is joined in Russia by the 'modernization paradox': accelerated modernization (defined in neo-liberal terms) can only be achieved by challenging the social gains of the population achieved during earlier eras of political struggle, and thus reinforces the insulation of the reforming elite, which undermines the political legitimacy of their rule. It means undermining the gains achieved in an earlier bout of (Soviet style) modernization. In other words, to 'become modern' the neo-liberal agenda for contemporary Russia forces it to dismantle the gains of modernity. The paradox can typically be overcome by a country when faced by an overwhelming crisis that necessitates harsh measures, or when the military or other modernizing elite can take charge, but in normal circumstances policy choices are mediated through representative institutions. The stultified development of these bodies in Russia allows the elite to insulate itself from social pressures and special interests (other than those generated within the governing elite), but this only reinforces the starkness of the modernization paradox. Calls for 'dialogue' in conditions in which structured interaction between the authorities and the people is missing is liable to fall on deaf ears.[26] More profoundly, the notion of modernization suggests some sort of agreement over the nature of the modernity to be achieved, but there is no such consensus in Russian society as it seeks to find an adequate way of implementing the 1991 agenda. At the root of such a discussion is examination of the type of capitalism that will operate and the level of welfare state that can be sustained.

Even though Putin was forced to row back on promises of reform during the 2011/12 campaign, in Babich's words, '[This] does not mean the "budget cutters" lost the sympathies of Putin and Medvedev, who are in fact both just trivial center-right politicians of an "emerging market" named Russia'. In other words, the political cleavage between regime and opposition is accompanied by a sociological split between the policy orientations of the elite, responding to globalization and other perceived challenges, and the 'moral economy' of the population, advancing a particular vision of fairness and justice. This is more than retrograde 'traditionalism'; in another era it was considered the acme of progressivism. Reforms of the Livanov type, as had already been seen in the mass protests against the monetization of social benefits in 2005, reinforce the stalemate that is evident at the political level. The deep unpopularity of 'reforms' that are seen to challenge the popular moral economy embedded in society is more than a reflection of tradition-alism or neo-Soviet sentiments, but reflects an inchoate yearning for a vision of justice independent of market forces.[27] From this perspective, discussion of 'inertial' or 'reactionary' scenarios needs to be supple-mented by more specific policy-oriented analysis in the framework of broader ideological debates about perspectives on what a 'modernized' just society would look like. These debates are usually mediated by an aggregative and representative political party, but United Russia has not been able to fulfill this role.

The actors involved in this debate are also changing. Although cowed by the attack on Yukos in the mid-2000s, big business remains a pow-erful player on Russia's political scene. This is fostered, in part, by the continuing problem of monopolization, accompanied by the emer-gence of a new generation of players in the energy sector. The tension between the liberal and conservative wings of the regime is moder-ated by a third group, the successful Putin-era entrepreneurs who are now emerging from the shadows to exert their political weight. Mikhail Prokhorov demonstrated the forms that their political ambitions could take, but others, like Gennady Timchenko and Oleg Deripaska, will no doubt be less fearful of exercising their political muscles in conditions of political stalemate and stalled modernization. They may emerge as a mediating power between the state and society. They do not only

challenge the dominance of state-controlled energy champio
as Rosneft or Gazprom; they also break the political monopol
regime as a whole.[28] However, unless this can take structured ~~p......~~
forms, Russia's new pluralism could emulate that already present in
Ukraine. A pluralism of politicized oligarchs would hardly represent a
step towards a more inclusive and universal democracy.

Looking at the future

In the light of the above, the scenario approach clearly has some major
shortcomings. The relationship between drivers and outcomes is potentially infinite. The scenario approach draws on sortal methodology, and
represents a form of undigested hybridity: in other words, it recognizes
the presence of incompatible features in a social order, but resorts to
typological solutions to resolve them. Scalar approaches find scenario
methodologies inadequate, and instead examine the forces that shape
an evolutionary process.

The Putinite system of rule has become a remarkably effective form
of governance. It was capable of dealing with major economic crisis
after 2008, and was also able to contain the worst pathologies of its
own system of rule. The networks on which the administrative regime
are based bypass the logic of operation of most formal institutions, yet
are careful not openly to challenge the normative foundations of the
state. By the time Putin returned to the presidency for a third term in
2012, the long period of stability had allowed the patronage networks
to become consolidated and to draw in ever new sections of society,
including the ability to co-opt potential competitors. As Heinrich and
Pleines put it, 'These networks, which transcend the constitutional institutions of the state and are based on a logic of mostly bilateral exchange
between patrons and clients, thus play a vital role for regime stability.'[29] The system was predicated on the continuing inflow of natural
resource rents, and thus Russia had become a distinctive type of *rentier*
state, and susceptible to the vulnerabilities of such a system. Nevertheless, Heinrich and Pleines are relatively sanguine about the durability of
such a system and its managerial capacities:

First, the real challenge for post-Soviet rentier states is not the lack
of government capacities, as the public good view would suggest. The
real challenge is the patronage system, which intentionally supports
weak governance so that elites can exploit the loopholes for their own
benefit. Second, the argument that the current government is not sustainable because it is inefficient and wastes financial resources on a large

scale is simply not tenable: the political leadership in the post-Soviet rentier states has in fact made extremely efficient use of resources to create vast, sustainable patronage networks that have the capacity to guarantee political stability.[30]

There is widespread consensus that Russia needs 'reform': in the social sphere (pensions, social welfare, rents, utilities, and so on); in the economic sphere (above all to improve the ease of doing business, reduce the weight of the bureaucracy and corruption, and overall to improve the business environment to foster a more competitive and open economy); and in politics to allow a more genuinely competitive and pluralistic order, characterized by free and fair elections, the rule of law, and the overall reduction of the 'emergency' character of political management. However, these three 'reforms' may not necessarily reinforce each other in the short term. Thus, the question of political strategy rises to the fore. Chinese experience after 1978 demonstrates that a new leadership can undertake swift and bold reforms that can change the whole national trajectory. Post-Mao China is one thing; Russia has been engaged in a long-drawn-out transformation for over a quarter of a century.

The dominant Russian strategy has been gradualism, punctuated by periods of accelerated change. The gradualist strategy has the advantage of trying to minimize social disruption, but it also means that entrenched social elites and the vast class of officialdom can act as a brake on necessary social changes. This could provoke crisis-led change, an acceleration of reform in certain sectors. This certainly now applies to the political sphere following the post-election protests. However, the Putin regime was weakened by the protests, with its very legitimacy questioned by the demonstrators, and thus the stability of the state becomes an issue, as does governance capacity. In that context, it would be easier to increase government borrowing, or even to print money, rather than undertake serious structural reforms.

There are profound methodological and substantive pitfalls in trying to outline a country's future. I have long argued that it is not the political scientist's job to predict the future (we leave that task to astrologers), but we are called upon to anticipate possible avenues of development.[31] This chapter argues that only by establishing an appropriate methodology can we hope to capture the evolving dynamics of state and elite development. I have argued that the historical situation in Russia remains open, and the dual state model suggests that the current stalemate in all probability will be overcome by reviving the democratic potential of the project of 1991. There is nothing automatic about this, and neither is the time-scale determined. Neither should we fall into the teleological trap of extrapolating a Western present onto Russia's future. The argument here is that 1991 represented a distinctive *Russian* attempt to meet the challenges of modernity, and Russia will have to find its own way to manage that modernity. The country in 1991 abandoned attempts to create an alternative modernity; now all it needs to do is to become modern in its own way.

Notes

1. For an excellent discussion, see S.V. Kortunov (2009) *Stanovlenie natsional'noi identichnosti: Kakaya Rossiya nuzhna miru* (Moscow: Aspekt Press).
2. For a discussion, see B. Kapustin (2012) 'Capitalism and Russian Democracy' in Per-Arne Bodin, Stefan Hedlund, and Elena Namli (eds) *Power and Legitimacy: Challenges from Russia* (London: Routledge), 75–101.
3. D.C. North, J. Wallis, and B.R. Weingast (2009) *Violence and Social Orders: A Conceptual Framework for Interpreting Recorded Human History* (Cambridge: Cambridge University Press).
4. On this, see T. Judt (2007) *Postwar: A History of Europe Since 1945* (London: Pimlico).
5. R. Sakwa (2012) 'Modernisation, Neo-Modernisation and Comparative Democratisation in Russia', *East European Politics*, vol.28, no.1, March, 43–57.
6. J. Gans-Morse (2004) 'Searching for Transitologists: Contemporary Theories of Post-Communist Transitions and the Myth of a Dominant Paradigm', *Post-Soviet Affairs*, vol.20, no.4, October–December, 320–49.
7. For an overview, see H. Balzer (2003) 'Managed Pluralism: Vladimir Putin's Emerging Regime', *Post-Soviet Affairs*, vol.19, no.3, 189–227.
8. For a collection of key articles, see N. Garadzha (ed.) (2006) *Suverenitet* (Moscow: Evropa).
9. D. Hutcheson, E. Korosteleva (2005) *The Quality of Democracy in Post-Communist Eastern Europe* (London and New York: Routledge).
10. G. O'Donnell, J.V. Cullell, and O.M. Iazzetta (2004) *The Quality of Democracy* (Notre Dame, IN: University of Notre Dame Press).
11. D. Lane (2008) 'The Orange Revolution: "People's Revolution" or Revolutionary Coup', *The British Journal of Politics & International Relations*, vol.10, no.4, November, 525–49.
12. P. Bernhagen (2009) 'Measuring Democracy and Democratization' in Ch. Haerpfer, P. Bernhagen, R. Inglehart, and Ch. Welzel (eds) *Democratization* (Oxford: Oxford University Press), 24–38.
13. D. Collier, S. Levitsky (1997) 'Democracy With Adjectives: Conceptual Innovation in Comparative Research', *World Politics*, vol.49, 430–51.
14. S. Levitsky, L. Way (2010) *Competitive Authoritarianism: Hybrid Regimes After the Cold War* (New York: Cambridge University Press).
15. R. Sakwa (2011) 'Transition as a Political Institution; Toward 2020' in M. Lipman and N. Petrov (eds) *Russia in 2020: Scenarios for the Future* (Washington, DC: Carnegie Endowment for International Peace), 233–54.
16. J. Møller, S.E. Skaaning (2011) 'Stateness First?', *Democratization*, vol.18, no.1, February, 1–24, at 2.

17. W. Adebanwi, E. Obadare (2011) 'The Abrogation of the Electorate: An Emergent African Phenomenon', *Democratization*, vol.18, no.2, April, 311–35, at 327.
18. V. Gel'man (2012) 'Treshchiny v stene', *Pro et Contra*, January–April, 94–115.
19. *Zur Aktualität von Karl Korsch* (1981) (Europäische Verlagsanstalt).
20. V. Inozemtsev (2012) 'The Cultural Contradictions of Democracy', *The American Interest*, Spring, March–April, 3–7.
21. A. Gat (2007) 'The Return of the Authoritarian Great Powers', *Foreign Affairs*, vol.86, no.4, July–August, 56–69.
22. V. Inozemtsev (2012) 'The Cultural Contradictions...', 10.
23. T.J. Clark (2012) 'For a Left With no Future', *New Left Review*, no.74, March–April, 53–75, at 56.
24. T.J. Clark (2012) 'For a Left With no Future', 73.
25. D. Babich (2012) 'Russia's Assess the Country's New Government', *Russia Beyond the Headlines*, 24 May.
26. See, for example, the report 'Obshchestvo i vlast' v usloviyakh politicheskogo Krizisa' (Moscow: Tsentr Strategicheskikh Razrabotok), May 2012, http://www.csr.ru/images/docs/doklad.pdf, commissioned by Alexei Kudrin's Civil Initiative's Committee, and presented by the Center for Strategic Research on 24 May 2012. It identified a genuine political crisis in Russia that could only be overcome by 'dialogue'.
27. The theoretical issue is discussed by M. Sandel (2012) *What Money Can't Buy* (London, Allen Lane).
28. See Sh. Yenikeyeff (2012) 'Big Business Under Threat in Putin's Russia?', 23 May, www.opendemocracy.net.
29. A. Heinrich, H. Pleines (2012) 'The Political Challenges of an Oil Boom: the Resource Curse and Political Stability in Russia', *Russian Analytical Digest*, no.113, 15 May, 2–6, at 6.
30. A. Heinrich, H. Pleines (2012) 'The Political Challenges...', 6.
31. R. Sakwa (1998) 'Russian Political Evolution: A Structural Approach' in Michael Cox (ed.) *Rethinking Soviet Collapse: Sovietology, the Death of Communism and the New Russia* (London and New York: Pinter), 181–201.

Bibliography

W. Adebanwi, E. Obadare (2011) 'The Abrogation of the Electorate: An Emergent African Phenomenon', *Democratization*, vol.18, no.2, April, pp. 311–35.

D. Babich (2012) 'Russia Assesses the Country's New Government', *Russia Beyond the Headlines*, 24 May.

H. Balzer (2003) 'Managed Pluralism: Vladimir Putin's Emerging Regime', *Post-Soviet Affairs*, vol.19, no.3, pp. 189–227.

P. Bernhagen (2009) 'Measuring Democracy and Democratization', in Ch. Haerpfer, P. Bernhagen, R. Inglehart, and Ch. Welzel (eds) *Democratization* (Oxford: Oxford University Press).

T.J. Clark (2012) 'For a Left With no Future', *New Left Review*, no.74, March–April, pp. 53–75.

D. Collier, S. Levitsky (1997) 'Democracy with Adjectives: Conceptual Innovation in Comparative Research', *World Politics*, vol.49, pp. 430–51.

J. Gans-Morse (2004) 'Searching for Transitologists: Contemporary Theories of Post-Communist Transitions and the Myth of a Dominant Paradigm', *Post-Soviet Affairs*, vol.20, no.4, October–December, pp. 320–49.

N. Garadzha (ed.) (2006) *Suverenitet* (Moscow: Evropa).

A. Gat (2007) 'The Return of the Authoritarian Great Powers', *Foreign Affairs*, vol.86, no.4, July–August, pp. 56–69.

V. Gel'man (2012) 'Treshchiny v stene', *Pro et Contra*, January–April, pp. 94–115.

A. Heinrich and H. Pleines (2012) 'The Political Challenges of an Oil Boom: the Resource Curse and Political Stability in Russia', *Russian Analytical Digest*, no.113, 15 May, pp. 2–6.

D. Hutcheson, E. Korosteleva (2005) *The Quality of Democracy in Post-Communist Eastern Europe* (London and New York: Routledge).

V. Inozemtsev (2012) 'The Cultural Contradictions of Democracy', *The American Interest*, Spring, March–April, pp. 3–7.

T. Judt (2007) *Postwar: A History of Europe since 1945* (London: Pimlico).

B. Kapustin (2012) 'Capitalism and Russian Democracy' in Per-Arne Bodin, Stefan Hedlund, and Elena Namli (eds) *Power and Legitimacy: Challenges from Russia* (London: Routledge).

S.V. Kortunov (2009) *Stanovlenie natsional'noi identichnosti: Kakaya Rossiya nuzhna miru* (Moscow: Aspekt Press).

D. Lane (2008) 'The Orange Revolution: "People's Revolution" or Revolutionary Coup', *The British Journal of Politics & International Relations*, vol.10, no.4, November, pp. 525–49.

S. Levitsky, L. Way (2010) *Competitive Authoritarianism: Hybrid Regimes after the Cold War* (New York: Cambridge University Press).

J. Møller, S.-E. Skaaning (2011) 'Stateness First?', *Democratization*, vol.18, no.1, February, pp. 1–24.

D.C. North, J. Wallis, and B.R. Weingast (2009) *Violence and Social Orders: A Conceptual Framework for Interpreting Recorded Human History* (Cambridge: Cambridge University Press).

'Obshchestvo i vlast' v usloviyakh politicheskogo Krizisa' (Moscow: Tsentr Strategicheskikh Razrabotok), May 2012, http://www.csr.ru/images/docs/doklad.pdf, Accessed 2 September 2013.

G. O'Donnell, J.V. Cullell, and O.M. Iazzetta (2004) *The Quality of Democracy* (Notre Dame: IN, University of Notre Dame Press).

M. Sandel (2012) *What Money Can't Buy* (London: Allen Lane).

R. Sakwa (1998) 'Russian Political Evolution: A Structural Approach' in Michael Cox (ed.) *Rethinking Soviet Collapse: Sovietology, the Death of Communism and the New Russia* (London and New York: Pinter).

R. Sakwa (2011) 'Transition as a Political Institution; Toward 2020' in M. Lipman and N. Petrov (eds) *Russia in 2020: Scenarios for the Future* (Washington, DC: Carnegie Endowment for International Peace).

R. Sakwa (2012) 'Modernisation, Neo-Modernisation and Comparative Democratisation in Russia', *East European Politics*, vol.28, no.1, March, pp. 43–57.

Sh. Yenikeyeff (2012) 'Big Business Under Threat in Putin's Russia?', 23 May, www.opendemocracy.net.

Zur Aktualität von Karl Korsch (1981) (Europäische Verlagsanstalt).

11

The Kremlin Turns Ideological: Where This New Direction Could Lead

Maria Lipman

Vladimir Putin's return to the presidency has brought to the fore the soul-searching questions that his regime had theretofore sought to avoid: what is Russia's post-communist identity; what are the origins of its new statehood, or the core values that hold the nation together; what is the desired direction of Russia's post-Soviet development?

His policy of evasiveness enabled Putin to marginalize those issues, which in the 1990s had caused societal discord and political turmoil. This policy worked well for Putin during his first decade in power. Combined with the high and growing price of oil, it provided the yearned-for stability. The Russian people readily stayed away from politics and focused on their daily lives. The general mood was that of acquiescence.

But then things began to change: in late 2011 the announcement of Putin's imminent return to presidency, jointly with the fraudulent parliamentary election, provoked mass political rallies unprecedented in post-communist times; tens of thousands took to the streets in Moscow chanting 'Russia without Putin.'

After some hesitation the Kremlin responded with a campaign aimed at quashing the protest movement. The government moved to discredit the protesters, then to intimidate and repress them. By way of discrediting the defiant minority in the eyes of their more conservative compatriots, the government branded them as immoral and unpatriotic, inspired, sponsored or otherwise abetted by evil forces in the West.

By pitting conservative Russians against their more modernized and defiant compatriots (a minority of the minority referred to as 'Russia-1' in the classification offered by Natalia Zubarevich in this volume), Putin abandoned the status of 'the leader of all the Russians' that he had built and emphasized throughout his earlier years in power.

Instead, he emerged as the leader of 'Putin's Russians'. This called for a more definitive ideological ground: if the newly defiant constituency was, to paraphrase the formula of the McCarthyist times, essentially 'un-Russian', what were the true values that good, patriotic, Putin's Russians stood for?

And, since the regime's opponents were mostly liberal and modernized, the government, its propagandists and loyalists inevitably shifted toward a conservative, anti-liberal and anti-Western stance. The need for a source of moral righteousness in its standoff with civic protesters pushed the government to draw ever more strongly on the Russian Orthodox Church, especially in the aftermath of the Pussy Riot affair in the summer of 2012.

This trend, which some analysts soon referred to as countermodernization,[1] while presumably accepted by a majority in Russia, faces a variety of limitations and pitfalls as it exacerbates intolerance of all things new, Other or alien, unleashes a range of angry and aggressive anti-liberal forces, and aggravates the existing societal divisions.

In the future the realm of ideas may become increasingly contested. The government's shift toward social and political conservatism (still not clearly defined, as will be shown in this chapter) may generate a broader national debate and even a clash of visions of Russia's past and future; a debate about ideas can play a bigger role in shaping the political and social life.

Should this happen, the challenge will be to avoid dangerous rifts and radicalization. A deterioration of the socio-economic conditions can generate the temptation of populist politics that would capitalize on more radical xenophobic, chauvinistic, or anti-capitalist sentiments.

Whether Russia will rise to this challenge is far from certain. Serious clashes are not unlikely; the eventual choice may not be consensual. There is little, if any, clarity as to what this choice might be.

This chapter outlines the current challenges and dilemmas as well as those that lie ahead.

The post-communist ideological void: All things uncertain

The political regime built in the course of Putin's leadership may bear some similarity to the late Soviet polity, such as the monopoly on state power, centralized governance, non-transparent decision-making, reliance on state security forces and police-state methods, as well as the dominance of the state over powerless society – but what it does not share with its Soviet predecessor is the latter's ideological backbone.

In the USSR the state had not just monopolized the political and the economic sphere; it also usurped the realm of ideas and imposed upon the Soviet people 'the one true' way of thinking.

After the collapse of the communist regime its ideology had been radically discarded, but even two decades later the identity and the foundations of the post-Soviet Russia have not been clearly articulated. There is no clarity on whether Russia has broken away from the communist past, or should even have this as its goal; the nation has not come to terms with its Soviet experience and does not show a desire to do so.

Uncertain direction of post-communist development

Russia's first president, Boris Yeltsin, built his leadership on anti-communism: after his victory over the coup plotters in 1991 he emerged as a conqueror of communism and thus a legitimate leader of the post-communist Russia. But the sense of triumph over the Soviet regime and its negative association with Stalin's terror, the late-Soviet police state and its economy of shortages promptly faded away – overshadowed by the collapse of the USSR, which to an overwhelming majority in Russia was by no means a desired or joyous event.

Some of the ex-USSR republics may celebrate the disintegration of the Soviet Union as a liberation from the oppressive imperial center (that is, Russia) and the long yearned-for reconnection with their European path or as a welcome beginning of a new independence. But Russia was a different story. The disintegration of the Soviet Union was a loss, not a gain in status for the post-communist Russian state, and this made the concept of independence hardly attractive ('from whom?' ran a commonly asked rhetorical question), even inappropriate for the Russian people.

Only a small minority in Russia rationalized the events that led to a collapse of communism in terms of liberation from the Soviet regime. In 2012 a plurality (41 per cent, the highest number in over 20 years) regarded them as a 'tragic event that had deleterious consequences for the country and the people'.[2]

To a majority the end of communism was far from beneficial – instead it was associated with the deprivations of the 1990s, the collapse of the habitual safety net and a painful transition to a market economy broadly seen as 'wild capitalism', or 'chaos of the 90s'. This perception left the nation without the sense of pride that is shared by most Eastern European nations, which commonly celebrate the shedding of the communist occupation. Nor has post-communist Russia developed a sense of national purpose, such as overcoming the aftermath of communism, that would bring the nation together and justify, at least to some extent, the concomitant hardship as a necessary sacrifice.[3]

Perception of the Soviet past: A lack of a narrative

In Yeltsin's Russia, politics was informed by the irreconcilable divisions between those who supported Yeltsin as an anti-communist leader and his vehement opponents in the Russian Communist Party. When he emerged as Yeltsin's successor, Putin was driven by a desire to secure himself and his regime from the hazards of political competition. In the legislature, he reached a compromise with the communists that for Yeltsin would have been inconceivable. In the public sphere, his administration sought to marginalize the ideological debate about the past. On the level of state symbols, he opted for an all-embracing message: a combination of the Soviet anthem, an imperial emblem, and an essentially anti-communist tricolor flag (in Yeltsin's Russia the tricolor flag symbolized his victory over Soviet communism). At the official level, mentions of divisive issues of the Soviet past were reduced to a minimum.

There is basically no discussion of the early Bolshevik period or the nature of Stalin's rule by terror[4] (or the police-state regime of the late Soviet decades that included persecution of dissidents and the political use of psychiatry). The historical political debate was not banned; it was just pushed to the margins (confined to academic/intellectual circles, nongovernment organizations, smaller-audience media, etc.). By avoiding the divisive subjects Putin calmed down the passions, demobilized the nation, and generated the appearance of a national agreement.

This is how, in the two post-communist decades, Russia has not generated a nationally accepted narrative on the origins of the Russian statehood or the causes and circumstances of the collapse of the USSR or, more generally, the Soviet experience.

Consensual historical memories are precious few in Russia, and by far the most important among them is the victory in the Second World War, which has indeed been celebrated with increasing pomp during Putin's leadership. The Second World War is referred to in Russia as the Great Patriotic War, and its history is reduced to 1941–45, and first and foremost to the Soviet victory. Arguably, the celebration of the victory comes as a compensation for Russia's loss of status following the disintegration of the USSR. Other episodes of Second World War-related history, such as cooperation with Hitler, the Ribbentrop–Molotov Pact, or the decades of Soviet occupation of Eastern Europe, are radically played down in the official discourse.

Many nations are split over certain events or periods of their histories; but few, like Russia, have experienced two major socio-political upheavals in the course of just one century. What makes Russia different is not so much a lack of national consensus, but more a dramatic historical discontinuity. This is why the need to define itself is especially urgent in Russia.

What does post-communist Russia celebrate?

Post-communist Russia does not have a 'liberation' or an 'independence' to celebrate as its main national holiday; nor is there a figure that could claim the fame of the founder of the post-communist state.

President Yeltsin introduced the Day of Adoption of the Declaration of State Sovereignty of the Russian Federation,[5] but since, as was mentioned above, the events associated with the disintegration of the USSR are seen as a negative development, the holiday failed to take root. As in the case of other moves associated with Yeltsin, Putin distanced himself from the 12 June holiday. He famously referred to the collapse of the USSR as 'the greatest geopolitical catastrophe of the 20th century'. Early in Putin's first tenure the holiday was renamed 'Russia Day' – but in this case, as in others related to the post-communist history, there is no narrative attached to it. 12 June is hardly seen by the citizens of Russia as a major national holiday.

Since there is no broadly accepted narrative regarding the substance or origins of Russia's new, post-communist statehood, there is no consensus on its age. During his presidency Dmitry Medvedev, on at least one occasion, referred to Russia as being 'only twenty years old' (apparently, dating back to the establishment of the post-communist Russia).[6] Shortly thereafter, however, he announced that 2012 would mark 1,150 years of Russian statehood.[7] In December 2012 Putin called for a return of 'the simple truth that Russia did not begin in 1917, or even in 1991, but rather, that we have a common, continuous history spanning over one thousand years'.[8] Putin's rhetoric emphasizes his desire to establish Russia's historical continuity, but, at the same time, to avoid a discussion of the causes and the meaning of the Soviet Union's collapse.

In 2004, 4 November was formally introduced as a new national holiday and called the Day of People's Unity (*Den' Narodnogo Edinstva*). It referred to the events of 1612 that had never been celebrated in the living memory of today's Russians. At its introduction the official interpretation of what we're actually celebrating was unclear; there was even less clarity on what we're supposed to do on that day: what slogans, decorations, or ceremonies should accompany it?[9]

As a result, 4 November was appropriated by ugly nationalist and xenophobic forces. Every year since 2007, on this day they have staged a 'Russian March', and the day has since become an annual headache for the authorities. In 2012, as Putin felt the urge to bring more clarity on the issue of Russian statehood, in his article on the 'national question' he emphasized the importance of the 4 November holiday as 'a day of victory over internal enmity and strife when... various peoples came to think of themselves as a single entity – one people'.[10] The number of those who took part in the Russian March that year by some estimates reached about 10–15,000 people, the highest number ever.[11]

Though the awareness of the 4 November as a state holiday has grown over the years (in 2012 43 per cent of Russians knew what the holiday is called, up from 8 per cent in 2005), a mere 16 per cent celebrate it.[12]

Heroes, invisible or ambiguous

A foreigner traveling around Russia would never guess whom the Russian people perceive as their greatest historical figure. Polls of the past decade have shown Iosif Stalin to be among the top three, and in 2012 he rose to the topmost position.[13] His images, however, are absent from Russia's physical space: there are no streets or squares named after him, and practically no monuments or portraits. Stalin's images had been radically scrapped back during the rule of Nikita Khrushchev (a figure hardly evoked in today's public discourse), who exposed and condemned Stalin's 'personality cult' and mass repressions. Another, broader de-Stalinization campaign was unfolded under Mikhail Gorbachev.

Stalin's status today as a 'hidden hero' is yet another reflection of post-communist Russia's vague identity. Even though he does not have a 'physical presence', Stalin is charged with a symbolic meaning: as an embodiment of the Russian state at its most powerful. Putin would not glorify Stalin, but neither would he oppose the rise of Stalin's 'popularity' that stems from the traditional paternalistic pattern that Putin has reinstated in Russia – that of the powerful state and powerless people. The discussions and analysis of Stalinism have been thoroughly marginalized. A modicum of mourning the victims may be accepted (though there is no national memorial site or a national museum), but the causes and nature of Stalin's brutal dictatorship are not broadly discussed, lest they stir the debate about the traditional nature of the Soviet/Russian statehood.

Among the top three most important figures of Russian history there are also the greatest national poet, Pushkin, and Peter the Great. Pushkin, the non-political figure, is unambiguous and universally accepted. Peter the Great is not broadly celebrated either, though, of course, St Petersburg bears his name and one can find a few of his statues elsewhere. Russia's 18th-century emperor Peter the Great was an unbending and merciless modernizer. His broad modernization effort, however, makes him a controversial figure, because he comes across as too much of a Westernizer: he unambiguously proclaimed Russia backward, insisted that it should learn from the West, and brutally coerced his subjects to adopt Western ways; he himself humbly and ardently learnt from – and in – the West.

Putin likes to mention and quote another historical figure, Pyotr Stolypin, Russian prime minister during a brief period between 1906 and 1911, who proceeded with progressive socio-economic innovations, yet mercilessly cleared the way for his reform initiatives by repressions and executions of the Russian revolutionaries. Putin had a Stolypin statue erected in Moscow in 2012 and attended its inauguration. Yet this attempt to endow post-communist Russia with a national hero was not followed through either. Stolypin had not been a historical celebrity before the erection of his statue, and there is still no consistent narrative about him or his failed reforms (Stolypin was assassinated before he was able to accomplish his ambitious goals). This still leaves Stalin as Russia's number one historical figure, if a controversial one.[14]

No longer an empire, but not a nation state either

Even after the collapse of the USSR, Russia did not – and could not – become a nation state. Its population is diverse, in terms of both ethnicity and faith, and its administrative structure includes about two dozen 'ethnic republics'. These factors leave Russia in a state of limbo: no longer a Soviet empire, but not a Russian nation state either.

What's the word for 'Russian'?

The collapse of the Soviet state and the ensuing disappearance of the Soviet identity thus left a gaping uncertainty in place of a new, non-Soviet identity. A striking illustration of this uncertainty is the absence of a *term* Russian citizens would use to identify themselves. The term *Russkie* refers to an ethnic identity and is, therefore, unacceptable to the dozens of ethnic groups inhabiting Russia, such as Tatars, Bashkirs, Chechens, Ossetians, Yakuts, and so on. President Yeltsin tried to introduce the term *Rossiyane* as a designation of a civic national identity. But *Rossiyane* failed to take root as a self-identification term. As soon as Putin took over, he dropped the term *Rossiyane* altogether, as part of his consistent effort to distance himself from everything associated with Yeltsin's highly unpopular rule. Putin would not adopt the ethnic term *Russkie* either – such a choice would have been highly divisive and dangerous, given the existing ethnic tensions between the predominantly Russian (Slavic) population and some ethnic minorities, especially those from Northern Caucasus. Instead Putin used the formal address 'citizens of Russia', hardly a phrase people would use to identify themselves.

In the Russian environment, where racism and xenophobic nationalism are not uncommon,[15] Putin is anxious not to aggravate the tensions; in his speeches he repeatedly emphasizes that ethnic and religious diversity is Russia's asset. This should imply a civic nationhood, but its foundation remains unclear. On several occasions Putin referred to the Soviet nation building as a successful experience,[16] yet he seems to realize that this experience is no longer applicable. In a meeting with Russia's regional ombudsmen in the fall of 2012 Putin basically admitted that the task of post-communist nation building remains unsolved.[17] Later that year he bemoaned the "deficit of spiritual ties" in Russian society.[18]

In his above-cited article about the 'national question' (see endnote 10), Putin offers some ideas of what a Russian multi-ethnic state should be, but the article is contradictory and well-wishing rather than practical.[19] The same applies to a new National Policy Strategy[20] which defines Russians as a 'many-nations people' (this term is borrowed from the Soviet political vocabulary). The strategy refers to ethnic Russians as a 'uniting force' that holds other ethnic groups together.

Putin's well-meaning and inclusive messages, however, can hardly be expected to soften the essentially racial bias against Northern Caucasus minorities or temper the sentiments of those ultranationalists who join the infamous Russian March chanting *Russia is for Russians, Migrants, go home*, or even *Sieg Heil*.

Russia and the West

Whether or not Russia is European, whether it belongs in the Western realm has been an issue of broad and deep controversy at least since the middle of the 19th century. The Bolshevik project was essentially 'Western', driven by European ideas of Marx and Engels and inspired by other European thinkers. In his time Stalin modified the modernist and cosmopolitan Bolshevik project launched by Lenin and replaced it with a more traditional one – imperial, socially conservative, and based on a strong and centralized state power (the earlier Leninist tenet was that the state was an outdated phenomenon and would gradually become extinct).[21]

In late perestroika the West was an almost universally accepted role model; emulating the West was widely seen almost as a silver bullet that would solve Russia's problems and transform it into a 'normal' (i.e. Western) country. Indeed, after the collapse of communism Russia adopted an essentially Western political arrangement with separation of powers, democratic checks and balances, and a multi-party system. It soon turned out, however, that Western models do not make miracles, Western standards remained unattainable, and after a while, in Putin's tenure, Russia returned to its traditional paternalistic pattern of statehood.

For a while statements of Russia's essential 'Europeanness' would be heard from Putin and others around him,[22] but gradually this rhetoric has faded away. Though Russia has long been a member of the G8, a club of Western-model market democracies, its relations with the West were often complicated. Ever since late 2011 government rhetoric regarding the West, and especially the US, has grown increasingly adversarial and isolationist. Rejection of Western values as inappropriate and unacceptable for Russia is implied in the official discourse.

Freedom of foreign travel and modern communications are still available in the Russian Federation, but in the course of Putin's leadership the government has increasingly – and especially since late 2011 – drawn on the besieged-fortress mentality in which the West is seen as a force that seeks to do harm to Russia, weaken or even destroy it.

The infatuation with the West that was a characteristic feature of the late 1980s had steadily subsided in the following decades,[23] while the concept of Russia's 'special path' once again was gaining popularity. A plurality of 41 per cent regarded Russia as a 'nation with a wholly special (political) organization and its own path of development'.[24]

But the West, and especially the US, even as an adversary, remains an important point of reference, and the controversial perception of the West thus remains in place. In seeking to justify its anti-democratic moves, Russian officials and loyalists commonly refer to 'Western experience'. For instance, as lawmakers frame bills imposing new constraints on rights and freedoms they often refer to 'similar' legal norms in Western countries. Even the outrageous trial of the Pussy Riot female band was accompanied by mentions of German and other norms that would allegedly have led to similar treatment of the Pussy Riot performance, should it have taken place in the West.

But, while Russia's values or its political organization are commonly referred to as 'special' and dissimilar from those of the Western world, they are harder to define in positive terms – except in a very general and essentially tautological manner, such as 'our own', 'traditional', and suchlike. Conservative, even fundamentalist discourse that has been on the rise as of 2012 may be accepted by the less modernized Russian majority, but it is also true that values such as traditional family, collectivism and solidarity, or emphasis on the spiritual as opposed to materialistic, are far divorced from the Russian reality – after all, Russia's breakaway from a traditional society was the making of Bolsheviks many decades ago.

Economic perceptions

Russia may have done away with the command and planned economy over two decades ago. A whole generation has grown that does not have the memory of chronic shortages and long lines even for staple food. In today's environment the value of money, income, and wealth has become overwhelming. Yet private entrepreneurship and money-making are hardly respected, big wealth is broadly regarded as ill-gotten gains, and the legitimacy of private property is questionable. When it comes to big-time properties, such as industrial enterprises and other business companies, a vast majority (73 per cent in 2011) believe that they should be owned by the state.[25]

Over half of Russians said in early 2013 that they preferred an economy based on 'state planning and distribution', with fewer than one-third in favor of an economic system based on 'private property and market relations'.[26] Putin's government, on the one hand, takes advantage of the negative attitude to the wealthy: it has drawn on this perception in order to keep the Russian rich under control, lest they evolve as an autonomous force and a potential rival to the government. On the other hand, a variety of government policies are conducive to egregious disparity of income, unlawful enrichment, and obscenely luxurious lifestyles.

While the official discourse is evasive and ambivalent, public perceptions are characterized by uncertainty and a lack of consensus on almost any issue. In his broad overview of the Russian economic developments, Thane Gustafson writes:

> There is no consensus among Russians about the most basic issues in economic or political life ... There is no agreement over who should own and run the essential assets of the country or which goods should be public or private ... At most there is a vague nostalgia for the Soviet past – not for communism as an ideology but rather for an era in which Russia was powerful and the state provided.... the overall story is one of a failure of consensus over the way ahead.[27]

Putin reinvents himself as an ideological leader

Established nations take their national myths for granted. They are accepted not because they are not questionable, but simply because they are part of the national tradition or habit. In Russia this 'habit' was broken twice in the past century – in 1917 when the imperial regime was overthrown and in 1991 when the communist regime collapsed. The task of an ideological legitimization of the new, post-communist nationhood and political order has not been solved; it has been barely addressed.

Early in his first tenure Putin gained legitimacy by providing relative stability. Soon thereafter, the steady rise of the price of oil enabled him to consolidate his legitimacy by delivering growing incomes. What he also offered was a 'non-intrusion pact'[28]: people would be kept away from policy-making, while the government would not intrude in their individual pursuits. The Russian people generally accepted this arrangement; an overwhelming majority remained unquestioning and quiescent. Even though the society was, in fact, divided on many issues – ethnic, social, religious, cultural, ideological, and so on – as long as the general mood was that of quiescence, these divisions did not make much difference socially or politically.

In late 2011 civic protests challenged Putin's legitimacy. A combination of repression and intimidation effectively suppressed the protest activity, but in order to stop the erosion of legitimacy these measures were insufficient. This task called for moral and ideological weapons, especially since the protest was essentially moral in nature.

Putin armed himself with an ideological message that boiled down to a Soviet-style patriotism built on the concept of an infallible state and unquestioning loyalty of the citizens to the ruling authority; state nationalism based on an anti-Western and especially anti-American stance with a distinct isolationist tint; political and social conservatism; a growing reliance on the Russian Orthodox Church as a pillar of statehood. The Church remains an external symbol of statehood, rather than an element of people's inner lives. The Church as a source of conservative values and radical anti-Americanism comes in handy for the government's new conservative shift. Besides, the Church is invariably loyal to the government. For its loyalty it is compensated with an ongoing expansion of property holdings, and a broader access to schools and armed forces. If sometimes its message becomes similar to Islamic fundamentalism, unlike Muslim clergy, Russian Orthodox churches are not an indispensable neighborhood presence; nor are they broadly seen as a friendly force that is always there to help the weak and the needy. Only a very small minority of Russians participate in parish life.

In Putin's heavily personalistic regime only he can assume the role of a chief ideologist. To entrust this function to somebody else (the Church is no exception) would be to share his authority, and this is something Putin could never afford.

Unlike his political talents, Putin's capacity as an ideologist is questionable. As the developments of 2012–13 have shown, he is capable of consolidating political control by switching to a more repressive mode, but there are several reasons to doubt that he can indeed build an ideological regime. To begin with, the nature of Russian statehood remains largely unclarified. Even the anti-Western and anti-American stance, which appears to be the most consistent of the new trends, is not fully unambiguous.

Putin's approach is likely rooted in his own experience with ideology. He matured in the Soviet Union of the 1970s, a period when Soviet people obediently paid lip service to the 'politically correct' ideological formulae, but the ideology was already dead and the regime's legitimacy was fast eroding.

Feigned consensus

Problems involved in Putin's ideological endeavor can be illustrated by the project of the 'single history book'. As of the early 2000s Russian officials repeatedly criticized excessive pluralism of the existing books, but in 2013, on Putin's firm suggestion, the effort went underway. Putin urged the creation of a unified line of history books for all grades based on a 'single logic of continuous Russian history'.[29]

But how does one write such a book in the absence of a national consensus? Putin has undertaken to fill the ideological void, bring the nation together, and solve the problem of missing 'spiritual ties' at a time when societal differences in Russia have become deeper and more pronounced. And, though Russian people at large may be generally acquiescent, today's Russia is a society with abundant sources of information and opinion. Putin, however, addresses the lack of public consensus Soviet-style: instead of building a consensus, he seeks to impose it. Meanwhile, an attempt to impose a uniform version of Russia's history risks deepening fragmentation along various lines, such as ethnic or ideological.

The Soviet Union had a firmly established national narrative on which school books as well as other ideological texts could draw. In today's Russia those entrusted with writing a uniform school book will have to invent their own narrative. There's little doubt that such a book, if accomplished, will be timeserving, driven, first and foremost, by political loyalty.

The end of the non-intrusion pact

By 2012 the pact of non-intrusion was largely abandoned. In response to the civic protesters' defiance, the Kremlin drew on conservative values that would justify the regime's righteousness and expose its excessively modernized opponents as morally reprehensible, unpatriotic offenders of the Russian tradition. The government has increasingly encroached on spheres related to family, sex, and faith, as well as physical and spiritual fitness, school curriculum, art and culture.

But the new trend of social conservatism has its own risks and problems. Throughout Putin's leadership he consolidated control by demobilizing the people; his regime made sure public passions remained unstirred. But his new ideological shift may undermine his own demobilization project. The emphasis on conservative family values, anti-gay sentiments, unchallenged authority of the Church, and so on may help discredit the excessively modernized and defiant minorities, but it is also bound to exacerbate the existing societal divisions and unleash undesired, radical forces and energies. In 2012 and 2013 a variety of such initiatives were launched by Cossacks, Orthodox vigilantes, and other morality mongers, ranging from attacks on gays, exhibits of contemporary art, theatrical productions or rock concerts to hunting for 'blasphemers' or harassing supporters of Pussy Riot.

Political conservatism has also pushed to the fore ultraconservative public figures who call for a revision of the constitution because it was written by foreigners[30] or propose a radically nationalist version of Russian history.[31] Increased reliance on the Russian Orthodox Church may alienate other denominations, such as growing Muslim minorities.

These risks may look marginal in the early 2010s, but, having unleashed such energies, the government at some point may turn out to be incapable of keeping them in check; especially since government resources are no longer as ample as they used to be and may continue to shrink in the future (see more on this in Boris Grozovsky's chapter in this volume).

Possible paths of ideological evolution

Putin's ideological pronouncements may look unconvincing and flawed; his proclamation of the state's primacy as Russia's perennial value leaves out the question of just how this primacy will be used at the current stage of Russian development. If it is a means to promote Russia's desired path, then what is the desired path? If Russia is on the move, whither is it moving? Or is the state primacy an end in itself?

In the short-term perspective, however, Putin's ideological shift has been effective. In 2012–13 it helped him discredit the defiant civic protesters. As polls show, by 2013 his conservative message was accepted by a majority: nearly all conservative, illiberal initiatives of the government, from a ban on American adoption of Russian orphans to censorship of the Web, enjoy broad public support. Putin may be unable to articulate a consistent legitimizing discourse, but he can still rely on an implicit consensus shared by a majority. This is a consensus of paternalism which accepts the notion of the government's omnipotence and lacks the notion of 'we, the people'. At the core of this paternalism lies a time-honored Russian strategy of adjustment to the will and whims of the state. One may demonstrate loyalty to the leadership, whatever its ideological shifts or policy initiatives, but at the same time deeply distrust it and figure out escapes and 'hiding places' should the government's initiatives encroach too much on one's life. In the framework of this paternalism, trouble-makers who openly defy the state, expose the government's wrongdoings, express independent political ambitions, or come up with ideological messages are regarded with suspicion and disapproval.

The question is just how long this traditional paternalism will work in Russia and what can replace it. In this 'intangible' sphere, as in any

other in Russia, an attempt to look into the future starts with the price
of oil (see Boris Grozovsky's chapter in this volume).

 Russia is heavily dependent on commodities exports as its major
source of national revenues. Should this resource significantly diminish, Putin's conservative ideological exercise will hardly help him keep
the people demobilized and quiescent.

 But, even without a dramatic economic decline, in the next decade
several factors can be expected to erode paternalism and drive broader
social debates and movements: the Soviet legacy will be fading and
paternalistic experience will diminish; social and regional diversity will
grow; migration to big cities will continue; group interests will begin to
take shape; popular causes and leaders are likely to emerge.

Looking from the early 2010s, several trends can be envisioned
to inform the ideological realm and have an impact on the Russian
identities in the next decade.

Regionalization – for a variety of political and economic reasons,
federal government will have to delegate more authority to the
regions (see Nikolay Petrov's article in this volume). A 'refederal-
ization by default' will encourage local patriotism and make less
relevant the Kremlin's ideological engineering. This may have the
effect of enlivening local politics and boosting local identities and
local cohesion. Just how local identities will be shaped and which
factors – religious, cultural, ethnic, economic, and otherwise – will
play a role, will vary depending on the particular region.

Russia's quest for its post-communist identity will continue regardless
of which ideological messages may be imposed from above. The rise
 of **state nationalism** is an undeniable trend. As Putin capitalizes on
this trend and deepens it, he is arguably under pressure from more radical nationalist groups among his elites. He may seek to preempt them
and move farther toward conservative nationalism. But he may also fail
to keep this trend in check, be pushed aside and eventually replaced
by more conservative forces, sometimes referred to in Russia as 'Orthodox Christian Stalinists' – those are proponents of hard state oppression,
isolationism, and ultraconservative values.[32]

Ethnic nationalism is another powerful trend. Putin regards ethnic
and racial xenophobia as a major threat, and this view is fully
justified. The government is constantly on the alert and takes a
range of measures to reduce the risk of ethnic clashes. Putin's

emphasis on state nationalism may be also seen as an attempt to inoculate the nation against race- or faith-based xenophobia. But, as was mentioned above, this inoculation is not innocuous and can make things worse instead of better. Growing ethnic minorities in large cities exacerbate interethnic clashes and crime. Russian ethnic nationalists are resentful of the government's reluctance to endow 'native Russians' with a higher status vis-à-vis unwelcome minorities. Such views, with varying degrees of radicalism, are commonly articulated on websites and have a sizable following. The emergence of 'nativism' or a similar nationalist program as a legitimate political cause is not hard to imagine.

The egregious corruption, injustice, and inequality is feeding **left-wing sentiments** of a more or less liberal strain. As long as the government continues to deliver, no force or figure in Russia can send a credible message to the nation that it will deliver better than Putin's government does. But, if resources shrink, social energies will become harder to restrain.

The above-listed ideological trends may develop all at the same time, with varying intensity in various regions. They may take the shape of street activism and outbursts of public energies, or – maybe in the longer run – evolve as rallying points for political organization and competitive politics.

Notes

1. K. Rogov (2012) 'Gimn otstalosti', *Novaya Gazeta*, no. 99; K. Rogov (2013) ' "On eto ser'yozno?", ili Novaya doktrina Putina', *Novaya Gazeta*, no. 22.
2. Levada-Center (2012) 'Putch avgusta 1991 goda', Press release, http://www.levada.ru/16-08-2012/putch-avgusta-1991-goda
3. Russia is the only country of the communist world that does not have the opportunity (or a narrative for that matter) of blaming outside forces (occupiers, invaders) for post-communist setbacks. Other ex-Soviet states build their narratives, to varying degrees, on the condemnation of the Russian/Soviet oppression and the celebration of national liberation.
4. M. Lipman (2013) 'Stalin Is Not Dead: A Legacy That Holds Back Russia' in Th. de Waal (ed.) *The Stalin Puzzle* (Washington, DC: Carnegie Endowment for International Peace).
5. This national holiday commemorates the vote for Russia's sovereignty held on 12 June 1990 by the legislature of the Russian Federation, then still a constituent part of the USSR.
6. President of Russia (2010) 'New Year's Address to the Nation', http://eng.kremlin.ru/transcripts/1560

7. The 1,150th anniversary has to do with the historically chronicled events related to the beginning of Russian statehood and associated with Scandinavian Varangians.

8. President of Russia (2012) 'Address to the Federal Assembly', http://eng.kremlin.ru/transcripts/4739

9. The events of 1612 have to do with the end of the Time of Troubles – a period when the Russian royal succession was suddenly broken and Russia lived through political turmoil and a series of impostors. The choice of 4 November for a new holiday, named the Day of People's Unity, was arguably determined by a desire to shift the focus away from the Communist holiday of 7 November that many in post-communist Russia continued to celebrate. The official narrative behind the newly introduced holiday was vague at best.

10. Prior to his return to the Kremlin in 2012, Putin published an article 'Rossiya: natsional'ny vopros' (Russia: the national question) (*Nezavisimaya gazeta*, 23 January 2012). In it he reiterated his adherence to the concept of Russia as a multi-ethnic state: 'I am deeply convinced that attempts to profess ideas of building a Russian "national" monoethnic state are in conflict with all our thousand-year history. Moreover, this is the shortest path to annihilating the Russian people and the Russian statehood.'

11. See, for instance, I. Varlamov (2012) 'Russkiy marsh', http://echo.msk.ru/blog/varlamov_i/947782-echo/

12. Levada-Center (2012) *Obschestvennoe mnenie–2012* (Public Opinion – 2012), Yearbook (Moscow: Levada-Center), 229.

13. L. Gudkov (2013) 'The Archetype of the Leader: Analyzing a Totalitarian Symbol' in Th. de Waal (ed.) *The Stalin Puzzle* (Washington, DC: Carnegie Endowment for International Peace).

14. Another universally and positively remembered figure is Yuri Gagarin, Russia's first cosmonaut. Russia's exploration of space is also broadly remembered as a major post-war achievement.

15. Polling data indicate that the line 'Russia is for Russians' is fairly popular. The xenophobic sentiments most often have 'people from the Caucasus' as the target, not surprisingly after two bloody Chechen wars in which Chechens were the enemy of the 'federal' soldiers. See: *Obschestvennoe mnenie–2012* (Public Opinion – 2012), Yearbook (Moscow: Levada-Center), 179.

16. President of Russia (2010) 'Transcript of joint meeting of State Council and Commission for Implementation of Priority National Projects and Demographic Policy', 27 December 2010, The Kremlin, Moscow, http://kremlin.ru/transcripts/9913 (in Russian). The Soviet 'peoples' friendship' was enforced by rigid constraints on individual or group self-expression that helped muffle ethnic tensions and prevent ethnic violence, while the government itself repressed and discriminated against various groups on the basis of their ethnicity.

17. President of Russia (2012) 'Meeting with Regional Human Rights Ombudspersons', 16 August 2012, The Kremlin, Moscow, http://kremlin.ru/transcripts/16260 (in Russian).

18. President of Russia (2012) 'Address to the Federal Assembly', http://kremlin.ru/transcripts/17118 (in Russian).

19. The article is a powerful denunciation of nationalism and xenophobia and a warning against ethnic bias. It calls for civic piece, tolerance, and respect for the Other. It ends with a pledge 'to live together as we have lived for ages' and warns against attempts 'to divide us'. It contains sharp criticism of Western experience of nation building and a glorification of pre-revolutionary Russia's experience of cohabitation of many peoples (without ever mentioning that the Russian Empire was based on religious rather than ethnic or civic identification and openly discriminated against certain denominations other than Orthodox Christian). Putin's piece gets murky and illogical when it comes to describing what 'Russians' are, if not ethnic.

20. National Policy Strategy of the Russian Federation through to 2025 (2012), http://kremlin.ru/news/17165 (in Russian).

21. This difference between Stalin's and Lenin's visions may explain the gradual decline of Lenin's popularity. (See: M. Lipman (2013) 'Stalin Lives', *Foreign Policy – Democracy Lab*, http://www.foreignpolicy.com/articles/2013/03/01/stalin_lives). Lenin's cosmopolitanism is inappropriate in Putin's conservative political design. In early 2013 Putin denounced Lenin's Bolshevik government's separate peace in Germany in 1918 and its withdrawal from the First World War as 'national treason' (see: *Izvestiya* (2012) 'Putin obvinil bol'shevikov v natsional'nom predatel'stve,' *Izvestiya*, 27 June). He later justified the Soviet 1939–40 invasion of and war with Finland as a rectification of that 'mistake' (see: *RIA Novosti* (2013) 'Putin: SSSR v voyne s Finlyandiey hotel ispravit' oshibki 1917 goda', http://ria.ru/society/20130314/927341148.html).

22. In 2006 Putin's chief 'ideologue' Vladislav Surkov said: 'Russia is a European country. However special it may seem to us, ... overall, we have gone through the same path as other European nations.' In a 2002 interview Putin said: 'Russia is, no doubt, a European country, because it is a country of European culture.' See: President of Russia (2002) 'Interview of Russian President Vladimir Putin with the Polish newspaper "Gazeta Wyborcza" and Polish TV channel "TVP" ', 14 January 2002, Moscow, The Kremlin, http://archive.kremlin.ru/text/appears/2002/01/28773.shtml.

23. O. Kuzmenkova (2012) 'Byli "sovetskie", stali "pravoslavnye" ', http://www.gazeta.ru/politics/2012/11/20_a_4860629.shtml

24. Levada-Center (2012) *Obschestvennoe mnenie–2012* (Public Opinion –2012), Yearbook (Moscow: Levada-Center), 19.

25. Sberbank of Russia (2012) 'Innovatsionniy i predprinimatel'skiy potentsial obschestva' (Innovative and Entrepreneurial Potential of Society), Survey by Levada Center commissioned by Macroeconomic Research Center, Sberbank, http://www.sbrf.ru/common/img/uploaded/files/pdf/press_center/2012/1/IPPS.pdf

26. Levada-Center (2013) 'Rossiyane o politicheskoy i ekonomicheskoy sisteme strany', Press Release, http://www.levada.ru/08-02-2013/rossiyane-o-politicheskoi-i-ekonomicheskoi-sisteme-strany

27. Th. Gustafson (2012) *Wheel of Fortune: The Battle for Oil and Power in Russia* (Belknap Press), 482–3.

28. N. Petrov, M. Lipman, and H.E. Hale (2010) *Overmanaged Democracy in Russia: Governance Implications of Hybrid Regimes*, Carnegie Papers No. 106 (Washington, DC: Carnegie Endowment for International Peace); M. Lipman

(2011) 'Russia's Non-Participation Pact', http://www.project-syndicate.org/commentary/russia-s-no-participation-pact.
29. President of Russia (2013) 'Meeting of Council for Interethnic Relations', 19 February 2013, Moscow, http://eng.kremlin.ru/transcripts/5017
30. M. Senchukova (2013) 'Arkhimandrit Tikhon (Shevkunov): o molodykh dushoy, igrakh na gryaznom pole i "tserkovnykh biznesmenakh"', http://www.pravmir.ru/arximandrit-tixon-shevkunov-o-molodyx-dushoj-igrax-na-gryaznom-pole-i-cerkovnyx-biznesmenax-video/
31. V. Bagdasaryan (2012) *Istoriya Rossii. Uchebnik dlya uchitelya* (Governance and Problem Analysis Center; Moscow: Nauchniy ekspert), Chapter 31 (Istoriosofiya Rossii (Historiosophy of Russia)), http://rusrand.ru/dev/uchebnik-istorii
32. For example, Orthodox Christian Stalinists as a potential alternative to Putin's elite of *chekist* (secret police) bureaucracy were mentioned by Leonid Radzikhovsky in March 2013: L. Radzikhovsky (2013) 'Chestnye vybory', http://www.echo.msk.ru/blog/radzihovski/1030072-echo/

Bibliography

V. Bagdasaryan (2012) *Istoriya Rossii. Uchebnik dlya uchitelya* (Governance and Problem Analysis Center; Moscow: Nauchniy ekspert).
L. Gudkov, (2013) 'The Archetype of the Leader: Analyzing a Totalitarian Symbol' in Th. de Waal (ed.) *The Stalin Puzzle* (Washington, DC: Carnegie Endowment for International Peace), 29–46.
Th. Gustafson (2012) *Wheel of Fortune: The Battle for Oil and Power in Russia* (Cambridge, MA: Belknap Press), 482–3.
Izvestiya (2012) 'Putin obvinil bol'shevikov v natsional'nom predatel'stve', *Izvestiya*, 27 June.
O. Kuzmenkova (2012) 'Byli "sovetskie", stali "pravoslavnye"', http://www.gazeta.ru/politics/2012/11/20_a_4860629.shtml, accessed on April 5, 2013.
Levada-Center (2012) *Obschestvennoe mnenie–2012* (Public Opinion – 2012), Yearbook (Moscow: Levada-Center).
Levada-Center (2012) 'Putch avgusta 1991 goda', Press release, http://www.levada.ru/16-08-2012/putch-avgusta-1991-goda, accessed on April 5, 2013.
Levada-Center (2013) 'Rossiyane o politicheskoy i ekonomicheskoy sisteme strany', Press Release, http://www.levada.ru/08-02-2013/rossiyane-o-politicheskoi-i-ekonomicheskoi-sisteme-strany, accessed on April 5, 2013.
M. Lipman (2011) 'Russia's Non-Participation Pact', http://www.project-syndicate.org/commentary/russia-s-no-participation-pact
M. Lipman (2013) 'Stalin Lives', *Foreign Policy – Democracy Lab*, http://www.foreignpolicy.com/articles/2013/03/01/stalin_lives, accessed on April 5, 2013.
M. Lipman (2013) 'Stalin Is Not Dead: A Legacy That Holds Back Russia' in Th. de Waal (ed.) *The Stalin Puzzle* (Washington, DC: Carnegie Endowment for International Peace), 15–28.
National Policy Strategy of the Russian Federation through to 2025 (2012), http://kremlin.ru/news/17165 (in Russian), accessed on April 5, 2013.
N. Petrov, M. Lipman, and H. E. Hale (2010) *Overmanaged Democracy in Russia: Governance Implications of Hybrid Regimes*, Carnegie Papers No 106 (Washington, DC: Carnegie Endowment for International Peace).

President of Russia (2002) 'Interview of Russian President Vladimir Putin with the Polish newspaper "Gazeta Wyborcza" and Polish TV channel "TVP"', 14 January 2002, Moscow, The Kremlin', http://archive. kremlin. ru/text/appears/2002/01/28773.shtml (in Russian), accessed on April 5, 2013.

President of Russia (2010) 'New Year's Address to the Nation', http://eng.kremlin. ru/transcripts/1560, accessed on April 5, 2013.

President of Russia (2010) 'Transcript of joint meeting of State Council and Commission for Implementation of Priority National Projects and Demographic Policy', 27 December 2010, The Kremlin, Moscow, http://kremlin.ru/ transcripts/9913 (in Russian), accessed on April 5, 2013.

President of Russia (2012) 'Address to the Federal Assembly', http://eng.kremlin. ru/transcripts/4739, accessed on April 5, 2013.

President of Russia (2012) 'Address to the Federal Assembly', http://kremlin.ru/ transcripts/17118 (in Russian), accessed on April 5, 2013.

President of Russia (2012) 'Meeting with regional human rights ombudspersons', 16 August 2012, The Kremlin, Moscow, http://kremlin.ru/ transcripts/16260 (in Russian), accessed on April 5, 2013.

President of Russia (2013) 'Meeting of Council for Interethnic Relations', 19 February 2013, Moscow, http://eng.kremlin.ru/transcripts/5017, accessed on April 5, 2013.

V. Putin (2012) 'Rossiya: natsional'ny vopros', *Nezavisimaya gazeta*, 23 January.

L. Radzikhovsky (2013) 'Chestnye vybory', http://www.echo.msk.ru/blog/ radzihovski/1030072-echo/, accessed on April 5, 2013.

RIA Novosti (2013) 'Putin: SSSR v voyne s Finlyandiey hotel ispravit' oshibki 1917 goda', http://ria.ru/society/20130314/927341148.html, accessed on April 5, 2013.

K. Rogov (2012) 'Gimn otstalosti', *Novaya Gazeta*, no. 99.

K. Rogov (2013) ' "On eto ser'yozno?," ili Novaya doktrina Putina', *Novaya Gazeta*, no. 22.

Sberbank of Russia (2012) 'Innovatsionniy i predprinimatel'skiy potentsial obschestva' (Innovative and Entrepreneurial Potential of Society), Survey by Levada Center on demand of Macroeconomic Research Center, Sberbank, http://www.sbrf.ru/common/img/uploaded/files/pdf/press_center/2012/1/IPPS. pdf, accessed on April 5, 2013.

M. Senchukova (2013) 'Arkhimandrit Tikhon (Shevkunov): o molodykh dushoy, igrakh na gryaznom pole i "tserkovnykh biznesmenakh" ', http:// www.pravmir.ru/arximandrit-tixon-shevkunov-o-molodyx-dushoj-igrax-na- gryaznom-pole-i-cerkovnyx-biznesmenax-video/, accessed on April 5, 2013.

I. Varlamov (2012) 'Russkiy marsh', http://echo.msk.ru/blog/varlamov_i/947782- echo/, accessed on April 5, 2013.

12
The World after Democracy Won

Fedor Lukyanov

The year 2025 is quite close at hand; hence, any attempts at predicting future developments automatically assume the absence of dramatic change and, upon making minor adjustments, project the current trends into the future. This approach underlies a number of studies. In 2008 and 2012, the US National Intelligence Council published reports on global trends for the years 2025 and 2030. In 2011, a similar project entitled 'Strategic Global Forecast 2030' was completed in Russia by the Moscow Institute of World Economics and International Relationships.

Meanwhile, a retrospective analysis that examines time segments of 12 to 13 years in length suggests that ordinary trend projections do not generally take into account and fail to predict sudden political change that alters the vector of political development. In 2000, as the 'carefree 90s' were drawing to a close, the West was still celebrating its Cold War victory, failing to observe many alarming trends. Almost no one could predict the events of September 11, the severe European integration crisis or the talk of decline of the West and the US that became commonplace in the early 2010s. Who could imagine that the leading states of the 'free world', while desperately trying to adjust to the sea changes across the globe, would end up on the same side as the powers they had been mercilessly fighting against until recently?

Let us take one more step back – this time into the years 1987 and 1988. No one could fathom that Europe and the entire world were on the brink of a genuine revolution that would herald a collapse of the world political order. In fact, Erich Honecker's statement that the Anti-Fascist Protective Wall (the term used in the East Germany to refer to the Berlin Wall) would be standing for another 100 years seemed quite reasonable in January 1989.

Futurology and science fiction, which were in their prime in the 1960s and 1970s, predicted scientific and technological change quite accurately but failed miserably when it came to describing social, and especially political, change. The political essayist Nassim Taleb encapsulated this inability to predict the political future in his concept of black swans.[1] In essence, this simply posits that anything may happen, causing everything else to go wrong. What a great analytical tool for predicting the future!

Indeed, looking into the future is a trying task when dealing with today's globalized world, where states and peoples representing different cultures, epochs, and social realities come into constant and close contact. The hierarchy of states on the global arena is being eroded, and with it the hierarchy of values that these states embody. In the past, we saw the competition of ideologies and economic systems in which one could clearly declare the winner. Now, we are witnessing another kind of competition that lacks criteria for declaring winners. For instance, lower indicators on military or economic scales can be offset by nimble reaction or an ability to accurately assess the current developments (the absence of ideological baggage allows such assessments).

This erosion of hierarchies is bound to affect changes in foreign relations, while the ever-increasing global transparency and interconnectedness may produce some strange configurations. The states that were previously satisfied with their secondary roles on the world stage will now aspire to an equal and more prominent place in the global system.

The fight against privileges

Let us take a peek into the near future. The Review Conference of the Parties to the Treaty on the Non-Proliferation of Nuclear Weapons is scheduled to take place in May 2015 in Vienna, the home of the International Atomic Energy Agency. The forum takes place every five years and has long stopped generating any excitement. For example, the 2010 conference agreed to a final document for the first time in many years, which was considered a major accomplishment despite the document's vagueness.

The 2015 conference, however, attracted a lot of attention. Ever since the Israeli air force attacked Iran's nuclear installations in the fall of 2014, the subject of the limits to non-proliferation has become especially relevant. The long-awaited and much-feared confrontation between Israel and Iran, in which the US supported the former militarily and politically, brought no resolution. Despite panic predictions, the attack did not thrust the world into global conflict, although the immediate terrorist response claimed many lives around the Middle East. However, the attack did not achieve its objectives. According to the intelligence reports, Iran did not sustain critical damage as a result of the Israeli strikes; in fact, the population of the Islamic republic had again consolidated around its theocratic government, quickly rebuilding the country's potential. Moreover, despite the extremely tense relations between Iran and the majority of Sunni Arab states (the Persian Gulf regimes silently approved of Israel's actions), massive popular unrest forced the Sunni Arab leaders to express their support for Teheran.

In this context, the Vienna forum started with a bang. Brazil, Turkey, and South Africa made a joint statement, demanding the revision of the Non-Proliferation Treaty (NPT). They assailed the treaty as discriminatory, since it stipulates that only five countries (the US, Russia, China, the UK, and France) should be granted the right to have nuclear weapons. India, a country that did not sign the treaty and thus acquired its nuclear weapons 'illegally', threw its full support behind the rebels. Brazil's former President Lula, who was present at the forum as his president's special representative, spoke on behalf of the 'revisionists'. In his passionate rebuke of the treaty, Lula called it discriminatory, antiquated, and blatantly hypocritical. 'The treaty violates every norm of equality in foreign relations,' said Lula. 'The hypocrisy is stunning. One country (Israel) that acquired its nuclear weapons illegally (in NPT terms) strikes another country to prevent it from doing the same. What is even more revolting, the sponsors of the treaty do nothing to stop the attack, and some of them even encourage it.'

Other speakers that represented small and medium states essentially supported the 'troika' and called for immediate discussions on revising the treaty. The representatives of the five 'legal' nuclear powers were shocked by this universal pressure and called an emergency meeting...

Such a scenario seems highly fictional at this time, but the criticism of inequality on the global stage is quite real and gaining popularity. Since the end of the Cold War, the question of reforming major international institutions to account for the new global balance of power has been raised numerous times. The discussion primarily revolves around the reform of the Security Council, whose permanent members have a right of veto obtained as a result of winning a war that ended almost 70 years ago, during a totally different era.

However, the Security Council reform is impossible for two reasons. First is the issue of selection criteria. The issue is easily resolved if the international governing body is being formed in the aftermath of a major conflict (the winner-takes-all criterion is adopted in this case). But there is currently no such conflict, so the question of selection criteria arises. What makes a country eligible to become a permanent member? Is it its economic might, population, leadership in the region, or perhaps military strength? The second obstacle is the current permanent members. They have to agree to the changes in the makeup of the Security Council, and they will never do so of their own accord. States do not simply give up their exclusive privileges; they tend to fight for them tooth and nail.

Nevertheless, this legalized inequality draws more and more criticism. The rights of the self-appointed world leaders are especially tenuous, since they are unable to perform their leadership functions and fail at conflict resolution. The Security Council either does nothing or makes decisions that accommodate the self-centered interests of major powers, primarily the US and Russia. In the meantime, the world is becoming less predictable and more dangerous. As a matter of fact, when the large countries do get involved in solving global and regional problems, these problems are quite often exacerbated. (Vladimir Putin has made a number of characteristically sharp remarks on this issue.)[2] First of all, due to global interactions and interconnectedness, cause-and-effect relationships are no longer linear; they are constantly affected by external factors that distort the projected outcome. Second, the US and other major global players increasingly resort to reactive politics, trying to adjust to sudden change. The Arab Spring events of 2011 and 2012 have clearly demonstrated that there can be no working strategy dealing with the turmoil that engulfed the region. The 'right side of history' rhetoric results in a paradox: the US suddenly finds itself aligned with the groups it had fought against just recently and is actually still fighting on different turf.

This state of flux has, in a way, benefited the midsize actors. Unable to effectively implement their grand strategies, the large states are forced to curry favor with the smaller states.

The Russian diplomats and political scholars often talk of democratization of foreign relations in the 21st century, saying that the global actors will no longer stand for the hegemony that they associate with the US. It is true that bloc discipline has long become a relic of the past, and the countries that had previously taken orders from the superpowers are now more independent. But the US is not the only country to bear the brunt of these changes; other countries are affected as well, and Russia is no exception.

Moscow finds itself in a strange predicament. It constantly stresses that most of its views do not agree with those of the West. It suggests alternative responses but offers no alternative model, nor does it stake any leadership claims in this department. Ultimately, Russia prefers to come to terms with the West rather than openly confront it. Nevertheless, it does not present itself as part of the West at the negotiating table and claims to protect the interest of the 'Third World' countries.

But, paradoxically, as the movement toward equality gains more ground, Russia will not be able to reap the reward of its advocacy efforts; it is most likely to end up in the minority camp and will be perceived as another usurper of majority rights. In the coming decades, the minority will have to justify its privileged status or come up with a power distribution arrangement that does not compromise it.

Will the General Assembly rule the world?

Ever since nation states appeared on the political map, the stable and generally accepted balance of power system has always been a product of large-scale armed conflicts. If a conflict had failed to produce such a system (as was the case with World War I), the tensions rapidly escalated again, sometimes culminating in a new war.

The Cold War marked a unique period in the history of international relations, since the standoff between the two equally strong superpowers ensured the remarkable stability of the entire system. This had never been done in the past, nor has it been possible since the arrangement collapsed. The end of the Cold War is no less amazing in historical perspective. The confrontation ended without ever reaching its 'hot' stage, and neither of the sides officially admitted defeat. Of course, everyone knows who ended up on the losing side, but there is still a debate over what caused the Soviet Union to collapse. Some say the country could not handle the pressures of the arms race, some see the devious American hand that sabotaged its adversary; others believe the elites' suicidal squabble destroyed the Soviet Union from within. There are also those who think that the country exhausted its social drive and simply gave up. Be that as it may, no peace treaty was signed as the standoff ended. There was no document that would outline the political contours of the new international system as the peace treaties of the 19th and 20th centuries had done.

In 1992 President Bush officially declared that 'by the grace of God, America won the Cold War'[3]; however, all the subsequent efforts to construct 'the new world order' (the term coined by Gorbachev, but adopted by Bush) were ad hoc. As it later turned out, this state of affairs was flawed mainly because it provided no incentive to alter the institutional design of the global political system. No agreement on the new principles of global governance was reached, and the perception that international structures would gradually evolve on their own prevailed. This did not happen, though. As a result, the world has changed beyond recognition, while the privileged global players still want to retain the antiquated system.

Why Russia, France, and the UK guard the sanctity of the current makeup of the Security Council is understandable – any reforms will reduce their relative powers, since their current role in the system is significantly smaller that it was in 1945. However, the US is just as reluctant to discuss possible change, although it hardly has reason to fear any loss of power, given the status it now enjoys on the global stage. The US was actually willing to discard the Security Council and the UN altogether in favor of some alternative institution. But this proposition was not feasible, the enormous influence of the US notwithstanding, so the Americans settled for the status quo. It is even more remarkable that China also opposes any reform, although it plays an incomparably greater role in today's international system than it did in the middle of the 20th century. However, Beijing understands that Japan and India are likely to gain permanent status in the reformed Security Council. These countries do not particularly trust China, to put it mildly, and are determined to contain it.

The deliberations in the Security Council became more substantive in the late 2000s–early 2010s than they were at the start of the new century, but the institution is not going to seriously affect international politics in the coming years. Nevertheless, both internal and external debate on the role and structure of the UN accurately reflect the state of the international system, and especially the international community's views on its change. In fact, there can be no other forum whose decisions are as legitimate.

This being the case, the UN's coordinating role in solving global problems has seriously weakened. The failure of climate talks is a clear example, although this issue has been among the most pressing challenges facing the international community since the mid-1990s. The UN failures cannot be attributed exclusively to the conflicts of interests and dysfunctional organizational structures. The problem is rooted in a qualitative change in the state of the international system. While we are constantly told that global problems have no local solutions in the era of universal and multi-vector globalization, the reality proves the opposite. The big treaties and universal conventions are on their way out as the number of views that can no longer be ignored grows, rendering any substantive compromise impossible or too amorphous to be meaningful.

The UN metamorphosis will continue in the next 15 years. The importance of the Security Council as the world government no longer reflects the real balance of power and will keep declining, while the role of the General Assembly as the most representative forum of this planet and the place for public debate will increase. So far, the calls for greater rights for the General Assembly and the end to privileges come from the most controversial public figures, such as Iran's President Mahmud Ahmadinejad.[4] But these calls are indicative of the growing sentiments on this issue.

While the General Assembly acts in an advisory capacity, and its resolutions are not binding, smaller states tend to use their numerical advantage to put pressure on the permanent members if their interests are ignored. As a rule, the General Assembly, which makes decisions by majority vote, does not support large states. For instance, the vote on Georgia's territorial integrity did not go Russia's way despite its efforts, and the resolutions in support of the Palestinian state were passed in the face of US opposition.

International relations are becoming more democratic, and once subordinate actors will inevitably come to play a more active role. The 'third world' countries traditionally hold the UN in higher regard than the superpowers do. This is perfectly understandable, since they represent the overwhelming majority of the UN members. So far, the numbers have not translated into influence, but this may happen at some point. While the binding decisions are still in the hands of the permanent members, the general organizational direction will shift in favor of the countries that have no veto powers but openly express an alternative point of view.

We could see the precursor of possible changes in 2010, when Turkey and Brazil made the surprising announcement that they had reached an agreement with Iran immediately before the Security Council voted on sanctions against this country.[5] Other members of the Security Council did not even deign to discuss the initiative, totally ignoring the upstarts, but the actions of such important players could not go unnoticed (Brazil and Turkey were the only members to abstain during the eventual vote).

A clearly delineated, albeit informal, division of labor existed in the UN at the time of the Cold War. The General Assembly provided impressive entourage and gave the entire international community a chance to let off some steam, while the Security Council was the forum for the political intrigue of the powerful members that actually affected the big politics. Currently, the Security Council still remains such a place, but the General Assembly will speak in a much louder voice, forcing the powerful states to take notice.

The impossibility of big wars

Although the start of the 21st century was marked by escalating tensions, they did not culminate in large-scale conflicts similar to those of the 20th century. Nuclear weapons, which still function as an important deterrent, largely account for the absence of such conflicts. Sergey Karaganov points out that the incredibly rapid shift in the balance of power away from Europe and toward Asia would not have been so smooth were it not for the deterrent effect of nuclear weapons.[6] Historically, such shifts have almost always been accompanied by wars. With further nuclear proliferation, states that are less capable of the delicate balancing act once performed by the USSR and the US are coming to possess nuclear weapons. Still, while the nuclear weapons remain under state control, the situation is manageable. However, as non-state actors get hold of them, the situation threatens to spin out of control. While this scenario is not as simple to implement as Hollywood blockbusters might suggest, it may not be completely ruled out.

Besides affecting the relations between world powers, the presence of nuclear weapons turns into a powerful instrument for smaller states. It allows them to guarantee their integrity and be heard on the global stage. The case in point is North Korea, the state of little power and influence that forced the international community to take it seriously because of its nuclear program. On the flip side are the examples of Saddam Hussein's and Muammar Kaddafi's collapsed regimes. Neither of them had weapons of mass destruction; in fact, Kaddafi voluntarily gave up his nuclear program. These examples suggest that the presence of WMD, even in its most rudimentary form, raises the risks of invasion to an unacceptably high level.

Great powers also benefit from having nuclear weapons. Russia's decline, much talked about in the last two decades, is offset due to the world's second largest nuclear arsenal. However, it does not substitute for other attributes of power, since the power phenomenon in the modern world is extremely complex and quite obscure.[7]

Nuclear weapons make world wars impossible by ruling out battlefield combat, the simplest and best-known method of determining strength.

At the same time, they encourage the use of other instruments of power. Drawing the red line does not only restrain parties, but also designates the safety margin, making for an intense and diverse confrontation before the line is reached.

The late 20th century brought about a belief that 'soft power' would gradually replace the traditional use of force. This belief has only partially materialized. Indeed, power is becoming a more complex, multi-layered phenomenon. It is comprised of military, political, ideological, cultural, religious, and economic components, whose proportions are constantly changing. The undisputed military dominance of the US often gives rise to a strange paradox. Militarily, the US is too far ahead of every other country, but the conflicts it is involved in do not require such an overwhelming advantage. Nuclear deterrence precludes the US from fighting against other major powers. But using high-tech contact-free warfare against Afghan rebels is either ineffective or counterproductive. For instance, the use of drones in Afghanistan or Pakistan has come to symbolize the blind brutality of the US.

In any event, the confusion around identifying the elements of power also complicates international relations. As Timofey Bordachev notes, 'the links and – most importantly – interdependencies between the states pegged on the power factor are getting loose. In other words, the fear of each other's power as the main bond keeping the international system together is vanishing.' He also reminds us that the international system cannot be managed; instead, 'it can generate the demand for a particular form of behavior on the part of participating states ... The young global community has only one clearly articulated wish, which is to oppose any form of domination and external restrictions on its members' freedom (sovereignty).'[8]

Russia in the middle

What does this all mean for Russia and its place in the world by the year 2025? The next 12 years are bound to bring change. Whether Moscow likes it or not, it will be unable to maintain the foundations of the foreign policy it conducted at the start of the 21st century.

What was the essence of 'Putin's doctrine'? The foreign policy of the 2000s and early 2010s has been reactive: it almost always responds to external impulses without generating its own. Putin's firebrand rhetoric notwithstanding, Russia's foreign policy has been generally characterized by caution. It placed the country's prestige at the center. There is always some value in bolstering a country's prestige, but it was particularly important to Russia in the second half of the 2000s as the country was failing to integrate into the West's institutional framework and facing growing external pressure. With the global situation growing more complicated in the 2010s, the offensive posture is giving way to the defensive one –external impulses are avoided and extinguished whenever possible.

Putin's Russia values its freedom and is maneuvering between the West and the East, trying to avoid commitment to any alliance. Thus, Russia's primarily anti-Western rhetoric is combined with working with mostly Western partners. Russians respect the fact that Putin was able to restore the national pride after the humiliating failures of the 1990s. So, in the 2000s and early 2010s, the country's foreign policy enjoyed overwhelming nationwide support.

There are two different perceptions of Russia on the world stage. In the West, it is generally looked at as an extremely obstinate partner that often acts as a spoiler. While Russia resists integration, the West still views it as a useful partner in certain cases. The East, on the other hand, sees, or would like to see, Russia – the successor to the Soviet Union, which played a role of system alternative – as a counterbalance to the overpowering dominance of the West. It was this combination of the international and domestic perceptions that enabled Russia to conduct a coherent, although not always consistent, policy. It factored in the inefficiency and errors on the part of other great powers that are experiencing a painful transition from absolute hegemony to being first among unequals. Using a limited range of instruments, Putin's Russia successfully capitalized on their weaknesses.

However, the consensus is now being eroded both internally and externally. Russia's universal drive for resurgence and greater prestige has reached its natural limit and also does not reflect the entire spectrum of interests. A more detailed and goal-oriented foreign policy that is no longer based on the absolute unity of opinions will be required. As the protests of 2011–12 have revealed, the maturing society will not toe the party line anymore, whatever that line may be. The changes inside Russia are likely to affect the country's foreign policy.

For instance, one can expect Russia's Muslims from Caucasus, Tatarstan, or Bashkortostan to be critical of Moscow's position on Arab Spring, Syria, and similar conflicts. Russia's Muslim community will hardly speak with one voice, but it will certainly demand that its views be given more respect than they have been in the past.

The international climate will meet internal social change. The internationalist and secular Soviet legacy has completed its life cycle; a new identity is being formed, generating new principles. With the Islamic world in turmoil, Russia's inter-faith relations and its foreign policy will become much more interrelated than they are today. In this respect, the role of the Russian Orthodox Church in shaping the country's foreign policy will be increasingly important. The Church probably has its own perspective on Russia's priorities on the global stage, and it intends to weigh in on this issue as political life becomes more diversified.

Post-imperial transformation is another uncertainty factor which leads to the weakening, or at least rethinking, of the past expansionist instincts. As the Soviet collapse fades from recent history, the nationalists of different stripes become more visible. Their ranks include both rabid hatemongers and sophisticated intellectuals from the 'New Right'. Neither group is impressed by Putin's intention to create the Eurasian Union. Rather, their goal is to prohibit the citizens of virtually all Eurasian states from entering Russia, which will probably happen in any case out of purely practical considerations. Nevertheless, as strange as it may sound, the nationalist outlook may still end up being quite pro-Western in the spectrum of Russian ideological thought, although the idea of 'white Europe' attracts them more than any other.

The new stage of Russia's development that came to replace the post-Soviet era has brought forth a salad bowl of culture and ideology where the components are too intermixed to permit the regime to conduct a policy that is clearly devoid of ideological overtones and based solely on pragmatism. Until now, Russia has been unencumbered by dogmatic restraints, which gave it the edge over the ideologically driven policies of the US and the European Union. However, there is a growing need for an ideal that would consolidate pluralistic society. Conversely, conducting mercantilist policies and disregarding values will rally different forces against the system. It is not accidental that the year 2012 was marked by the discussion of values (though for the most part quite strange and distorted). The Presidential Address to the Federal Assembly was also replete with allusions to ethics and morality.[9] The emerging protective and traditionalist values will certainly influence foreign policy. Perhaps it will become more cohesive and consistent, but the detached, flexible approach used until today will be lost.

After Vladimir Putin's return to presidency, the discussions of Russia's foreign policy acquired a new element. It is called 'soft power', and the head of state instructs the diplomatic corps to work on strengthening it while counteracting Russia's negative image.[10] The president is primarily concerned with counterpropaganda, although the counterpropaganda of today is substantially different from its Soviet version.

At that time, the information transmitted to the West did not have to take into account the reality inside the country. With the current informational transparency, such behavior is impossible. The countries that possess significant soft power and are able to affect others without apparent pressure or coercion thus display their own political order and norms.

The normative approach has not characterized post-Soviet Russian politics. The brief period that followed the collapse of the Soviet Union was perhaps the only exception. At that time, Russia and other post-communist countries were trying to join the rank of liberal democracies. But the emphasis on the belief system was quickly replaced by pragmatism, expediency, and avarice.

The situation is beginning to change as the Soviet Union is buried deeper in history. Until recently, the debate on ideology had mostly revolved around the Soviet legacy and the consequences of the country's collapse. But this debate has exhausted itself and cannot produce any new ideas. The mercantilist and valueless politics is also a thing of the past. Therefore, both the regime and society feel that an ideological base for the current policies and a vision for the future are needed. However, the vision is lacking, so the void is being filled haphazardly.

It is quite logical, then, that the demise of the Soviet values prompts explorations of the pre-Soviet era in an attempt to find 'Russia that we lost'. After all, the Eastern European and Baltic states had restored their pre-communist statehood. Such impulses were common in the late 1980s and early 1990s, when the descendants of the Romanov dynasty frequented Russia and quasi-imperial pop culture trimmings abounded. But the attempts to re-create the historical narrative quickly faded, leaving the eclectic and arbitrarily selected array of fragments taken out of historical context.

The newfound return to tradition points to confusion. When Putin talks of 'moral ties', he is not simply being rhetorical; he actually does view them as a necessary condition for further development. But where these ties come from remains unclear.

Russia's domestic and foreign policies are clearly drifting toward conservatism. Domestically, Russia positions itself as the keeper of traditional values, while internationally it portrays itself as the guardian of the status quo. (Those who like to draw historical parallels may remember Russia as a pillar of legitimism and the Holy Alliance during the reign of Nicholas I.) On the global arena, the country unambiguously denounces any revolution as a source of instability and insists on the sanctity of national sovereignty. Inside the country, the regime emphasizes traditional values, sharply contrasting them with liberal ones. Religion is gaining a more prominent place in social life, and moralizing sermons – almost non-existent until very recently – are becoming more common.

While the Eastern European countries did not spend enough time under communist rule to lose tradition completely, Russia had its traditional life destroyed during the Soviet era. Any attempts to restore it are impossible. The best the regime can do is imitate it. Moreover, the development that Russia so desperately needs is incompatible with conservative and archaic approaches to social and political life. A few years ago, the premise of stability inspired the United Russia Party to come up with the concept of 'conservative modernization'. Now the situation is considerably worse: we can talk of 'reactionary modernization', modernization that leads to deceleration.

What about 'soft power'? Clearly, it will not work in the West. The described approach contradicts liberalism and opposes the US and Europe. It will have a limited impact in the East as well, since a positive image should feature a progressive agenda. The most conservative regimes, such as those in the Persian Gulf, will not be interested either – for geopolitical and religious reasons.

At any event, the era of political consensus is drawing to a close. In the future, the Russian authorities will have to deal with a much greater variety of views. As Russia becomes more democratic, its foreign policy will grow more complex, but its responses will be less predictable.

And, as the world becomes more democratic and pluralistic, Russia's image in the eyes of the world will become more ambivalent. In essence, the traditionalist Russia that is distancing itself from Western normative standards will be increasingly viewed by the West as drifting toward the 'alien' East. On the other hand, the East will resent Russia's inconsistency in opposing the West and the privileged status it gained at the time of Western dominance (for example, its Security Council Permanent membership, the NPT terms). So the East will treat Russia as part of the West, which is paradoxically the complete opposite of what Russia will need in the coming years. The country has to strengthen its cultural, historical, and normative ties to Europe, since it has no alternative self-identification and is not likely to develop one. At the same time, Asia is moving to the center of the global stage, and Russia has to reorient itself toward this part of the world both economically and politically. The dilemma may play itself out in the coming years as the competition between the US and China intensifies. Russia will have to formulate the right response to it. Ideally, Moscow needs to play an active but neutral role, although both sides will try to take advantage of it.

When it comes to other existing or growing power centers, Russia will have to come up with far more nuanced policies and priorities. This will not be an easy task, especially given the perceptions that Russia is declining, which the Russian leadership will have to counter. The West already treats Russia as a waning power, despite being proven wrong by Putin's diplomacy a number of times. The rising and rapidly developing states of the East will contrast Russia's development with their own. Russia's inability to reform itself, diversify, and accelerate its growth – absent a sudden turn for the better – will not look good when compared with the flexible and dynamic East. In short, Russia's woes will cast doubts on the country's future. Besides, Russia's colonial and superpower past will hold it back from joining the chorus of those demanding equality and institutional reform on the world stage. On the other hand, being ready and able to act independently will be an asset under any scenario, especially in the ever more chaotic global picture.

* * *

The Economist's deputy chief editor Norman Macrae wrote a book entitled *The 2025 Report: A Concise History of the Future, 1975–2025*, published in New York in 1985. The author, who, as one might expect, was a devout market liberal, predicted many of the next century's economic breakthroughs and innovations. He was quite accurate in assessing the fate that befell the Soviet Union: he thought the state would not survive in the absence of serious reform. He expected the Soviet Union to be a market economy, but not a Western democracy, by 2025. Generally speaking, the prophesy came true (but for the fact that the Soviet Union disappeared, and Russia took over in part), although there might be some changes in the next 12 years.

Almost 40 years will have passed between the time reforms started and the year 2025. This is a long enough period for the old system to finally vanish and for the new institutional order to form in its place. Besides, this period was incredibly saturated with events. The previous system demolition that took place in the first half of the 20th century also took roughly 40 years – from the prelude to war to creating a relatively stable global system. At that time, two world wars had to take place to stabilize the system. As was described above, such wars are hardly possible nowadays, so the processes that are accelerated by globalization are somewhat blurred. Therefore, one cannot guarantee the appearance of a clear picture by 2025, even though all the institutions of the previous era will probably have ceased to function. The challenges that Russia is currently facing do not allow it to separate domestic and international concerns. Russia is actually not the only state that is facing such challenges. Every single state is now forced to act globally on a local level and vice versa. In Russia's case, the situation is exacerbated by its own transformation. The imperial state with the global agenda and ambitions is morphing into another formation, which is still vast and incapable of a limited regional or subordinate role but is trying to narrow the sphere of its immediate interests and ambitions. The society is also losing its multi-national character, but cannot afford to exist as an ordinary nation state. Geopolitical pluralism on the global arena, as well as political and religious diversity inside the country, requires harmonization, but so far no one knows how it can be achieved.

Notes

1. N.N. Taleb (2007/2010) *The Black Swan: The Impact of the Highly Improbable* (New York: Random House and Penguin).
2. Valdayclub (2012) *Vladimir Putin on Foreign Policy: Russia and the Changing World*, http://valdaiclub.com/politics/39300.html
3. Wikisource (2011) *George Herbert Walker Bush's Fourth State of the Union Address*, http://en.wikisource.org/wiki/George_Herbert_Walker_Bush%27s_Fourth_State_of_the_Union_Address
4. Council on Foreign Relations (2012) *Ahmadinejad's Remarks to the UN General Assembly, September 2012*, http://www.cfr.org/iran/ahmadinejads-remarks-un-general-assembly-september-2012/p29153
5. J.E. Sweig (2010) 'A New Global Player. Brazil's Far-Flung Agenda', *Foreign Affairs*, November/December 2010.
6. Terra America (2013) *Yadernoe oruzhie – eto nechto poslannoe nam Vsevishnim*, http://terra-america.ru/yadernoe-orujie-eto-nechto-poislannoe-nam-vsevishnim.aspx
7. Council on Foreign and Defense Policy's assembly (2012) 'Russia in the World of Power. Power of Money, Power of Arms, Power of Ideas and Images', The conference materials, 1–2 December 2012 (Moscow).
8. T. Bordachev (2010) 'Foreign Policy Comeback', *Russia in Global Affairs*, 15 October 2010.
9. President of Russia (2012) *Address to the Federal Assembly*, 12 December 2012 (Moscow), http://eng.kremlin.ru/news/4739
10. Ministry of Foreign Affairs of Russia (2013) *The Foreign Policy Concept of the Russian Federation*, 12 February 2013, http://www.mid.ru/brp_4.nsf/newsline/6D84DDEDEDBF7DA644257B160051BF7F

Bibliography

T. Bordachev (2010) 'Foreign Policy Comeback', *Russia in Global Affairs*, no. 3 (July–September), 2010, pp. 6–12.

Council on Foreign and Defense Policy's assembly (2012) 'Russia in the World of Power. Power of Money, Power of Arms, Power of Ideas and Images', The conference materials,1–2 December 2012 (Moscow).

Council on Foreign Relations (2012) *Ahmadinejad's Remarks to the UN General Assembly, September 2012*, http://www.cfr.org/iran/ahmadinejads-remarks-un-general-assembly-september-2012/p29153, accessed 15 May 2013

Ministry of Foreign Affairs of Russia (2013) *The Foreign Policy Concept of the Russian Federation*, 12 February 2013, http://www.mid.ru/brp_4.nsf/newsline/6D84DDEDEDBF7DA644257B160051BF7F

President of Russia (2012) *Address to the Federal Assembly*, 12 December 2012 (Moscow), http://eng.kremlin.ru/news/4739, accessed 15 May 2013

J.E. Sweig (2010) 'A New Global Player. Brazil's Far-Flung Agenda', *Foreign Affairs*, November/December 2010, pp. 173–184

N.N. Taleb (2007/2010) *The Black Swan: The Impact of the Highly Improbable* (New York: Random House and Penguin).

Terra America (2013) *Yadernoe oruzhie – eto nechto poslannoe nam Vsevishnim*, http://terra-america.ru/yadernoe-orujie-eto-nechto-poislannoe-nam-vsevishnim.aspx, accessed 15 May 2013

Valdayclub (2012) *Vladimir Putin on foreign policy: Russia and the changing world*, http://valdaiclub.com/politics/39300.html, accessed 9 March 2013

Wikisource (2011) *George Herbert Walker Bush's Fourth State of the Union Address*, http://en.wikisource.org/wiki/George_Herbert_Walker_Bush%27s_Fourth_State_of_the_Union_Address, accessed 25 April 2013

13
Russia and the World: The Path to 2025

Thomas Graham

For the 300 years before 1991, Russia was a consequential country. That was a remarkable achievement for a country that in comparison to other great powers was poor, poorly administered, and technologically backward. Despite its obvious weaknesses, Russia was the dynamic core of Eurasia, pressing outward and extending its sway into Europe, the Caucasus, Central Asia, and the Far East. It repeatedly managed to catch up sufficiently in technology, military organization, and mobilization capabilities to play a major role in European (and, by extension, global) affairs. Twice it drove its troops to the center of Europe, in 1814–15 and 1944–45, in response to first Napoleon's and then Hitler's strategic blunders. In the 20th century, as the other European powers disappeared (Austro-Hungary) or descended into the second echelon by reason of crushing defeat (Germany) or the devastating costs of victory and burdens of empire (Great Britain and France), Russia emerged as the other superpower in a global existential competition with the US. Even the collapse of the Empire in 1917 led to continuing world-historical significance, as the Bolsheviks inspired revolutionary movements and anti-colonial national liberation movements in the decades after they seized power. For better or worse, Russia mattered.

Russia's consequentiality, however, has been in question since the new Russia emerged from the wreckage of the Soviet Union a generation ago. In the 1990s, Russia suffered a socio-economic and political collapse and national humiliation unprecedented for a great power not defeated in a great war. It offered no new, promising model of political and socio-economic organization to inspire the oppressed as it sought to adapt to the requirements of the then dominant Western liberal free-market democratic model and integrate into the West. By the end of the decade, many Russian leaders feared that Russia was on the path to becoming a failed state, that it would break up, much as the Soviet Union had. In the 2000s, Russia may have engineered a remarkable political and economic recovery that returned it to the world stage as a major player – at least in its leaders' eyes – but the global financial crisis of 2008–09 has raised questions once again about Russia's future role in world affairs. Today, Russian leaders themselves, from Putin downwards, acknowledge that the economic model that produced the recovery has exhausted itself and that Russia needs a new approach to sustain economic growth and back up claims to great-power status. As the eruption of anti-Putin protests at the end of 2011 and the continuing political discontent demonstrate, many also question the viability of the political model behind the recovery.

Russians' own doubts meet similar – and perhaps greater – doubts abroad. The West appears more concerned about Russia's continuing capacity for mischief than hopeful of its ability to bring something important and concrete to the resolution of global problems. And, while Western leaders still talk of Russia's significance and treat it with a certain deference, they harbor doubts about its long-term future, uncertain as to whether 'Russia's demographic crisis, political corruption, outdated and resource-driven economic model, and social retardation' will not drag it down to the second or third echelon of global power in the next few decades, as Zbigniew Brzezinski, one of America's leading strategic thinkers, has put it.[1] Chinese leaders also harbor doubts. In spring 2012, they took the unusual step, albeit indirectly, of publicly warning Russia about the deficiencies of its economic model.[2] As a leading expert on Sino-Russian relations wrote, 'In many respects, for the Chinese Russia represents the past: a former superpower harking back to earlier glories and living off its natural assets; an erstwhile ally of suspect reliability whose relevance to China's domestic and foreign policy goals is restricted to a few sectors only.'[3]

Nevertheless, few expect Russia's imminent collapse, or even a collapse in the long term. Rather, the vision is one of a slow decline to lesser relevance. Given the challenges Russia now faces at home and abroad, the next decade will be critical in determining whether that expectation is correct or whether Russia can confound it and reliably recapture its historical reputation as a country of strategic consequence.

* * *

Taking a world-systems approach in *Russia in 2020*, Georgi Derluguian and Immanuel Wallerstein tend toward pessimism. In their view,

Russia will remain on the periphery of the world's capitalist core as a 'semi-peripheral' state, having squandered the organizational advantages of the Soviet period that could have moved it closer. The reason lies in the emergence of what they call a 'sovereign bureaucracy' in post-Soviet Russia, a bureaucracy that is 'sovereign from foreign dictates and any domestic elite interests' and satisfied with the status quo and its ample rent-seeking opportunities. Derluguian and Wallerstein doubt that this bureaucracy can be tamed – that is, rationalized and disciplined – from above or below for the purposes of modernization. The rulers – including Putin and his possible successors – lack the tools, the people (workers and members of the intelligentsia), the imagination, and the daring. The only hope they see lies in the return of Leninism, not as an official ideology, but as a political model of successful state building and modernization that lies between the extremes of reactionary imperial nationalism and global neo-liberalism.[4]

Even without the evocation of Leninism, Derluguian's and Wallerstein's argument is a curious read. There is something quaint about a neo-Marxist world-systems approach when the world itself has entered a period of great turbulence that will end at some unknown point in the future when a new equilibrium emerges. About the only thing that can be said with confidence is that the new equilibrium will not be dominated by the West, economically, politically, or intellectually. The capitalist core Derluguian and Wallerstein write of is itself degrading under great stress. The US has to come to terms with straitened circumstances. Europe has to decide whether it has sufficient will to move its grand project of integration forward. The historic transformation underway in the Arab world marks a rejection of Western norms, regardless of the earlier raptures about a democratic transition. Meanwhile, global dynamism has shifted from the core to what Derluguian and Wallerstein would call the periphery in South and East Asia. Looking forward, the issue is not what new states or regions will rise to the top spots in a global structure shaped by the norms and rules of Western liberal democracy and capitalism, but what new states and regions will rise to the top as they reshape those rules and norms. Under these circumstances, what is the core on the periphery of which Russia lies?

That question might generate an entertaining academic debate, but it is of little use to practitioners, for whom the question is a practical one: Will Russia matter? The answer lies in Russia's ability to accomplish the four central strategic tasks before it:

- Restore primacy in the former Soviet space
- Balance and link Europe and East Asia
- Defend itself from the unrest in the Muslim South
- Come to terms with the US.

* * *

The sine qua non of Russia's successfully handling those strategic tasks is rebuilding itself as the dynamic core of Eurasia. Economically, that requires some form of modernization and diversification that would allow Russia to compete successfully in a broad range of sectors, including those based on cutting-edge technology. It needs to master the challenges of the information–communications revolution, ease its reliance on commodities, and rebuild and upgrade its infrastructure. At the same time, Russia needs to bring its educational and public-health systems up to world-class standards. Russian leaders understand this. Government officials, business leaders, and experts have worked separately and together in drafting innumerable programs and initiatives to achieve those goals. What has been lacking is the political will to choose among them and to execute them in a reasonably effective and timely fashion. This is not to say that there has not been some progress toward the goals – Russia is without doubt better off economically now than a decade ago – but much more needs to be done; otherwise, Russia will fall further behind the leading powers.

What political changes are necessary to return the needed dynamism is another matter. The requirements of economic modernization would suggest that the political system has to open up to encourage the creativity, innovation, and risk-taking that lead to economic dynamism. There are various ways this could be done well short of the full embrace of liberal democracy. But one thing should be clear: if Russia has not engineered a generational change in leadership by 2025, it will have failed. Today's dominant figures, starting with Putin and including major opposition figures, are all products of the Soviet period. In the next few years, they need to begin to retire, to make way for a generation of new leaders who came of age in the new Russia, who are better educated, with more experience with, and greater confidence in, dealing with the outside world, and who are more in tune with the possibilities of modern information–communications technology. Putin's return to the Kremlin at a minimum retarded the process of elite renewal; it could eventually lead to stagnation.

Rebuilding Russia as the dynamic core will clearly take time. But the eruption of anti-Putin protests and the clear manifestation of widespread discontent, particularly among middle-class professionals, present an immediate challenge. The professionals are critical to any effort to rebuild Russia. As a result, Putin cannot simply crack down on the protest or ignore the discontent; he must find a way to assuage the professionals' concerns and co-opt them. Indeed, handled properly, that is, with a significant opening up of the political system, the resolution of this issue could give a major boost to the generation of the needed dynamism. Whether it will turn out that way remains to be seen.

* * *

Beyond recapturing its historical dynamism, Russia will have to develop a clear sense of the stakes in each of the four strategic tasks it must accomplish, the obstacles to success, and the most promising ways forward. In addition, Russia will have to examine and adjust some deeply held views, particularly about Europe and the US.

The former Soviet space

Historically, primacy in the former Soviet space has been critical to Russia's geopolitical heft, but today that primacy is hardly assured, even if Russia remains by far the pre-eminent power among the former Soviet states. An economically robust and increasingly assertive China is penetrating into Central Asia. It is on the verge of becoming the region's main commercial partner, ahead of Russia, if it has not done so already. It has built an oil and a gas pipeline from the Caspian Basin to its markets, circumventing Russian territory, and thereby eroding the control over the exit routes for Central Asian oil and gas that has been a major source of Russian leverage in the region. Radical Islamic movements are active in Central Asia and the Caucasus, including Russia's own North Caucasus, and have added another major element of instability to regions marked by fragile states, aggressive criminal groups, and pervasive poverty. Europe, despite its current disarray, continues to act as a magnet at least to Ukraine, Georgia, and Moldova. And the US has been active throughout the region, but especially after the terrorist attacks of 11 September 2001, more often than not in competition with Russia.

Not surprisingly, Putin has made reasserting Russia's position throughout the region a top foreign policy goal. He has aggressively used economic levers (particularly control over gas pipelines) and encouraged Russian investment in an effort to reassert Russia's influence. He has pushed institutional arrangements, such as the Collective Security Treaty Organization (CSTO) and the Customs Union (Russia, Kazakhstan, Belarus), as integrating forces. In September 2011, he announced wide-ranging ambitions to create a Eurasian Union, along the lines of the European Union (EU), that would build on the Customs Union and eventually include at a minimum all the former Soviet states, minus the Baltic countries.

But his plans for a Eurasian Union will run into two main obstacles: Ukraine and Uzbekistan. In the absence of these two countries, the union does not make economic or strategic sense. Ukraine is the former Soviet state with the greatest economic potential, after Russia itself, and located in a key strategic position along the Black Sea's northern coast. Uzbekistan has by far the largest population of the five Central Asian states and lies at the heart of the region. Neither country wants to part of a Russian-dominated economic entity. Ukraine – even under the supposedly pro-Russian President Yanukovich – sees its future in Europe and is actively pursing an Association Agreement with the EU, notwithstanding continuing EU concerns about Ukraine's backsliding on democratic reforms. Uzbekistan will continue to maneuver among Russia, China, and the US to enhance its independence. In the past year, it has rebuilt its relations with the US after the rupture over the Andijon incident in 2005 and withdrawn, for the second time, from the CSTO.

Europe and East Asia

Europe and East Asia are the two strategic poles between which Russia must balance to defend and advance its own geopolitical interests and the two major economic zones into which Russia must integrate to prosper economically.

At the moment, Europe is more important by a wide margin for historical, cultural, political, security, and commercial reasons. Since Peter the Great built St Petersburg as a window to Europe, Europe has provided the standard by which Russia measures itself. Russia has followed the European trajectory of political development toward greater liberty, albeit with a considerable lag of about 100 years behind England and France and 50 years behind Germany, as the eminent historian Martin Malia once argued.[5] Russia demonstrated its prowess as a great power on the battlefields of Europe, in the great European diplomatic conferences, and in competition with European great powers, especially

Great Britain, along its southern periphery. As Putin has said more than once, Russians are Europeans, and Russia is a part of European civilization. What is also true is that they are not Asians, and Russia will never become a part of Asian civilization.

East Asia, however, provides a potential counterweight to Europe as a commercial partner. Today, Europe is Russia's leading commercial partner by a wide margin. It accounts for over half of Russia's overall trade and some 75 per cent of cumulative foreign direct investment in Russia, while East Asian countries (China, Japan, and South Korea) account for less than 20 per cent of Russia's overall trade. Nearly 100 per cent of Russia's gas exports and 80 per cent of its oil exports flow to European markets. Asia as whole accounts for about 12 per cent of Russia's oil exports.[6]

With the hosting of the Asia-Pacific Economic Cooperation (APEC) summit in Vladivostok in September 2012 Russia sent a clear signal of its determination to become a major commercial partner in the region, and with the creation of a Ministry for the Development of the Far East in May 2012 Russia put a focus on the implementation of the strategy it announced in 2009 for that region. The strategy lays out the right goals: geographic diversification of Russian trade (read counterweight to Europe), reinforcement of Russia's sovereignty over the Far East (by reversing the population outflow, strengthening economic links between the region and the rest of Russia, and building regional infrastructure so that it helps to bind the region together as it integrates into the Asian-Pacific economic zone), diversification of the region's economy (so that it does not simply become a natural resource appendage), and reinforcement of transportation links from the region across Russia (so that Russia becomes a commercial link between East Asia and Europe).[7]

Not surprisingly, China will figure large in this strategy, but it must be treated with care. While it is true that Russia's relations with China have never been better, certainly not in the past 50 years, and it makes sense to increase bilateral trade (from the current $80 billion to $200 billion in 2020, as now planned[8]), Russia has no interest in the region east of Lake Baykal becoming captive to Chinese markets. As the Russians have discovered in their negotiations with China over oil and gas deals, China drives a hard bargain and is not about to make concessions, especially on price, to curry favor with Russia. As a result, Russia's interest lies in infrastructure development that gives it greater access to the entire Asia-Pacific region and in attracting investment from as many countries as possible, but particularly from Japan, South Korea, and the US, to balance commercial relations with China.

Beyond commercial ties, Russia will also have to carefully manage its strategic relations with Europe and East Asia. Russia is already working closely with China as a counterweight to the US on global issues (witness the close coordination of Russian and Chinese positions in the UN Security Council during the past two years, especially on Middle Eastern issues) and in Central Asia (through the Shanghai Cooperation Organization). But Russia also needs a close strategic relation with Europe to act as a counterweight to China in Eurasia and to gain leverage in its relations with the US. In this regard, Russia would benefit from a unified Europe, and the current disarray in Europe with the mounting questions about the future of European integration endangers Russia's interests.

This, however, is not the current view in Moscow. Russia prefers to deal bilaterally with European states, rather than with the EU as an institution, and seeks to play on differences among European states to advance its perceived interests in Europe. This is most evident in energy politics, where Russia has sought to prevent the emergence of a unified European position and to work with Germany to gain leverage over Poland and the Baltic States. But it is also evident in Russian efforts to weaken NATO in the name of equality in security matters inside Europe.

This approach is embedded in a traditional view that no longer corresponds to the strategic realities Russia now faces in a multi-polar world in which the major powers are not individual European states, but the US, China, India, Japan, and (potentially) a unified Europe. Moreover, a unified Europe would also go a long way toward easing Russian concerns about NATO, because it would lead to the creation of a European pole inside that organization that would balance the US and, in fact, create more opportunities for involving Russia as the third pillar in managing European and transatlantic security matters.

The Muslim south

The Muslim south, stretching from the Middle East through Afghanistan, is a growing threat to Russia. There are two related long-term problems Russia must manage: (1) the spread of radical Islamic movements and (2) Afghanistan.

Radical Islamic movements continue to gain power and influence in the North Caucasus and could eventually endanger the strategically more important Muslim provinces in the heart of Russia, Tatarstan, and Bashkortostan. Despite Moscow's claims of victory against Chechen

terrorists nearly a decade ago, the North Caucasus has not been stabilized. Running conflicts between radical Islamists, criminal groups,
and local authorities ebb and flow but never go away, especially in
the ethnically complex Dagestan. The attack on Tatarstan's mufti in
July 2012 by radical Islamists underscored the dangers in a region that
prided itself on its moderation and good relations among different
religious confessions. Radical Islam is not necessarily the primary cause
of the unrest – corruption, poverty, and chronic unemployment plague
the North Caucasus – but it thrives on it, creating potentially larger
problems in the future.

In 2010, then-President Medvedev created a North Caucasus
Federal District and appointed a presidential representative, Aleksandr
Khloponin, who simultaneously served as deputy prime minister, to
oversee it. The focus has been on developing the region economically to deal with the fundamental causes of the unrest, so far without
much visible success. That Putin after his return to the Kremlin retained
Khloponin in this capacity indicates that Moscow has not yet given up
on this strategy. To increase the chances of success, Russia must also
manage the instability in the South Caucasus. Although Russia has given
no indication that it is prepared to change policy, its recognition of
Abkhazia and South Ossetia as independent states has done nothing
to contain the instability; on the contrary, it has absorbed time and
resources that could probably be put to better use in the North Caucasus.
Russia must also work with the other co-chairs of the Minsk Group,
France and the US, to ensure that the Karabakh problem does not lead
to outright warfare between Armenia and Azerbaijan.

In addition, Russia needs to forge a civic national identity, not one
based on ethnicity. This should be the natural inclination of a ruling
elite that is multi-ethnic, as Russia's ruling elite has been for centuries,
governing a country in which over 15 per cent of the population is
not ethnically Russian. But within the population as a whole ethnic
Russian nationalism is gaining strength, with calls for a 'Russia for ethnic Russians' or jettisoning the North Caucasus as an alien body in the
ethnic Russian state. This sentiment will likely only grow if Russia does
not master the economic challenges it now faces.

Finally, the growing unrest in the Arab world threatens to invigorate
radical Islamic movements throughout the world, including in Russia's
Muslim regions. The radical Arab transformation is only in its early
phases, and it will play itself out over the next decade and beyond. It has
already empowered radical Islamic movements, and it will almost certainly lead to new political structures in which Islamic parties dominate

the secular forces. The only question is the nature of the Islamic parties, moderate or radical, democratic or authoritarian. Ensuring an outcome that does as little damage as possible to Russia's interests, or, better yet, one that advances them, will require greater cooperation among the world's major powers than we have seen to date. At a minimum, these powers need to sit down to determine the realistic scenarios for the evolution of Arab unrest and then decide what should be done to nudge developments into the more moderate, constructive channels.

With regard to Afghanistan, the American determination to withdraw from the military conflict by the end of 2014 raises the risk of instability. There is no way the corrupt Afghan central government or the national security forces will be able to cope on their own with a complicated security challenge that includes the Taliban, regional war lords and narco bosses, and other insurgent groups, in addition to likely meddling by outside forces, especially Pakistan. The challenge for Russia will be to work with other regional states to stabilize the country, prevent the reemergence of the Taliban as the dominant force with ambition to extend their sway into Central Asia, and to contain the drug trade. The Shanghai Cooperation Organization includes the key states for successful management of the Afghanistan problem (Russia, China, and Uzbekistan as full members, India, Iran, and Pakistan as observers), but it has shown little inclination to engage in a serious fashion, at least as long as the US is involved. That will have to change, if Afghanistan is not to deteriorate further in the years ahead.

The US

Russia continues to see the US as the most severe challenge to its international standing. This no longer makes sense, if it ever did in the post-Soviet period. The US Russia faces now is not the one it faced a dozen years ago when Putin rose to power. It is not coming off the longest period of uninterrupted economic expansion in its history; rather, it is still struggling to overcome the effects of the global financial crisis of 2008–09. It may remain the world's pre-eminent power, but its margin of superiority has shrunken considerably, particularly vis-à-vis China, since 2000. It is no longer in an expansionary mood; it is retrenching as it rethinks its role in a rapidly changing world. Most importantly, it is no longer flowing into the strategic vacuum created by the breakup of the Soviet Union and a decade of profound crisis in Russia; if anything, it is slowly withdrawing from Central Asia and the Caucasus.

This situation should create the basis for closer Russian cooperation with the US. Every American administration since the breakup of the Soviet Union has believed that a weak Russia is not in America's interests (even if Russian leaders find that hard to credit), although each has also harbored lingering fears about a Russia that was too strong. Ironically – and contrary to what Russia's national security documents suggest – the greater threat to Russia now comes from a weaker, not a stronger America, from America's retrenchment, not from its alleged hegemonic designs.

The reason is straightforward. The US is a factor in all the central strategic challenges Russia will face over the next decade; its cooperation – even if its power has declined in relative terms – could play a key role in helping Russia meet those challenges. It could increase Russia's leverage in its relations with China without undoing them. It could help contain the destructive forces emanating from the Arab world. It could help build a European security architecture with Russia as one of the three key pillars along with Europe and the US. And, as strange as it might appear to Russians now, the US could also help advance Russian interests in the former Soviet space (because, contrary to prevailing opinion in Washington, a cogent argument could be made that a robust Russian presence there would help advance American interests throughout Eurasia). Under these circumstances, the anti-Americanism that continues to play such a prominent role in Russia's political discourse and that is often fanned by the Kremlin works against Russia's own national interests. That situation needs to change to a more balanced assessment of America's role in the world, for Russia's own good.

* * *

The years to 2025 are likely to prove some of the most consequential ones in recent history. The forces that have gained strength and eroded the foundations of the Western-dominated international system since the breakup of the Soviet Union will continue to play themselves out. There will be many surprises ahead, but it is possible that these forces could by 2025 produce a new equilibrium, one that would define the international system well into this century. These will be challenging years for Russia, as they will be for all other major powers. To succeed, Russia will have to see clearly the ways things are tending, define its strategic tasks and goals, and then pursue them vigorously. In any event, that is what a country hoping to be a consequential country would do.

Notes

1. Z. Brzezinski (2012) *Strategic Vision: America and the Crisis of Global Power* (New York: Basic Books), 139–40.
2. A. Bashkatova (2012) 'Pekin postavil Putina v bezvykhodnoye polozheniye', *Nezavisimaya gazeta*, 17 April.
3. B. Lo (2008) *Axis of Convenience: Moscow, Beijing, and the New Geopolitics* (London: Chatham House), 167.
4. G. Derluguian, I. Wallerstein (2012) 'Russia in World-Systems Perspective' in M. Lipman and N. Petrov (eds), *Russia in 2020: Scenarios for the Future* (Washington, DC: Carnegie Endowment for International Peace), 25–43. The quoted material is on page 39.
5. M. Malia lays out this argument in detail in M. Malia (1999) *Russia under Western Eyes: From the Bronze Horseman to the Lenin Mausoleum* (Cambridge, MA: The Belknap Press of Harvard University Press). See in particular 17–39, 418–19.
6. Trade data are available at http://ec.europa.eu/trade/creating-opportunities/ bilateral-relations/countries/russia/. Data on oil and gas exports are available at http://www.eia.gov/countries/cab.cfm?fips=RS
7. *Strategiya sotsial'no-ekonomicheskogo razveitiya Dal'nego Vostoka i Baykal'skogo regiona na period do 2025 goda*, approved 12 December 2009.
8. K. Hille, J. Anderlini (2012) 'Russia and China to strengthen trade ties', *Financial Times*, 5 June 2012.

Bibliography

A. Bashkatova (2012) 'Pekin postavil Putina v bezvykhodnoye polozheniye', *Nezavisimaya gazeta*, 17 April.

Z. Brzezinski (2012) *Strategic Vision: America and the Crisis of Global Power* (New York: Basic Books).

G. Derluguian, I. Wallerstein (2012) 'Russia in World-Systems Perspective' in M. Lipman and N. Petrov (eds), *Russia in 2020: Scenarios for the Future* (Washington, DC: Carnegie Endowment for International Peace).

K. Hille, J. Anderlini (2012) 'Russia and China to Strengthen Trade Ties', *Financial Times*, 5 June.

B. Lo (2008) *Axis of Convenience: Moscow, Beijing, and the New Geopolitics* (London: Chatham House).

M. Malia (1999) *Russia under Western Eyes: From the Bronze Horseman to the Lenin Mausoleum* (Cambridge, MA: The Belknap Press of Harvard University Press).

Strategiya sotsial'no-ekonomicheskogo razveitiya Dal'nego Vostoka i Baykal'skogo regiona na period do 2025 goda, approved 12 December 2009.

Trade data are available at http://ec.europa.eu/trade/creating-opportunities/ bilateral-relations/countries/russia/. Data on oil and gas exports are available at http://www.eia.gov/countries/cab.cfm?fips=RS

The Stalinization of Putinism: A Doomed Effort

Russia in 2013 is on the threshold of serious changes, which could happen at any moment, with or without sanction from the top. In fact, these changes have already begun with the political crisis of the fall and winter of 2011/12. The interests of the principal actors – the regional elites, the business sector, civil society – are more and more frequently coming into sharp conflict with the interests of the federal government. And in Russia today there are no institutions or even accepted frameworks for reconciling these different interests.

The principal actors

The federal government

State governance still hinges on rigid centralized control over all spheres of life – from politics and economics to the administration of Russia's regions and society in general. But, in the context of growing conflict and contradictions within the federal government, this model of administration has begun to run into serious difficulties.

There is no unity within the federal government: it is characterized by corporate and departmental divisions that only grow deeper with the further weakening of the figure of the chief executive. At the same time, the radical weakening of democratic institutions – the result of a concerted campaign throughout the Putin era – has created a state in which there is virtually no separation of powers. There are no effective mechanisms for reconciling the interests of various clans and groups. Instead, there exists a complex system of communication through the chief executive, to whom all of the main government players still swear allegiance. A shrinking global market for energy suppliers, together with a decrease in administrative efficiency, has led to a drop in federal income, resulting in a smaller 'economic pie' for Putin to divide among the various groups within the elite. This has lead to increased intra-elite competition that has, with growing frequency, begun to spill over into public space. A short planning horizon lowers the possibility of national development. This creates a vicious circle: long-term investments in economics and politics are impossible in the context of a short planning horizon, and, in the absence of long-term investments, the planning horizon inevitably shrinks.

Resources of the federal government: Putin remains fairly popular. A large majority of Russians (including those who do not support him) still feel that there is no alternative to Putin's leadership. Popular support (even with reservations) allows Putin to maintain the loyalty of the elites, and significant financial reserves make it possible to continue the current populist policies and delay the adoption of harsh and unpopular reforms for at least another year and a half to two years. The Kremlin still has absolute control over the entire law enforcement system, including the police, the Investigative Committee, the Prosecutor's Office, the Federal Security Service, and the courts. It also still wields a powerful propaganda apparatus, including all of the leading electronic media outlets. And the elites, despite increased internal competition, remain relatively consolidated and loyal to the Kremlin. But this loyalty is increasingly enforced by the stick (in particular, threats of criminal investigations of corruption and a prohibition on holding assets abroad). Although tactics of intimidation and asset 'freezing' are quite effective in guaranteeing loyalty and obedience, they hinder, rather than promote, the possibility of reform and national development.

Society

Russian society has experienced significant shifts over the past few years. The more modern segments of the population – in Moscow, St Petersburg, and a number of other large cities – have gained considerable experience with social activism, primarily in the form of charitable and other volunteer work. At the same time, these groups, who have rejected paternalism and become focused on achievement and success, are growing increasingly dissatisfied with Putin's regime, which they view as corrupt, mendacious, and immoral. This attitude spilled out into the streets during the protests of 2011/12. Although the protestors represented only a 'minority of the minority', their *mood* was shared by approximately one-third of the Russian population in

2013. Government authorities categorically refuse to engage in dialogue with the activists, correctly considering them to be a weak and disorganized opponent. Instead, the government has been attempting to neutralize these groups by discrediting leading activists, labeling them as immoral, unpatriotic figures trying to undermine traditional social norms or as agents of hostile forces in the West. At the same time, the government has begun to resort to repressive police tactics with ever-greater frequency, increasing dissatisfaction and deepening the divide between the authorities and the most progressive segments of the Russian population, as well as between more modern Russians and their conservative compatriots. In this way, the authorities are deliberately provoking a confrontation with the politically active part of the population and creating divisions within society (including between the post-industrial capital and the 'blue-collar' cities).

Resources of the federal government: Although the government still has an enormous advantage in power resources compared with the public (see above), **social resources** should not be underestimated. The private sector of the economy and, specifically, its post-industrial component contribute to the public's liberation from traditional paternalism, bolstering, and in the long run expanding, the segment of non-Soviet Russians who reject the traditional model of an all-powerful government and a powerless society. A significant amount of social capital had been generated by the end of the 2000s – not only in connection with the protests, but also as a result of the experience of effective cooperation, the success of a variety of social initiatives, and the explosive growth of social networks. Of no small importance is the fact that a significant portion of the Russian population shares in resentment over the immorality of the current regime.

Business

Big business directly depends on the natural resource economic model that it serves. The success of big companies is based in large part on the preferences that result from government connections. This, in turn, strengthens the bond between business and the state. As a result, big business essentially opposes free competition and supports the maintenance of the political status quo, since the current regime guarantees favorable operating conditions. At the same time, business interests are seeking both greater independence from the authorities and the strengthening of property laws, which creates tension with the government, especially since loyalty to the regime is not limited to a simple oath of allegiance. Instead, it entails the subordination of for-profit and non-profit activities (of all investment generally) to the interests and directions of the political leadership. The increase in clan conflicts within the current political regime not only affects the business world, but also ensures that it is a direct participant in the struggle. On the one hand, business interests increase path-dependence, but, on the other, they restrain the government from taking steps that would destabilize the situation, therefore lengthening the planning horizon.

These circumstances lead to a contradictory role for business as an agent for change. Innovative business, as well as small and medium business, is weak, and, in the context of a natural resource economy and increased government interference, its share of the pie is only shrinking, making it an ineffective lobby incapable of shaping the future course of events.

> **The resources of business** – Though they do not hold any official positions, 'Putin's oligarchs' engage directly with the planning and implementation of high-level government decisions. The Russian political leadership, in other words, operates as if it were the board of directors of Russia Inc. Business shares a large portion of its resources (especially its media outlets) with the government. It can only use its own resources freely on a very limited scale (this is true of the relatively small number of media outlets that have maintained an independent editorial policy), but this independence is not at all guaranteed, and business as a whole is vulnerable to pressure from the government.
>
> **Resources of the federal government:** Many government officials are deeply engaged in business–political clans and use their authority to further the interests of these clans. Business serves as 'government's wallet' and pays for expensive political projects, including elections. In the event of an escalation of political conflict, big business could become an important player, as it did in 1996, for example, when it played a key role in helping to elect Yeltsin to a second term.

The regional elites

The regional elites have been weakened as a result of the increased centralization of the past ten years and the sharp constriction of public political space. At the same time, the separation of powers and the system of checks and balances often works better at the local than at the federal level. The absence of dominant leaders – a role occupied in the 1990s by the heads of the regions – hinders opposition to the center, but helps generate political competition at the regional level. The weakening of the natural resource economy and the resulting decrease in centralized financing of the regions will contribute to the emergence of a more powerful regional elite, leading to inevitable tensions with the federal government. Contrasts and conflicts among the different regions will also increase.

> **Resources** – Most important for the regional elites is the electoral resource, which has been somewhat strengthened with the partial return of direct gubernatorial elections and the planned shift to a mixed system of electing representatives to the State Duma. This new electoral system for the State Duma and the Federation Council may also contribute considerably to the consolidation of the resources of the regional elite. Finally, in regions that are important for big business, the regional elites could benefit from a connection to business interests.

The situation

Politics

The political system, built on centralization and a monopoly of power in the federal center, restricts development and requires reform. At the same time, political reform since December 2011 has been following the pattern of 'one step forward – a half-step back' – in other words, reform has been accompanied by counter-reform.

- State Duma elections: There is a proposal to abandon the majority electoral system in favor of the old, mixed system of electing representatives to the State Duma (one half of the seats would be filled on the basis of party slates, while the other half would come from single-mandate districts). However, the proposal includes a 'criminal filter', forbidding the nomination of candidates convicted of certain crimes (this filter, it seems, will be used in the interests of the regime, in order to completely close off a path into politics for the most notable members of the social protest movement – see page 276 below). In addition, party coalitions will remain forbidden.
- Gubernatorial elections have been formally restored (they were abolished in 2004), but they will also be accompanied by a system of 'filters', which provides the incumbent with a number of important advantages. A 2013 proposal for indirect gubernatorial elections at the discretion of the regions has already been adopted in a number

of Northern Caucasus republics. Finally, the announced reform of the Federation Council has yet to be implemented, although there are now plans to transform the quasi-representative Civic Chamber into a sort of Upper House for civil society with representatives from each region.

- The widely advertised reform to make the creation of new parties much simpler will lack any real effect in the absence of changes to the electoral system in particular and the political system more broadly. Parties have almost no place in the current political system. They are not transmission belts or mechanisms for cooperation between the government and the public; rather, they are elements of a political show. Dozens of phantom parties have already been registered, but even the few that are able to play a real role in the elections are unable to seriously affect political decision-making (this is true not only of parties, but of the representative branch in Russia generally). Subjected to the will of the Executive, 'United Russia' – the so-called 'party of power' – has also seen its role diminish.

By betting on a fragmented party landscape, by forbidding parties from uniting in coalitions, and so on, the government is, in effect, sawing off the branch it is standing on: in the event of a serious crisis, it will be impossible to transfer power from one party to another – it will be necessary to change the entire political system. In other words, the very survival of the Russian political system will be in question.

The economy

The former model of economic development has run its course and Russia has entered a phase of stagnation, characterized by decreased economic growth and an outflow of capital. Without a new model capable of generating economic growth, both the country and Putin's current politics of social-populism have no future. But, in contrast to the modern highly qualified economists who developed the liberal 'Strategy-2020' in the period immediately preceding Putin's return to the presidency, the current regime's economic gurus are old Soviet state academics led by a group of *dirigistes*.

Development is currently following a number of different vectors: on the one hand, there have been proposals for massive privatization programs; on the other hand, the oil and gas sector is effectively being nationalized. The government has raised taxes on small and medium-sized businesses, decreasing their share of the economic pie significantly, while, at the same time, developing programs for their support. Welfare expenditures are being cut, while huge sums are being spent on unproductive 'image' mega-projects and the military industrial complex.

In an attempt to curb the outflow of capital and attract vital investment, the Kremlin is using both the stick of forcing the return of financial assets from abroad ('de-offshorization') and the carrot of making technical improvements to the tax and custom system as a means of attracting potential investors. However, this strategy has, so far, been unable to reverse the current negative trend.

A crisis of legitimacy

The Putin government is a hybrid regime, from both an economic and a political perspective. Russia has a hybrid economy because, despite the nominal existence of a free market, the economy is under the mostly informal control of the government. Russia has a hybrid political system because the democratic institutions defined by the Constitution have been neutered and the whole political sector is under the rigid control of the Putin regime. In order to maintain this hybrid regime, it is constantly necessary to reconcile the interests and conflicts of various sub-systems 'by hand'. If this is not done, internal conflict could accumulate until it reaches the surface, potentially destroying the entire system.

The weak point of a hybrid regime is the juncture between the real and the decorative. Elections are a prime example of this difficulty. Even the decorative procedure of voting can give rise to the 'sprouting' of new growth – for example, the work of independent observers – that needs to be 'clipped' to prevent decorative elections from becoming real and preclude the uncertainty that characterizes democratic elections. The overpowering of the semi-democratic component of the system by its authoritarian component is driven by the mechanism of self-preservation: the hybrid system seeks to preserve itself against the 'corrosive' effect of democratic elements upon the authoritarian ones. As the regime gets weaker, so does its ability to keep the balance and maintain its hybrid quality – this is what is happening with Putin's regime entering its second decade.

In December 2012, just as Putin gave his presidential speech, supporting, essentially, the maintenance of the status quo, Russia passed a point of bifurcation and set out on a path of increasing authoritarianism.[1]

It is not as if the Kremlin fundamentally changed its position. Instead, a series of steps, each of which separately could be considered a tactical maneuver in response to some challenge or other, come together to form a general authoritarian trend.

The key problem of the Putin regime is a *crisis of legitimacy*. Putin won the presidential elections of March 2012, but was unable to reinforce his legitimacy: his result of 63.6 per cent (47 per cent in the capital!), which would be good for any democratic leader, does not add anything to the authority of the 'father of the nation' who picks his own opponents. The tens of thousands of people chanting 'Russia without Putin' in the streets of Moscow make up a tiny percentage of Russia's population, but the very fact that they took part in the first mass political protests in all the years of the Putin regime inescapably diminishes his legitimacy as a leader. In April 2013, Putin's ratio of approval/disapproval stands at around 63:37 – a significant shift from its peak of 88:10 in September 2008.[2] Overall support has decreased substantially: about half of the country's population does not want Putin to be president after 2018,[3] and a growing number of Russians see him as representing the interests of big business, top managers, the power agencies, and the bureaucracy, and not common people.[4]

In May and June 2012, the Kremlin launched an active campaign against the protest movement. It is possible that at the beginning the goal was to clamp down on the street protest and take the edge off of the political crisis so that the government could enact a new strategy of socio-economic development. But, by the beginning of 2013, it became clear that there was no strategy for Putin's third term except to consolidate his power.

With Putin's return to the presidency, the Kremlin has launched a campaign on three fronts:

- Against politically active citizens expressing their displeasure with the current situation
- Against the remainder of organized and autonomous social activism in the form of non-governmental organizations (NGOs)
- Against political elites potentially capable of playing their own game.

Scare tactics and demonstratively harsh punishments are employed in all three cases. The Kremlin's objective is to avoid a fragmentation of the elites and a unification of these 'splinter groups' with dissatisfied citizens.

The first front: The struggle with the protesters and politically active segment of society

The new policies of repression employ methods developed earlier – discrediting political opponents, tightening legislative screws, limiting rights and freedoms, harassing specific activists. All of this was in use in the 2000s, but, beginning in mid-2012, these policies became harsher and more unforgiving: discrediting campaigns were no longer limited to propagandistic television segments; TV reports became the basis for criminal investigations; administrative detention and minimal jail time of up to 15 days were replaced by months-long pre-trial detention and real sentences with long prison terms.

In this context, the trial of Pussy Riot, the 'May 6' affair, and the continued harassment and investigation of the most visible figures of the protest movement – Sergei Udaltsov and Aleksei Navalny – are particularly noteworthy. The trial of Pussy Riot combined medieval obscurantism with gross violations of the letter and spirit of Russian law and procedure and culminated with a harsh sentence for the members of the punk group, despite considerable international attention. The mass rally of 6 May 2012 was the first in five months to end in clashes with the police. There is serious reason to believe that these clashes were intentionally orchestrated (members of an independent investigation came to this conclusion[5]). All told, around 30 rally participants were arrested. They were accused of mass disturbance and, as of this writing, many of them have been in confinement for approximately one year. In all likelihood, they will face an extended court case and lengthy prison terms. Sergei Udaltsov, a leftist political activist, is under house arrest and is practically cut off from any contact with his supporters. Aleksei Navalny, who has the best claim to leadership of the protest movement, is under investigation for several economic crimes simultaneously. The accusations against him appear fabricated and are not practically supported by facts. Guilty verdicts for both activists seem predetermined and the probability of long prison sentences is high, but even suspended sentences would preclude them from running in any elections.

The second front: Containment of the elites

In the fall of 2012, the Kremlin launched an anti-corruption campaign and imposed a ban on state officials holding assets abroad. The campaign was designed to fulfill several functions at once:

- To demonstrate that legal investigations can be a threat to any member of the elite, so that nobody would feel secure; to pre-empt the risk of disobedience and minimize the risk of a schism among the elites
- To create a system of 'soft purges' necessary for the maintenance of a minimal level of administrative efficiency
- To engage in a financial maneuver to carve out a portion of the 'pie' for new elites
- To 'isolate' the system, lessening its vulnerability to and dependence on the West.

But the role of the anti-corruption campaign is of questionable value in reinforcing the legitimacy of the regime. On the one hand, the exposure of corrupt public officials serves to satisfy the wishes of the citizenry (surveys show that a considerable percentage of Russians are unhappy about corruption), but, on the other hand, it undermines the already weakening legitimacy of the Putin regime. An anti-corruption campaign waged by a political regime that has been in power for the last ten years discredits the regime as a whole as much as it does its individual members. The increased pressure on the elites has brought about a series of resignations, a rise of nervousness with intra-elite conflicts spilling over into public space, and an incipient exodus of business representatives from the governing apparatus (especially at the regional level).

The soft purges are carried out 'by hand' – in other words, the targets of anticorruption investigations are hand-picked by the Kremlin. As a result, the administration of the president and its personnel department have seen their power grow tremendously, as they now have the right to check the income and expenses of any member of the million-strong bureaucratic army and of any candidates for positions within it.

This strategy of purges cannot help overcome the crisis within the administrative system – a system that constitutes a hybrid of Soviet-style *nomenklatura* and new elites and is incapable of reproducing itself. At the same time, the increase in public competition, which pushed the system toward an elite-type model, has been blocked.

Third front: The struggle with civil society

The most consistent and massive campaign is the one against NGOs. The targets of the campaign are NGOs with foreign sources of funding. Two political trends are combined in this attack: isolationist, anti-Western policies and an absolute rejection of autonomous civic activity.

Over the years of post-Soviet development, NGOs gained skills and experience in implementing a variety of watchdog functions. It was precisely foreign funding that enabled them to act independently of the government, but, similarly to other public actors, they remained at the government's discretion. Foreign-funded NGOs have been under government pressure at least since the mid-2000s, but in 2012, when the government realized that civic awakening was eroding the regime's legitimacy, the Kremlin opted for a policy of essentially eliminating these NGOs.

Russia's eviction of United States Agency for International Development (USAID), which used to be a source of funding for many prominent NGOs, dealt a radical blow to their activities. This was followed by across the board inspections of almost all foreign-funded NGOs by a variety of government agencies. One after another, they have been subject to administrative penalties, and many of them are likely to curtail their operation by the end of 2013. This would eliminate the last remains of public accountability, such as election-monitoring (and thus facilitate the government's election rigging); monitoring of human rights and the free legal defense of victims of human rights violations (and thus give the government an ever freer hand in unlawful activities); anti-corruption efforts (Transparency International is among the likely victims; the Kremlin wants to secure full control over anti-corruption probes, including the choice of their targets).

The government will thus purge public space of the 'enemy within' funded by outside 'hostile forces.' The availability of information about domestic developments will thus be radically reduced and police-state operation will expand unhampered by autonomous watchdogs. The latter are being replaced by GONGOs, government-funded and therefore loyal organizations imitating genuine civil society. This replacement has gone on since the middle of the previous decade, and has been given a new boost in 2012–13: government funds allocated for this purpose have been significantly increased and a trusted official, formerly a Kremlin staffer, was put in charge of distributing these funds.

Another reason for neutralizing and eliminating unwelcome activists and organizations is to minimize the risk of future protests. The urgency of this goal may rise in the coming years: socio-economic protests can become a real threat, since there is no way to keep in full the present model of paternalistic populist politics at a time of economic stagnation or even recession.

Multi-faceted nationalization

The first year of Putin's most recent term has been defined by government expansion and a 'nationalization' of a variety of spheres, from economics to ideology.

- In the economy, this new wave of nationalization was epitomized by Rosneft's purchase of TNK-BP and the transformation of the company, headed by Putin's close ally, Igor Sechin, into a giant monopoly along the lines of Gazprom.
- The enactment of a whole packet of legislation that clamped down on the administrative and political elites and made them more dependent on the president's administration has experts talking of a 'nationalization of the elites'.
- The 'nationalization' of the population's income is evidenced by the fact that the government has become the country's largest employer. Putin's first decrees in his latest term contained strong demands for raising the salaries of teachers and medical workers to regional averages; these demands reached down to the regions, where their implementation is obligatory.
- The nationalization of civil society can be seen in the rooting out of autonomous social activism and the co-optation of NGOs by planting new 'non-governmental' organizations answerable to the regime (discussed above).
- The nationalization of the ideational realm: the government is once more attempting to conduct ideological indoctrination after two decades of essentially keeping clear of ideological matters. The state ideology supplied by the Kremlin in 2013 can be described in general terms as a form of state nationalism/patriotism of a conservative, protective nature based on an intolerance to foreignness (the West, the new, the modern) and a perception of Russia as a 'besieged fortress' whose opponents constitute a 'fifth column'. Putin's demand for the swift creation of a single Russian history textbook serves as an explicit example of this claim to ultimate truth.

A simultaneous attack on the bureaucracy (by launching an anti-corruption campaign), on parties (by depriving them of any real political role), and on business (by following a policy of informal nationalization) can only be justified politically if the regime definitively decides to further centralize state administration and transform Russia into a police state.

Putin chooses 'Stalin-lite'

In our 2011 report analyzing development possibilities till 2020, we addressed the scenario described above, calling it 'Stalin-lite'.[6]

'Stalin-lite' as defined in our previous scenario exercise:

Political Institutions	Degradation of institutions and an increase in personalist elements in the political system
The Party System	A one-and-a-half-party system plus other imitation parties
Elections	Neutered, ritualized elections
Government	Strengthening of the power verticals and increased cooperation among them; the institutionalization of a 'politburo' for reconciling the interests of the main business–political clans; a growing role for the security forces
The Government's Role in the Economy	An increased role for state corporations and 'business among friends'
Federalism and Regionalism	Further centralization and standardization; a potential enlargement of the regions; the transformation of federal districts into an additional layer of state administration accompanied by a weakening of regional government; risk of secessionism
Society	Increased paternalism in the relationship between the government and society; an inculcation of the 'besieged fortress' mindset together with the mass emigration of the opponents of this ideology; a growth of nationalism and ethnic tensions
Foreign Policy	A slow turn toward isolationism; an anti-Western perspective shaping foreign policy decisions, pushing Russia to become a junior partner to China

A quick glance at our description of the 'Stalin-lite' scenario shows that, in essence, we described the general trend correctly, but were unable to foresee specific events and the Kremlin's reaction to them. In part of the political system, elements of a corporatist government have become stronger than we had supposed in our Stalin-lite scenario. Also, instead of the one-and-a-half-party system with the party in power and a cloud of satellites, we can now observe an evolution toward a pseudo-party system, where the bureaucracy has all of the real power.

In contrast to what we believed in 2011, an anti-Western orientation has not been the only important element of Russia's foreign policy positioning in a context of continuing global economic crisis. Russia has also attempted to create its own 'global power center' – be it with the Eurasian alliance, the Customs Union with Belarus and Kazakhstan (and, ideally, Ukraine as well), or the totally ephemeral BRICS (Brazil, Russia, India, China, and South Africa).

But the most important phenomenon, which we could not have foreseen, was the beginning of the mass protests in December 2011, the regime's subsequent shift toward becoming an authoritarian police state, the 'ghettoization of the opposition', the repression of protestors and NGOs, and the soft purges of the elite. This shift has been enforced by the Kremlin's turn to ideology with a focus on Soviet-style state nationalism and social conservatism sowing intolerance toward those perceived as Other, alien, or unpleasantly modern, as well as Putin's positioning as the 'father of the nation', edifying his subjects on issues ranging from patriotism to family values to school curriculum and language style. All this makes the scenario of authoritarianization, defined as 'Stalin-lite', significantly worse than we envisioned back in 2011.

Summing up

Putin's apparent bet on a policy of maintaining the socio-economic status quo cannot possibly pay off in the long run. The system has almost completely exhausted its resources from the Soviet period (its transportation and engineering infrastructure, its industrial potential, and its education and health care systems), from the Yeltsin period (renewed elites), and from the early Putin years (the first-term economic liberalization and an increase in available funds). Putin's system is impotent and incapable of reproducing itself. Its own effectiveness is plummeting as external conditions change all around it. Megaprojects – both completed and planned – serve as perfect examples of the system's colossal ineffectiveness. Vladivostok-2012 and Sochi-2014 have proven many times more expensive than originally projected, despite the extremely poor quality of the work (newly built roads began to deteriorate before construction was even complete). A similar fate awaits all other extremely costly projects, including the overhaul of the military, the 2018 World Cup, 'Northern Caucasus Resorts', and the development of Siberia and the Far East. Whatever is not stolen is shoved into the ground, with minimal benefit for the economy or people's lives.

Rather than maintaining the status quo, Russia must modernize. But economic modernization is impossible without political modernization. The Kremlin is capable of blocking development (for a little while, at least), but is unable to provide alternative scenarios or mechanisms. And the longer it stalls and plays for time, the more turbulent and unpredictable the inevitable changes will be in the end. Revolution provides an alternative and accelerated path of evolution. Either the regime decides to lead the process of radical political and economic modernization itself or it will lose control of the situation and be replaced by a new regime, potentially even worse than the current one – more authoritarian, repressive, and isolationist, but more effective at maintaining power.

The idea that 'putinism' – a Russian iteration of a hybrid regime with elements of traditional Soviet paternalism – might last much longer is as ill-conceived as the earlier idea that Russia would see a swift transition to democracy. Putin's regime is rapidly deteriorating and transforming from a hybrid system into a more standard authoritarian regime.

The effects of this are felt differently in different parts of the country – a divergence that will only grow in the long run. Although Moscow is a global, post-industrial city that differs little from the large capitals of the West, the human resource in the surrounding regions is severely compromised and cannot serve as a major building block for modernization efforts. A few national republics look like semi-feudal princedoms, while Chechnya is probably most similar to the authoritarian regimes of the Middle East.

At the same time, Putin is seeking the support of this non-modernized majority and is essentially creating a course of anti-modernization, reinforcing resistance to change and blocking any possibility for the government to propose serious reforms in the future.

Over the next few years, the growth of heterogeneity in Russian society will lead to an increase in tensions among the various regions, as well as between the regions and the center. If, before, recentralization was based on the natural resource model of economic growth, then, now, decentralization will follow a non-natural resource model. This significantly increases the danger of soft, or perhaps even hard, territorial disintegration, which would be provoked by the clumsiness of the center, incapable of accounting for vast regional differences and unable to predict the regional consequences of decisions made on the federal level.

An escalation of the political crisis in Russia is likely in the following years next few months as a result of increased economic difficulties, incorrect government action, and government inaction when action is necessary. The system will face its first test in September 2013, when widespread regional elections demonstrated growing support for opposition leaders, at least in Moscow and Yekaterinburg, one of Russia's biggest cities will inevitably result in an intensification of existing tensions and serious defeat for the party in power in a number of regions. Next come the Sochi Olympics in 2014, the almost inevitable destabilization of the Caucasus, and, that same year, city council elections in Moscow, where opposition feelings are strongest. In store for 2015 are the mayoral elections in Moscow and the preordained failure of investment programs in the military–industrial complex. Elections to the Duma and a widespread replacement of the country's governors will take place in 2016–17. This list can also be expanded to include unfavorable external conditions caused by the global economic crisis and the likely political destabilization of neighboring countries, as well as the serious risk of massive internal technological and infrastructural failure.

It appears that, in the foreseeable future, there are two possibilities for further development: one characterized by a series of systemic crises, each leading to significant changes to the system, and the other by a single powerful crisis that would result in its total replacement. Figuratively speaking, the first would develop according to the laws of an internal combustion engine, provided that the current regime of personalist hands-on administration began to institutionalize, and the second according to those of a powder keg, if the prevailing trends continue.

Notes

1. President of Russia (2012) 'Address to the Federal Assembly', http://eng.kremlin.ru/transcripts/4739. date accessed 5 April 2013.
2. http://www.levada.ru/indeksy
3. http://www.levada.ru/07-05-2013/obshchestvennoe-mnenie-o-vlasti-i-4-m-sroke-putina
4. http://www.levada.ru/11-04-2013/vladimir-putin-god-posle-izbraniya-prezidentom
5. http://6may.org/rassledovanie/
6. N. Petrov, M. Lipman (2012) *Rossiya-2020: Stsenarii Razvitiya*, Carnegie Working Papers (Moscow: Carnegie Moscow Center), 48.

Index

"aggressive immobility" of Russians, 46

All-Russian Center for the Study of Public Opinion (WCIOM), 50

'angry urbanites', 72, 74, 78

anti-corruption campaign, 130, 276–7, 279

anti-modernization, 282

'Arab Spring', 129, 131–2, 152, 204–5, 243, 249

Arab world, Arabs, 258, 264

arms race, 244

Asia, 247, 253

authoritarianism, 23–5, 35–7, 144, 148, 152–3, 157, 274–5, 281, 282
  benevolent, 35–7
  bureaucratic, 163–6
  electoral, 18–19, 43, 144, 146, 153–4, 210
  repressive, 144, 148, 151

automotive market, 110

Babich, Dmitry, 213

'Beslan' political reform, 194–6

birth rate, 92–4, 97, 98

Bolotnaia Ploschad, 47, 276

Bordachev, Timofei, 248

Brezhnev, Leonid, 22, 149

Brie, Michael, 189

Bush, George W., 244, 245

business culture and corporate management, 110–11

business-political elites relations, 198

business-state relations, 182, 270

cadres rotation system, 194, 196

Center of Human Demography and Ecology, Russian Academy of Sciences, 98

center-periphery model, 67, 69, 79

Center for Political Technologies, 11

center-regions relations, 181, 192, 194, 196–7

Central Asia, 10, 256, 260–1, 263, 265

centralization, 20, 23, 25, 27–30, 32, 35–6, 193, 268, 271–2
  decentralization, 10, 21
  overcentralization, 38
  recentralization, 282

Chechen war (Second), perception of, 63

Chechnya, Chechens, 11, 13, 89, 204, 282

'Chekist' corporation, 182–3

China, 156, 242, 245, 252, 257, 260–3, 265

Civic Chamber, 273

civil services, low quality of, 113

Clarke, Harold, 63

Clarke, T.J., 212

Cold war, 240, 242, 244, 246

Collective Security Treaty Organization, 10

Colton, Timothy; Hale, Henry, 20, 57, 58, 63

communism, 152, 157–8
  end of communism, perception of, 222, 224

Communist Party of the Russian Federation (CPRF), 165, 174–5, 211

Communist Party of the Soviet Union, 158

Concept of Demographic Policy of the Russian Federation until 2025, 86, 97, 101–2

Concept of the State Migration Policy (2012), 87

conservatism, 15, 221, 229, 231–3, 281

constitution, 150, 158

corporate federation, 181, 197

corporate political machinery, 184, 189

corporate state model, 12, 181–3

Printed and bound in Great Britain by
CPI Group (UK) Ltd, Croydon, CR0 4YY

Plan

* Our view on sanctions / conflict → how long will they last.

* Our view on how Russia will perform
  → more detail on how will upp will sanctions

* Longer term outlook * some thoughts +
  assumptions. Avenues of possible development.

* Sanctions → wipe out service / consumer
  sectors of economy

Tatu ⇒ authoritarianism
           for Russia)
           → subsidies for Russia
                2

read all
amul by
Kirill Rogov &
Petrov & Inozemtsev

* Intensify

* This could mult